THE GUID

Yellowstone
Waterfalls
and Their Discovery

Paul Rubinstein

Lee H. Whittlesey

and Mike Stevens

"Yet where does water ever
fall with such incomparable
loveliness as here?"
—ALMON GUNNISON,
1883 visitor to Yellowstone

WESTCLIFFE PUBLISHERS
www.westcliffepublishers.com

For more information about other fine books and calendars from Westcliffe Publishers, please contact your local bookstore, call us at 1-800-523-3692, write for our free color catalog, or visit us on the Web at www.westcliffepublishers.com.

PLEASE NOTE:
Risk is always a factor in backcountry and high-mountain travel. Many of the activities described in this book can be dangerous, especially when weather is adverse or unpredictable, and when unforeseen events or conditions create a hazardous situation. The authors have done their best to provide the reader with accurate information about backcountry travel, as well as to point out some of its potential hazards. It is the responsibility of the users of this guide to learn the necessary skills for safe backcountry travel, and to exercise caution in potentially hazardous areas, especially on snowfields and avalanche-prone terrain. The authors and publisher disclaim any liability for injury or other damage caused by backcountry traveling or performing any other activity described in this book.

COVER PHOTO: Dunanda Falls; Photo by Mike Stevens

BACK COVER PHOTO: Lower Falls; Photo by Paul Rubinstein

OPPOSITE: Union Falls; Photo by Mike Stevens

INTERNATIONAL STANDARD BOOK NUMBER:
1-56579-351-X

TEXT AND PHOTOGRAPHY COPYRIGHT:
Paul Rubinstein, Lee H. Whittlesey, and Mike Stevens. 2000. All rights reserved.

EDITOR:
Jennie Shortridge

DESIGN AND PRODUCTION:
Rebecca Finkel, F + P Graphic Design, Inc.; Boulder, CO

PRODUCTION MANAGER:
Craig Keyzer

PUBLISHED BY:
Westcliffe Publishers, Inc.
P.O. Box 1261
Englewood, Colorado 80150
www.westcliffepublishers.com

Printed in Hong Kong by H & Y Printing, Ltd.

LIBRARY OF CONGRESS CATALOGING-IN-PUBLICATION DATA:
Rubinstein, Paul, 1961–.
　　The guide to Yellowstone and their discovery / by Paul Rubinstein, Lee H. Whittlesey and Mike Stevens.
　　　p. cm.
　　Includes bibliographical references
　　ISBN: 1-56579-351-X

　　1. Waterfalls—Yellowstone National Park—Guidebooks.
2. Yellowstone National Park—Guidebooks. I. Whittlesey, Lee H., 1950– II. Stevens, Mike, 1946– III. Title.

GB2423.R83 2000
551.48'4'0979447—dc21　　　　　　　00-027461

Cave Falls; Photo by Paul Rubinstein

While doing research for my book *The Spirit of Yellowstone,* I came upon the following passage in an 1897 Northern Pacific Railroad promotional pamphlet entitled *Wonderland '97:*

> *Yellowstone Park is the realm of the water-nymph. It revels in rills, mountain brooks, rivers, and lakes. It leaps about the cataracts, disports itself in the rapids, flits through the veils of spray that gracefully sway hither and thither, and haunts the hundreds of cool trout streams that wind from sunlight to shadow, from cañon to meadow. But it finds its chief delight in the waterfalls. And what wonder, when such cataracts, falls, and cascades are there. There is apparently no extended area in the park without them.*

The author of this piece, Olin D. Wheeler, revealed his own amazement and glee at finding such a number and concentration of waterfalls in Yellowstone National Park. Anyone who has driven through eastern Montana and Wyoming to the park knows of the seemingly endless, arid grasslands that must be crossed en route, and, after passing through such dry country, Yellowstone's well-watered landscape does seem to be a world apart, a wonderland.

Yellowstone may be the world's oldest national park, but, geologically speaking, it is a young landscape. Glaciers receded only recently from the Yellowstone plateau. Their imprint combined with ongoing volcanic activity has created a landscape in transition, where rivers and streams are active agents still shaping the land. Hence, from the perspective of geologic time, the waterfalls Mr. Wheeler described in 1897 are fleeting. Yet from the human perspective, Yellowstone's waterfalls are part and parcel of what makes the place unique.

In July 1997, 100 years after Olin Wheeler encouraged people to gaze upon Yellowstone's waterfalls, NASA landed the Pathfinder on Mars and Americans saw the Martian landscape. That same century brought changes that allowed us to gaze into the depths of space and time as well as into living cells the human body. And, with satellites constantly orbiting Earth and computers instantaneously digesting information, now we can know more about where we are and where we are going. There seems to be no limit to what we can see, where we can go, and even what we can explore, if only as virtual travelers. It is easy, therefore, to assume that there are no more blank spaces on the map to intrigue the curious and lure the adventurous. The known world and the unknown world seem, finally, to have merged.

"Not so!" say Paul Rubinstein, Lee Whittlesey, and Mike Stevens, who tell of their discovery of 240 heretofore unknown, unmapped, or unphotographed waterfalls in Yellowstone National Park in this book, *The Guide to Yellowstone Waterfalls and Their Discovery*. But how can this be? Yellowstone is one of the best known, most visited, and most studied landscapes on the planet. Surely, every nook and cranny of this grand old park has been poked, prodded, sampled, categorized, mapped, and photographed! How could so many waterfalls have remained "undiscovered" for so long?

One reason lies in the idea of "discovery." The title of "discoverer" is not necessarily bestowed on someone who sees something for the first time. A discoverer discloses information to others. Christopher Columbus was not the first to see America any more than Captain Cook was the first to see the Hawaiian Islands; there were already people living there. However, Columbus and Cook discovered these places for their culture and their people by making the places known, giving the places names, and drawing the places on a map. In the same way, Yellowstone's official discoverers, the men credited with discovering the region that was to become Yellowstone National Park, were not the first to see it. Native Americans had long occupied the region and scores of white men had hunted, trapped, and prospected for gold there. But Yellowstone's discoverers publicized the region and made it recognizable. Correspondingly, many of the waterfalls described in this book may have been seen by human eyes before, but Rubinstein, Whittlesey, and Stevens, made these waterfalls known to the public for the first time.

In the park's earliest years, there were few roads and most visitors wound their way haphazardly across the landscape. It is foolish to suggest that no one saw any of the waterfalls pictured and described in this book during those years. Similarly, scientists and park personnel have long collected data in the Yellowstone backcountry on a wide variety of topics touching every branch of scientific inquiry. How could these individuals not have stumbled on some of the waterfalls described here? But, because no one noted the existence or location of the waterfalls in their reports or in some other way publicized their existence, the waterfalls remained undiscovered until now. Hence, Rubinstein, Whittlesey, and Stevens can honestly be considered discoverers of some of the most incredible of Yellowstone's waterfalls: incredible in their size and beauty as well as the fact that they have remained hidden for so long.

The publication of this book comes at an exciting time in terms of our knowledge of planet Earth as well as our understanding of our relationship to it. Just months before this book on Yellowstone's waterfalls went to press, news arrived of the discovery of a long-sought-after but always elusive great waterfall on Tibet's Tsangpo River.[1] And, members of the National Geographic Society team who discovered the falls expressed the same sense of enthusiasm mixed with disbelief expressed by the Yellowstone waterfall team: "How could such a large natural feature remain hidden for so long?" News of this similar discovery yields two geographic lessons for our time. The first is that despite our sophisticated satellite imaging and computer mapping capabilities, without explorers down here on the ground to enter information into the system and interpret what comes out, geographic knowledge of our planet is, at best, incomplete. Second, from the far reaches of the Himalayas to the backyard of our own national parks, we still have much to uncover, to explore, and to learn! If natural features as grand and obvious as waterfalls still await our discovery in a public park hosting millions of people every summer, one can only imagine what we might find if we look carefully in our own backyards, on the outskirts of our towns, under the seas, or in places beyond earth. Of course, there is always the chance that with exploration and discovery will come exploitation and destruction, but let us hope we have learned from the past.

In 1873, a Yellowstone tourist named Edwin J. Stanley hiked with friends down steep canyon walls to reach the banks of the Yellowstone River. Of his reaching the bottom of the canyon, he wrote, "Proudly we walked along the banks of the river and slaked our thirst from the emerald-tinted stream, feeling that we were explorers in this region, and the first to set foot upon these mystic shores."[2] The desire to be first to do something or to discover something may be a characteristic of our humanness. We are intrigued by the novel and the new. It remains to be seen what impact the discovery of so many new waterfalls will have on our image of Yellowstone and our behavior toward it. Certainly, our understanding of the park's topography has improved, as has our ability to locate missing persons or simply navigate in the backcountry. The publication of this book, too, adds to our knowledge of the amazing features found in this unique place and why it is so important to protect and preserve it. If nothing else, this book should encourage each of us to look around with eyes wide open and realize there is still much to discover, much about which to wonder, and much to be the first to accomplish.

— DR. JUDITH L. MEYER
Geographer, Southwest Missouri State University

Silver Cord Cascade; Photo by Paul Rubinstein

ACKNOWLEDGMENTS

Iris Falls; Photo by Paul Rubinstein

In today's complex world, almost no one can produce a book without help from many other people, and we are no exception. It took years of Yellowstone hiking by many persons to amass the photographs for this book. While the three of us did the majority of hiking to produce this work, many others went along at various times and provided us with important information and support.

Paul Rubinstein and Mike Stevens took the majority of photographs however, others contributed various photos: Chris Benden and Julie Gayde Benden, Bob Berry, Darla Choquette, Reagan Grau, Tracey Jelly, Dr. John Landrigan, Joe Mangiantini, Rocco Paperiello, Zachary Park, David Rothenburger, Michelle M. Serio, Joanne Sides, James Spanglet, Josh Steele, Patrick Wherritt Jr., Lee Whittlesey, Steve Wiechmann, Jed Winkelman, and Mike Yochim.

A number of folks were kind enough to review the book and make valuable suggestions: Orville "Butch" Bach, Sue Consolo-Murphy, Dick Ferguson, Bob Flather, Bob Jackson, Steve Lieurance, Tom Mazzarisi, Dr. Judith Meyer, Andrew Mitchell, Betsy Schissel Mitchell, Tom Olliff, Rocco Paperiello, Leslie J. Quinn, Mike Ross, Paul Schullery, Michelle M. Serio, Joanne Sides, Bob Siebert, Dunbar Susong, and Mike Yochim.

Several others provided valuable information used in our book: John Alley, John Barber, Doug Berringer, Tom Carter, Collette Daigle-Berg, Bob Gresswell, Katarina Gvozdić, Stan Hoggatt, Rick Hutchinson, Kristen Legg, David Lentz, John Lounsbury, Dan Mahony, Sharon McGee, Jerry Mernin, Chuck Mohr, Lee Silliman, and John Varley.

The following people also participated in the field (some accompanying us and some on their own) that led directly to photographs and information in this book, and we thank them for their efforts: Dell Abelein, Anthony Akin, Stephanie Anderson, Washo Ashley, Jessica Baker, Dave Berry, John Billington, Kate Billington, Laura Caldwell, John Camp, Sara Clancey, Maureen Clifford, Karen Connelly, Ted Davenport, Jim Davidson, Michael DeWitt, Kirk Dietz, Dave Disney, Bill Dooley, Michael Doran, Sarah Dykes, David Fabricant, Josh Fahl, Matt Ferner, Jamie Foster, David Frahm, Melissa Frost, Charity Geffers, Stacey Graham, Leah Grossman, Julie Guarino, Jack Hade, Melissa Haslauer, Doug Hatfield, Julie Hecktmann, Kristina Hendrix, Scott Hensley, Claire Hilger, Kirk Hill, Sarah Hoadley, Shannon Holmes, Marek Hrebicek, Jennifer Huggins, Keith Humphrey, Tom Hurtzel, Garrett Jones, Matt Jordan, Cynthia Keller, Kurt Keller, Mike Keller, Debbie Kohn, Kristin Koutnik, Andy Krumm, Ryan Krymbourg, Chris Laninfa, Mark Lee, Mark Lehman, Phil Lerman, Brian Lesko, Gil Lesko, Linda Lesko, Chuck Mackie, Jen McArdle, Louise Mercier, Judith Metzger, Coy Miller, Ashea Mills, Ryan Morgan, Jeremy Muraski, Tom Murphy, Dennis Nervig, Treg Nichols, Dave Nixon, Jeanne Nuechterlein, Bill Patten, Brian Payne, Nels Peterson, Marc Phillips, Bruno Carmine Picinich, David Powell, Carissa Powley, Lee Ramella, Chris Reis, Celso Reyes, Gail Richardson, John Richardson, Dave Richerson, Brian Ronstadt, Greg Sandberg, Jane Saunders, Rick Saunders, George Shabel, Casey Sheehan, Joni Shenefield, Adina Smith, Angela Smith, Steven Smith, Marian Steffes, Danny Strong, Sarah Szofran, Kim "Rufus" Taylor, Matt Tekiela, Keri Thorpe, Tina Toth, Barbara Totschek, Tim Valentine, Chris Van De Ven, Aaron Vigneault, Melissa Vines, Evan Volk, Adam Wagner, Helyn Wallace, Pete Wardlow, Kristie Wiederholt, Geoff Wilson, Mindi Wilson, Wendy Winkelman, and Tracy Winter.

The following people were indirect contributors to the book: Colin J. Aro, Leslie Burgess, John Bunker, Katherine Doane, Courtney Fehn, Nettie Isaacson, Whitney Latham, Patty Lewallen, Wayne McNeely, Mary Miller, Lee Neel, Lenny Pawlak, Paul Rothenberg, Phil Thomas, and Phil Victoria.

And finally, we thank our parents: Pamela Marks, Bonnie Paull, Dr. Martin Rubinstein, Jim and Dolores Stevens, and Charles and Dorothy Whittlesey.

THIS BOOK IS DEDICATED TO RICK HUTCHINSON, Yellowstone explorer extraordinare, who saw many of these waterfalls while hiking alone, and who let his love of the place flow to everyone he touched.

TABLE OF CONTENTS

TABLE OF CONTENTS

Lower Falls; Photo by Paul Rubinstein

YELLOWSTONE MAP

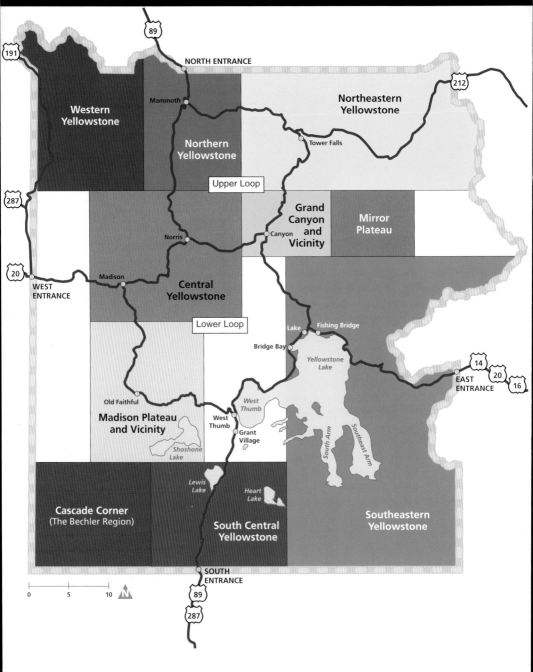

NORTH ENTRANCE

Western Yellowstone

Mammoth

Northern Yellowstone

Northeastern Yellowstone

Tower Falls

Upper Loop

Norris

Grand Canyon and Vicinity

Canyon

Mirror Plateau

Madison

WEST ENTRANCE

Central Yellowstone

Lower Loop

Lake

Fishing Bridge

Bridge Bay

Yellowstone Lake

EAST ENTRANCE

Old Faithful

Madison Plateau and Vicinity

West Thumb

West Thumb

Grant Village

Shoshone Lake

South Arm

Southeast Arm

Lewis Lake

Heart Lake

Cascade Corner
(The Bechler Region)

South Central Yellowstone

Southeastern Yellowstone

0   5   10

SOUTH ENTRANCE

"Mist of the Trident Falls;" Photo by Patrick Wherritt, Jr.

Waterfalls mesh with—indeed almost capture—our spirits in some wild, romantic way. In 1869, naturalist John Muir acknowledged this fact when he wrote of one of his favorite waterfalls: "The water does not seem to be under the dominion of ordinary laws, but rather as if it were a living creature, full of the strength of the mountains and their huge wild joy."[3]

"Enchantress Falls;" Photo by Mike Stevens

In writing this book, the three of us have confronted our collective senses of beauty, for beauty is what we think most people see in and love about waterfalls. There is a little-known word for this; it is "philocaly," which means "love of beauty." We believe this love of beauty is what drives the human desire to visit waterfalls.

Early visitors to Yellowstone agreed with this assessment. We have included many of their poetic, even musical, comments about the waterfalls they saw. It seems a shame those nineteenth century tourists did not see the many other waterfalls that Yellowstone had preserved in its deep fastnesses, for then we would have even more of their pastoral musings.

But they did not see them. Captivated by the geysers, the canyons, the lakes, the wild-flowers, and the animals, visitors did not seek out the waterfalls. Only a few of the park's waterfalls commanded attention. Even in the early 1920s, when W.C. Gregg and Jack Haynes found, protected, and promoted the numerous waterfalls in the park's Bechler region (Cascade Corner), most others remained undiscovered.

This book shows, describes, or mentions roughly 290 waterfalls. Until we started this project, common knowledge had it that Yellowstone housed only about 50 waterfalls. It is difficult to believe that, as late as 1999, nearly 240 of the falls remained essentially unknown; nevertheless it is so. A number of them are far from the park's main roads, far even from established trails. In many places in the world, any one of these idyllic natural features might be enough reason for an entire park. But here, in the "Wonderland of the World," most do not even have names. It is a comfort to know there are still places in our overdeveloped country that have not been claimed by mankind.

Why would so many world-class natural features remain undiscovered until the 1990s? There are numerous reasons:

• The Organic Act, signed by Ulysses S. Grant, took this large tract of land out of circulation very early. The preservation of Yellowstone in 1872 kept it forever free "from settlement, occupancy, or sale...for the benefit and enjoyment of the people." That ensured the lock-up of beauty and protected the features from the inevitable, gradual discovery by settlers, which would have occurred anywhere else.

• The place is geographically remote. Even today, the park remains far from urban centers.

• The area is huge, larger than some states. Travel around and through it even today is slow and not very complete; its road and trail system still covers only a small portion of it—less than one percent.

• It is locked in snow much of the year.

• Early explorations by Folsom, Washburn, Hayden, Jones, Ludlow, and Hague failed to cover the mass of the park; they simply missed a lot of features.

• The park's other attractions eclipsed its waterfalls. In a place with a surfeit of beauty, no one looked farther than "the ends of their noses." Why should they? There were so many other interesting features in Yellowstone.

• The park's backcountry system allows camping in designated sites only and restricts (or closes) other areas, thus limiting exploration to a significant degree.

But wait. Didn't anyone see these waterfalls from airplanes or helicopters over the years? Yes. A few folks did see some of them. Most of them failed, however, to write reports on the waterfalls they saw from the air, or photograph them, or even map them. It is truly unfortunate that these privileged individuals missed their chance at credit for their discoveries.

About the Waterfalls We Chose

The following text discusses approximately 290 waterfalls, and includes their heights, histories, and some early visitor reactions to them. All waterfalls previously documented by books, journals, diaries, maps, and photos are featured. Those falls with no previous documentation are listed only if they are at least 15 feet high and on permanent streams. Where two falls of less than 15 feet are located very close to each other, and together total 15 feet or more, we sometimes added them as a single feature if they seemed truly allied.

Dozens if not hundreds of falls and cascades that are less than 15 feet high are not included, although we have included a few of these shorter waterfalls where we have deemed that special circumstances (such as the existence of a historic name) warrant it. Also not included are the hundreds of Yellowstone waterfalls that are temporary. These exist in the spring and early summer on streams that originate mostly from snowmelt. Those streams usually dry up by mid-July or early August, and their waterfalls disappear. The many ephemeral streams that flow off the east side of Barronette Peak are good examples. Four seasonal falls we included are the beautiful, tall-but-temporary waterfalls that appear each spring from the plateau just west of Old Faithful, at the summit of Sylvan Pass, and two falls west of the Pebble Creek Campground on Pyramid Mountain (see "Unfaithful Falls," "Talus Falls," "Zephyr Falls," and "Tempest Falls"). Unfortunately, if we were to try to include all of these evanescent features, we would be dealing with what John Muir called "a thousand dashing waterfalls with their marvelous abundance of irised spray."[4]

Accurately judging whether a specific falls is permanent or seasonal can be a formidable task. Even if one were to view these falls for an entire year, a small number would appear to be seasonal in some years and permanent in others. Then too, even minor changes in climate can change a falls' status. We have selected the falls in this book based on our best guesses as to their current statuses.

Naming the Waterfalls

We have included all Yellowstone waterfalls with official names (about 50) and around 240 others that essentially never had names. For most of these latter falls, we use "working" names, which we indicate by placing them in quotation marks. With this many waterfalls, names are necessary in order to simply differentiate the features for our project. Can you imagine the difficulty of our task without these suggested names? ("Boy, waterfall number 56 is neat, but you really should see number 109!")

In some cases, our names are formulated from proximity to nearby natural features (e.g. "Robinson Canyon Falls"). In other cases, we chose names based upon our impressions (usually descriptive of the feature itself or its surroundings, or based upon the area's birds, beasts, plants, minerals), upon the long history of Yellowstone, or upon folklore, of which Yellowstone is an entrenched part.

Where place names are concerned, folklore has played an important historical role in Yellowstone. Place names such as Minerva Terrace, Prometheus Spring, Tantalus Creek, Undine Falls, Treasure Island, River Styx, and Narcissus Geyser represent only a few of the many park names that come from mythology and literature.

With our name proposals, we have to be careful to not only follow established history but also to make them as suitable as possible for a place as beautiful and magical as Yellowstone. This idyllic place evokes for us metaphorical comparisons

"Citadel of Asgard Falls;" Photo by Paul Rubinstein

to Shangri-La, the Garden of Eden, the Elysian Fields, Valhalla, Zion, Mount Olympus, and of course Heaven. It is a land full of wonders such as jagged mountains, "haunted" forests, clear blue and emerald green rivers, fields of flowers, and wild animals like "lions and tigers and bears." Like Oz, it has been called a land where your every wish can come true, whether it be for a brain, a heart, a home, or the courage. Its wonders, especially its heretofore-overlooked waterfalls, deserve beautiful, mythological, enchanted names. It is, after all, Yellowstone: the first national park in the world, cornerstone of conservation history, icon of wilderness preservation, linchpin of early tourist travel to the American West, and a member of the first family of mythical places. Thus we have tried hard to keep our suggested names within the framework of the history of names in Yellowstone and within the rules of the U.S. Board on Geographic Names (USBGN).

Long a tradition in Western America, discoverers or first documentors have the right to propose names. Members of the 1870 Washburn expedition knew this tradition well and gave names in recognition of it.[5] Dr. F.V. Hayden, one of the great surveyors of the American West and discoverer of many western land features, mentioned this fact in 1871:

> In attaching names to the many mountain-peaks, new streams, and other geographical localities, the discovery of which falls to the pleasant lot of the explorer in the untrodden wilds of the West, I have followed the rigid law of priority, and given the one by which they have generally been known...but if...no suitable descriptive name can be secured from the surroundings, [others] may then be attached.[6]

Roger Payne, chief of the USBGN, recently confirmed to us this history and tradition of first documentors and the giving of names. Of course only Yellowstone National Park itself has final authority to affirm names and submit them to the USBGN; our names are merely suggestions and the world has the right to ignore them. But as we thought of them, especially the names that evoke folklore and beauty, we were reminded over and over of how truly high Yellowstone is on the list of the world's most special places.

Some wilderness advocates hate the idea of official names in wilderness areas and love the idea of large spaces on maps where there are no names. While we sympathize with this idea in theory, a number of reality-based reasons illustrate why historians recognize that it will not and cannot work.

First, trying to leave a place unnamed usually causes it to become named in a de facto manner. When queried on the subject, our friend Paul Schullery, author of more than 25 books on Yellowstone and the West, noted to us that "bare spots" on the map are theoretically wonderful. But as soon as you try to consciously keep something unnamed, you've named it. It quickly becomes known as "The Bare Spot," "The Unnamed Area," "The Place With No Name," or something similar. Whether one likes it or not, once a place has come to someone's—anyone's—attention and there is a need to discuss it, it is going to be named. Existing examples are two Yellowstone streams: Unnamed Creek and No Name Creek.

The fact that trying not to give names often *causes* names, leads to our second argument: that trying to avoid giving names goes against American history and culture. In the history of the American West, discoverers (or first documentors) have always given names to unnamed places; if they did not do it consciously, they generally did it unconsciously simply by discussing such places. A place will be named one way or another, whether purposefully or through happenstance.

It is interesting to note that Yellowstone's caretakers have always named its natural features, beginning with the earliest park superintendents and employees. Starting in 1886, Army protectors chose names, then in 1916, Yellowstone rangers began the practice as well. Today, rangers routinely give names in Yellowstone—in their reports, on hand-drawn maps, and in backcountry logbooks. Anderson Mountain and Chaw Pass are two examples of ranger-given names now entrenched in local usage. While we sympathize with those who do not share our naming philosophy, we do not share their views on this sensitive subject.

The Discovery Process

While we do not claim to be the absolute discoverers of these waterfalls (we believe in a handful of cases that we may be), we do claim that many have never before been written about or photographed, and many more have never been mapped. How did we find so many new waterfalls? We looked at historical park maps and, in some cases, we found notations such as "falls" or "cascades." We read various U.S. Fish and Wildlife Service (USFWS) fishery reports. As those scientists surveyed streams for fish-study purposes, they often noted where waterfalls occurred, because waterfalls represent critical barriers to upstream fish migration. We interviewed many of those fishery researchers, read their reports, and looked at their hand-drawn maps. We spoke to park rangers and longtime employee-hikers who knew of unsung backcountry waterfalls. Finally, we examined park maps for relief lines and spent years hiking up streams where it looked as if there might be waterfalls.

How did we deal with the hundreds of permanent streams in the park that have no names but have many waterfalls on them? Using the park's System of Numbering Yellowstone Waters (SONYEW, originated by John Varley and the USFWS in the 1970s), we identified and occasionally proposed names for streams

Morning Falls; Photo by Mike Stevens

with significant waterfalls. Streams in the park that do not have names are generally assigned a number by the USFWS. We adopted this little-known but effective tracking system for our own.

How did we acquire our numerous photographs? The three of us worked on the project for more than seven years. We made repeated hikes to upgrade photos. Many of these treks were long, strenuous, difficult, and time-consuming without guarantees of better weather or complete success, which often led to multiple trips. We put ourselves into repeated precarious situations and positions that we would not suggest for anyone. We encountered trouble with weather, light and shadows, camera malfunctions, deadfall obstructions to the views, processing errors and precious rolls of film lost by developers, bad water-flow conditions, dangerous grizzly bear encounters, and failure to find some waterfalls on the first effort. In our photos, we try to offer a blend of familiar, traditional perspectives with more imaginative, ambitious views from different positions.

In particular, master-hiker Mike Stevens deserves credit for obtaining photos of some of the more distant locales. For example, he hiked three times for a total of 45 miles to get the photo we finally used for "Peterson Falls." He hiked into the Three River Junction area on six separate occasions in 1979, 1990, 1992, 1996, 1997, and 1999. The trips, which averaged 40 miles apiece, were largely rainy. He estimates that after six visits to this remote region, he still hasn't had more than a couple days of sunlight. In the end, we were not too proud to utilize the photographs of some very generous friends whom we have gratefully acknowledged.

How did we measure the heights of the previously unmeasured waterfalls? The short ones were simple: for some, we measured them with ropes or string. The taller ones were more difficult. Where we could not actually measure them because of difficulty of approach, the three of us, along with our numerous hiking partners, made "eyeball" estimates based upon our long experience in the park.

We should also clarify some definitions here. We believe that the words "waterfall" and "cascade" have long been used carelessly and sometimes interchangeably. Dictionary definitions make it clear that this is the case; there is not much delineation between the two words, and sometimes they are synonymous. Some of the established names of Yellowstone waterfalls even refer to falls as cascades and vice versa. In this book we try to make the two words mean entirely different things. We use waterfall to mean a plunge or a horsetail, while we use cascade to mean water flowing at an angle with too many small leaps or segments to count. Even with this plan, we have had difficulty being consistent.

Another problem we faced is that United States Geological Survey (USGS) maps do not make a clear distinction in their map marks between waterfalls and cascades. They use the terms "falls" and "rapids" for these and use one mark for falls and two marks for rapids. This is confusing where there is a sequence of such features, because when these marks are tightly grouped together, one cannot tell, for example, whether there are six falls or three rapids. In addition, these maps are not infallible; USGS topographers make errors just as the rest of us do.

The Effects of Discovery

What are the ramifications of revealing such features to the world? We certainly have had second thoughts about exposing some of these places to more visitors. It brings to mind Ashleigh Brilliant's humorous comment: "Why wasn't I told about this wonderful place, and how can I prevent others from discovering it?"[7] However, aside from the usual if-we-don't-do-it-someone-else-will sentiment, we think we may actually help the situation by adding to the record yet another reason (or 292 reasons!) why Yellowstone is one of the Earth's most special places and thus deserving of special protection. Control of public lands is continually up for grabs in America. Government policy will ultimately dictate what happens to pristine places in future years. We hope the revelation of these beautiful natural features will spur city dwellers, who need these places for mental health and restoration more than anyone else, to use every wherewithal to protect them—by voting for the environmental candidates rather than the developers, by yelling loudly whenever there are threats to these places, and by supporting the regulations of agencies such as the National Park Service (NPS) in their attempts to protect such places.

As Bill Schneider notes in his book *Hiking Yellowstone National Park,* some locals whisper that books like this are a bad idea because they reveal locations of backcountry features. He does not agree with that sentiment. Like Schneider, we believe that experienced backcountry users tend to have a loftier attitude about preserving wilderness than do inexperienced ones and that books like this help people become experienced. Moreover, inexperienced folks usually don't go to these places, especially the more difficult locations. As evidence, we note the dozens of Yellowstone's backcountry waterfalls that have been on park maps for more than 100 years, yet are rarely visited even today.

Some NPS employees also have reservations about a book such as this one. Like the locals, they fear the more people who know of such places, the more likely those places are to become spoiled. Frankly, a few irresponsible members of the public have given them good reason to fear this possibility. On the other hand, to quote one district ranger, the NPS is "not in the business of keeping secrets." There have been many occasions when heavy public support has actually resulted in better protection for sensitive places.

These debates within the NPS, between those who want to keep things secret and those who believe that public support actually helps protect special places, will no doubt continue. They illustrate the NPS's own dichotomous mandate: allow the public to use and enjoy park resources while simultaneously preserving them for future generations. It is an inherent conflict, and one that is reflected in the philosophies of two different NPS divisions: law enforcement rangers have a duty to protect park resources while interpretive rangers have a duty to give people information to aid in their use and enjoyment of park resources.

We subscribe to George Wuerthner's statement in his book *California's Wilderness Areas, Vol. 1:* "Most people will only defend something they believe is personally important, and without direct and repeated experience with our wild lands, people can't be expected to rally around the need to protect them." We believe our book will reinforce public perceptions regarding the need to preserve these special places. Our goal is to provide enjoyment through pictures and through the knowledge that these beautiful falls are out there in the wilderness, in their natural, untouched state. This comes under that area of appreciation known as "existence value": the waterfalls have value for their very existence even if one never sees them.

In 1920, when the Bechler region of Yellowstone was threatened by Idaho developers who wanted to inundate the entire Cascade Corner with a reservoir, a private individual named W.C. Gregg took it upon himself to explore the region, looking for specific reasons why the area should be preserved. He discovered dozens of waterfalls and thereafter spearheaded a drive to defeat the reservoir-developers by publicizing the place in national magazines such as *Saturday Evening Post* and *Outlook*. We want to align ourselves with the historic efforts of W.C. Gregg at a time when Yellowstone is similarly threatened by developers outside its boundaries. With our documentation of approximately 240 "new" waterfalls, it is clear that, now more than ever, we must all work together to protect this region that is home to many of Earth's most special wonders.

We would be fools to believe we have found every waterfall in Yellowstone. The park is too rich in such treasures. There are still dozens of streams that we ache to explore, canyons with rapids where we have told each other, "I'd bet a week's pay that there will be a waterfall on that stretch." Undocumented and unphotographed, they are still out there for anyone to discover. For all our efforts to bring the waterfalls and cascades to light, we have not affected one incredible aspect of Yellowstone—its mystique. If you find a waterfall in the park that is 15 feet high or higher, permanent, and largely vertical, please contact us at the Yellowstone Center for Resources, c/o Lee H. Whittlesey, P.O. Box 168, Yellowstone National Park, Wyoming 82190.

We like to think there is considerable magic in this book—magic in the first documentation of these wonderful features, magic in the beauty of the waterfalls themselves, magic in the new names proposed here, and (we hope) magic in your reactions. We are happy to share this magic with you. It is our desire that you will be able to value our book for its photographs and its stories. But we have also tried to create something you can relish for its historical and geographical contributions. Yellowstone is so rich in both of those aspects that perhaps you the reader will share our sense of discovery of these treasures.

Meriwether Lewis recorded for posterity how he felt at the time of his expedition's 1805 discovery of the Great Falls of the Missouri River. We relate closely to his description, for it mirrors the way we feel every time we find a new waterfall in Yellowstone: "To gaze upon this sublimely grand spectacle forms the grandest sight I've ever beheld . . . I wished that I might be enabled to give the enlightened world some just idea of this truly magnificent and sublimely grand object which has from the commencement of time been concealed from the view of civilized man."[8]

In a world rapidly becoming too urban, it is exciting to think that as late as 1999, most of these waterfalls remained hidden and unknown even to the most experienced Yellowstone backcountry hiker.

Yellowstone is too large, too wild, and too magical for anyone to ever know everything there is to know about it. One can spend a lifetime in the Grand Old Park and still see only small portions of the place.

And that is why we love it.

—PAUL, LEE, AND MIKE
1999
"Red Rock Cascade;" Photo by David Rothenburger

Maps

In this book, area maps showing waterfall locations introduce each region. The waterfalls shown on the maps correspond to their assigned numbers, which are given in the waterfalls headings and sometimes in the "factboxes" in boldface type within the text. Features 1–32 (The Frontcountry) are located within a mile of a paved highway. Features 33–250 (The Backcountry) all require some degree of hiking in order to view. Features 251–292 (Best of the Rest) are listed in Appendix A. Most of them have been documented previously in places such as aquatic reports or ranger logs, or have undoubtedly been seen by numerous backcountry hikers, but did not quite meet our criteria for inclusion in the main text.

All features on these maps appear in three colors. Features shown in blue represent those falls that have appeared in previous publications. Those features shown in red represent "new" and "rediscovered" falls. Although some of the "new" falls have certainly been visited over the years, to the authors' knowledge they have not previously appeared—either in writing or in photographs—in any books or magazines about Yellowstone National Park. The "rediscovered" falls are those features that have not appeared in any documentation since the late nineteenth century. Features 136–137 and 287–292 are rumored falls that the authors believe exist but have not yet been able to locate. They are shown on the maps in yellow.

Factboxes

An informational "factbox" accompanies each waterfall entry. Each factbox is divided into six sections:

1. LOCATION

Each waterfall's location is given in coordinates using the Universal Transverse Mercator system (UTM), which was developed by the National Imagery and Mapping Agency. These coordinates are based on estimates provided from research in the field and were not obtained using a Global Positioning System (although they may be plugged into GPS units), thus they are only approximate. They were hand-calculated using the 1986, 1987, and 1989 USGS 1:24,000 quadrangle series of Yellowstone National Park.

UTM numbers run along the borders of USGS 7½-minute and 15-minute maps. The 7½-minute map series is one of several standard series maps produced by the USGS. One inch on a 7½-minute map represents 2,000 feet on the ground. Paper prints of this series are approximately 22x27 inches. Roughly 80 individual quads make up the entirety of Yellowstone National Park.

2. FALL TYPE

There are three basic types of waterfalls and four modifiers of these three types described in this book. We have adopted these categories, with some modifications, from Gregory Plumb's *A Waterfall Lover's Guide to the Pacific Northwest*. Our descriptions refer to the predominant type for each feature, although some waterfalls may exhibit pieces of several types.

Plunge—Water free falls for some or all of its height without coming into contact with the underlying rock or is nearly vertical in its descent.

"Birdseye Falls;" Photo by Paul Rubinstein

Horsetail—Water descends rapidly down a near-vertical wall, continually maintaining some contact with the underlying rock.

Cascade—Water flows at an angle over a series of rocks or down a broad rock face with too many small leaps or segments to count. A cascade is often the result of a waterfall either eroding upstream or breaking down into smaller components through erosion.

FALL MODIFIERS

Fan—Water stays in contact with the underlying rock, but gets wider as it approaches the bottom of its descent.

Segmented—Falling water divides into two or more falling streams, the divisions sometimes increasing as the water approaches the bottom of the falls. The segments may themselves be classified separately.

Tiered—The length of the water's drop is broken into two or more distinct falls, one succeeding another down the drainage, and both or all are visible from a single vantage point. An upper limb of a tiered falls may be one type and a lower limb another.

Serial—Where the "limbs" of a tiered falls are not all visible from one vantage point, where limbs are separated from one another by a long run of stream, or where there are many limbs.

3. HEIGHT

All waterfall heights are given in feet. They are taken from previous documentation where available. Where no previous documentation exists, they were measured using rope and string or approximated.

4. STREAM

We have listed either the official stream name, our working or proposed stream name (in quotation marks), or where unnamed, the tributary system and drainage.

5. MAP

If a particular waterfall has appeared in any form on a documented map it is indicated. This documentation may have been by waterfall name, by the designation "falls" or "cascade," or by the standard waterfall tick mark. In cases of waterfalls that have appeared on multiple maps, we have included the official USGS 7½-minute quadrangle on which the waterfall is shown. If the waterfall has not appeared on any USGS quad, then the waterfall data will be from the most recent map on which it has been shown. If the particular waterfall has never been officially mapped in any form, it is listed as "unmapped."

6. ACCESS

Each waterfall has an accompanying icon indicating difficulty of access to view. The reader should be aware that these ratings can and do vary based on selected routes, weather conditions, and chosen vantage points. They are based solely on our experiences at each of these falls. The definitions are as follows:

The waterfall is accessible by car or a short walk. It can be seen with little difficulty.

An easy to moderate hike is required. The waterfall is visible from an established trail or a short off-trail excursion and is limited to relatively easy walking. The hike can be reasonably expected to take one day or less. (Ten miles or less round-trip.)

A moderate to difficult hike is required. Significant off-trail hiking or long distances are required to view these waterfalls. While they can be done as day-hikes, they may test the limits of even strong hikers. (Up to 20 miles round-trip.)

A multiple-day hike is most likely required. These waterfalls require appallingly long day-hikes or multiple days to view. Any off-trail hiking will be easy to moderate and navigation should not be extreme. (More than 20 miles round-trip.)

An extremely strenuous hike is assured. Severe or extensive off-trail hiking is required. Distances may not be lengthy, but the hiker will encounter slow travel, poor footing, extreme deadfall, swamps, deep fords, steep grades, or a combination of the above. Navigation will be difficult and terrain will pose special challenges.

The hike is not recommended. In these cases, very real and extreme dangers exist to the hiker. These hikes pose great risk to personal safety even when proper off-trail hiking techniques are followed to the letter. We do not advise travel to these waterfalls.

The access information to the right of the icon indicates whether the waterfall is visible "on-trail," or requires an "off-trail," hike to view. Please note that these designations refer to the waterfall's location, not to the entire hike. Also, some waterfalls designated as "off-trail" require a walk of 100 yards to view, while others demand miles of off-trail travel.

Additional location information is provided in the factboxes for "Part I: The Frontcountry," as this section generally includes the most accessible waterfalls in this book.

Naming Key

Officially and previously named waterfalls appear in the text without quotation marks:
   Cascade Falls

Unnamed waterfalls for which we are proposing names appear with quotation marks:
   "Unfaithful Falls"

Because many waterfalls listed in this book are off-trail, we believe that special pre-hike instructions are in order. Off-trail hiking in Yellowstone presents different challenges than routine on-trail hikes. Greatly varying conditions are assured and therefore extra preparation is required. Before setting out on any extended off-trail exploration, we strongly recommend the following:

Know exactly where you want to go. You would be surprised how many people get into trouble in the backcountry due to poor preparation. Hikers who are vague about routes or reference points can easily become disoriented, especially off-trail. Know your route before you leave.

Bring the best maps available. Always carry some kind of map on your hike. For mapped waterfalls we suggest the standard USGS 7½-minute quadrangles that are listed in the waterfall factboxes. If the feature you are attempting to view is unmapped, bring the corresponding topographic map(s) that covers the entire area you anticipate passing through.

Tell someone where you are going. The single most important thing you can do before attempting any type of off-trail trek in Yellowstone is to tell someone where you are going. Even better, show them on a map. If a friend knows your planned route, then park rangers may find you that much faster if you need assistance. We recommend going directly to the source and notifying a ranger at any park backcountry office about your plans. (Any park visitor center can direct you to the nearest backcountry office.) In addition, backcountry office personnel can provide current conditions for many backcountry areas of the park.

Have a group of at least four for off-trail travel. Conditions will vary to a great degree once you leave the trail. By having at least four people in your party, should a group member become incapacitated for any reason, two can go for help while one stays behind with the injured party. Also, you virtually eliminate the chances of a dangerous grizzly bear encounter.

Carry the proper items. The following list is what the authors carry on day-hikes when searching for new waterfalls. We have had to use every item on this list and strongly recommend bringing all of them. Obviously, extended backpacking trips will require additional resources. This is only a day-hike checklist.

1. **Compass**—With few reference points once you are in deep forest, this is the first item to have on any hiking list.

2. **USGS 7½-Minute Topographic Map(s)**—As stated previously, at least one group member should carry all maps needed and have studied them thoroughly beforehand.

3. **Food**—Bring more than you think you'll need. Fatigue creeps up slowly. We find that if you snack continually rather than eating a big meal your stamina will stay consistent.

4. **Water**—Drink all day, even if you are not thirsty. Dehydration is common at high altitudes.

5. **Water Filter**—Never drink unfiltered water in the Yellowstone backcountry. No creek or river is a sure thing. Bacteria are present in Yellowstone's streams. It's better to play it safe. Plus, you are virtually guaranteed to never run out of water.

6. **Raingear**—Yellowstone's weather is never predictable. Always bring rain protection no matter what the forecast or how good the sky looks.

7. **River Fording Shoes**—We prefer rubber, tight-fitting "aqua boots."

8. **Insect Repellent and Mosquito Netting**—This is especially important in the month of June when falls are full. The mosquitoes can be horrendous.

9. **Head Protection**—We've seen the strongest hikers wilt under continuous hours of direct mountain sunlight. Wear a hat or cap of some type.

10. **Flashlight**—Walking speed can be very difficult to predict for off-trail hikes. Often the hiker runs out of daylight with just a few miles to go. Having one or several flashlights in your group can mean the difference between getting to the car a bit late or spending a cold, uncomfortable night in the woods.

11. **Space Blanket**—If you become lost in the back-country, a space blanket could save your life. On many summer nights, temperatures in Yellowstone drop to near or below freezing. Without some protection from the cold, hypothermia is almost assured.

Dunanda Falls; Photo by Paul Rubinstein

12. **First-Aid Kit**—Obviously you want to have some remedies for cuts and bruises. Even more common in the backcountry are blisters. Always carry Band-Aids and/or moleskin for blisters or they may quickly become severe.

13. **Extra Batteries**—Extra flashlight and camera batteries are always a good idea. We have had to use both on several occasions.

14. **Sunscreen**—Sunburn can be a problem in the thin air of Yellowstone. Sunscreen should be used liberally and often.

PART I: The Frontcountry

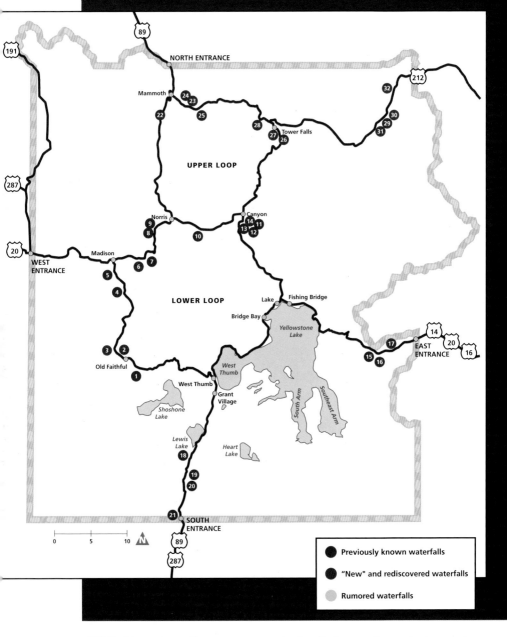

While "frontcountry" may not appear in the dictionary, those who love and enjoy Yellowstone are familiar with the term. For our purposes, frontcountry means those parts of Yellowstone within a mile from a paved, main road. Most of the waterfalls listed in "Part I: The Frontcountry" are accessible by automobile and/or a short, easy, popular walk.

1 KEPLER CASCADES

LOCATION: 515460 4921222

FALL TYPE: Tiered Cascade

HEIGHT: 100–150 feet

STREAM: Firehole River

MAP: Old Faithful, Wyoming - 1986

ACCESS: 2.7 miles east of the Old Faithful Interchange between Old Faithful and West Thumb. Overlook and parking available.

Mike Stevens

This enchanting tier of cascades and waterfalls above Old Faithful was named in 1881 by park superintendent P.W. Norris for Kepler Hoyt, a twelve-year-old boy who toured Yellowstone that year with his father, Governor John Hoyt of Wyoming Territory.

In 1870, members of the Washburn party passed the cascades. Lt. G.C. Doane wrote: "These pretty little falls if located on an eastern stream would be celebrated in history and song; here amid objects so grand as to strain conception and stagger belief, they were passed without a halt."[9]

Later visitors found the falls equally lovely and did stop for a look. William M. Thayer, probably in 1887, thought they were "really quite bewitching in their loveliness, the harmony of the picture leaving nothing to be desired, as the romantic is here picturesquely perfect, the colors of the vegetation on the rocks in contrast to the foaming water delighting the eye. The visitor reluctantly leaves this idyllic spot."[10]

An 1894 visitor described them as follows: "In the dark denseness of a pine forest Kepler's Cascades, a series of ten or more falls foam through a rocky rent, until their wild white witchery blends with the blackness of the pine-gorge below."[11]

2 CASCADE FALLS

Paul Rubinstein

LOCATION: 512470 4924431

FALL TYPE: Plunge/Cascade

HEIGHT: 5 feet

STREAM: Firehole River

MAP: "Map of the Upper Geyser Basin" - 1872

ACCESS: 1.1 miles west/northwest of the Old Faithful Visitor Center in Upper Geyser Basin adjacent to East Sentinel Geyser. No auto access; walk is required to view.

Although the effective height of this waterfall is only five feet and normally would not meet our criterion for height, it is included here because the name is an old and accepted one. In 1871, Captain John Barlow noticed this waterfall, located on the Firehole River on an eastern split of the stream just above East and West Sentinel Geysers. Barlow noted "the rapids here are 200 yards in length, with a fall of 30 feet," and those rapids are probably the reason for the name Cascade Falls.[12] Gustavus Bechler seems to have given the name to the "falls" in 1872, for his map of that year, published in the Earl of Dunraven's book *The Great Divide,* shows "Cascade Falls 25 ft." Little noticed by most park visitors, this small falls is easily viewed because it is so close to the Morning Glory-Artemisia Trail.

In giving their height figures, it appears Barlow and Bechler were talking about the entire loss in elevation of the river. One version of Bechler's 1872 map includes the notation "Cascade Falls, 25 feet, in 250 feet of run."[13]

3 UNNAMED FALLS SOUTHWEST OF BISCUIT BASIN "Unfaithful Falls"

LOCATION: 510320 4924426

FALL TYPE: Plunge/Cascade

HEIGHT: 100+ feet

STREAM: Unnamed Tributary of the Little Firehole River

MAP: Unmapped

 ACCESS: 2.8 miles north/northwest of the Old Faithful Interchange between Old Faithful and Madison Junction Visible on cliffs to the west from Biscuit Basin and vicinity.

Mike Stevens

This peculiar falls is one of the few seasonal or temporary waterfalls presented in such detail. We include it because it is seen annually by thousands of park visitors and because it exhibits curious behavior.

Located just west of the village of Old Faithful, the falls is easily visible from the park's main road near Biscuit Basin on a short-lived branch of the Little Firehole River, and most prominent in late June and early July. It is substantial in both height and beauty, dropping for at least 100 feet and then cascading for a great deal more. Sometime between 1989 and 1992, area employee Mike Stevens began referring to it as "Unfaithful Falls" for its proximity to Old Faithful and because it is temporary.

Around the same time, Paul Rubinstein noticed a peculiar aspect of the falls. He wondered why it did not seem to flow during the height of spring runoff but instead appeared later in the snowmelt season. He questioned whether or not there was some sort of natural "valve" that diverted the water elsewhere earlier.

Stevens then expanded on this natural valve theory based on the glacial dam thought to have once diverted the waters of Yellowstone Lake into the drainage of the Snake River. In 1995, he hiked up the unnamed stream to try to settle the matter. About two-thirds of the way between "Unfaithful Falls" and Summit Lake, he found a spot where the stream's flow constricted into a narrow streambed. This critical spot was in deep shade where the forest pinched together. He believes this shade preserves a seasonal "snow dam," which does not usually melt until mid-June. Only at that time does the stream begin to flow to the northeast, thus creating the abrupt appearance of "Unfaithful Falls."

4 CASCADES OF THE FIREHOLE

Mike Stevens

LOCATION: 511515 4940171

FALL TYPE: Tiered Cascade

HEIGHT: 20 feet

STREAM: Firehole River

MAP: Lower Geyser Basin, Wyo. - 1986

ACCESS: 2.3 miles south of Madison Junction between Old Faithful and Madison Junction. Best viewed from Firehole Canyon Drive.

This popular, tumbling series of cascades is located at the head of Firehole Canyon, just below an island used as a camping spot by Yellowstone's earliest visitors. These cascades are easily seen by visitors at the end of the one-way Firehole Canyon Drive.

Cascades of the Firehole seem to have been so designated in 1879 by park super-intendent P.W. Norris, but others wrote about them as well. Topographer Frank Bradley mentioned the Firehole Canyon in 1872 and noted that it contained "two long successions of rapids, with many points of artistic beauty."[14] A 1908 traveler stated that these cascades were "energetic and tossed and foamed with a vigor highly attractive."[15]

5 FIREHOLE FALLS

LOCATION: 510858 4941739

FALL TYPE: Plunge

HEIGHT: 40 feet

STREAM: Firehole River

MAP: Madison Junction, Wyoming - 1986

ACCESS: 1.5 miles south of Madison Junction on Firehole Canyon Drive between Old Faithful and Madison Junction. Overlook and parking available.

Mike Stevens

No one knows who actually named Firehole Falls, but members of the 1872 Hayden Survey took note of it. Dr. Frank Bradley wrote that the river "for about five miles above its mouth . . . passes through a succession of small cañons with precipitous walls, which render the stream inaccessible in most places. At one point there is a fine fall of about thirty feet." Dr. A.C. Peale also saw this waterfall, calling it "a very fine fall of about forty feet" located "in a gloomy gorge."[16] Peale's height figure was more accurate than Bradley's.

The falls is located in the spectacular Firehole Canyon, a place characterized by jumbled cliffs of rhyolite breccia. Motorists can easily see this 40-foot drop of the Firehole River from a turnout and parking area on the Firehole Canyon Drive. Numerous unnamed cascades are also visible downstream.

6 GIBBON FALLS

LOCATION: 518230 4944351

FALL TYPE: Horsetail/Fan

HEIGHT: 84 feet

STREAM: Gibbon River

MAP: Madison Junction, Wyo. - 1986

ACCESS: 4.7 miles east/northeast of Madison Junction between Madison Junction and Norris Junction. Overlook and parking available.

William Henry Jackson and John Merle Coulter of the second Hayden Survey discovered this waterfall of the Gibbon River in 1872. Its name seems to have come into general usage from the river; by 1877, park superintendent P.W. Norris was using it.[17] In addition, several early park maps used the name "First Cañon Falls."

Gibbon Falls from its original viewpoint

Mike Stevens

In those early park days, travelers viewed Gibbon Falls from the east side, as the stagecoach road passed that way and then dropped steeply to nearby Canyon Creek. In celebration of those early visitors, our photo is taken from the same vantage point on the east side, as the water drops over the rim of the park's ancient caldera.

For such a commonly viewed and striking waterfall, Gibbon Falls seems to have had few poetic reactions written about it. In 1895, road engineer and historian Hiram Chittenden called it "a water-fall of very irregular outline, but withal one of much beauty."[18] Dr. A.C. Peale noted in 1872 that the stream "strikes upon a sloping ledge of rock and is shot out at an angle of about 45 degrees. The scene is the more impressive from the fact that it bursts upon the view so unexpectedly, and without the least warning . . ."[19]

In 1889, Private Lewis of A Troop, First Cavalry, Ft. Yellowstone, bet his fellow soldiers $800 that he could scale the cliff at Gibbon Falls 10 times in 10 hours. The soldiers took him up on the wager and he "commenced his trial at once." He accomplished his feat and won his money in four hours and forty-nine seconds.[20]

7 UNNAMED FALLS DOWNSTREAM FROM GIBBON FALLS

ACCESS: *3.8 miles east of Madison Junction between Madison Junction and Norris Junction*
Alert motorists will easily spot this 20-foot waterfall from the main road at a point about one-half mile below the picnic area at Gibbon Falls. Its stream emerges as a cold spring from the bluff called Earthquake Cliffs and runs for perhaps a few dozen yards before dropping into the Gibbon River on the south side of that stream. From the road, it appears as if the water springs up at the brink, however, this is not so. The unnamed spring-fed stream has several sources.

The majority of the water bursts out of solid rock in the cliff face behind and to the west of the falls. That ultimate source forms a steep descent of its own of 13 or 14 feet.

8-9 GIBBON RIVER RAPIDS

LOCATION LOWER (#8):
520795 4950755

LOCATION UPPER (#9):
521017 4950872

FALL TYPE: Serial Cascades

HEIGHT: 50 feet (in two drops)

STREAM: Gibbon River

MAP: Norris Junction,
    Wyoming - 1986

ACCESS LOWER: 2.7 miles south of Norris Jct. between Madison Jct. and Norris Jct. No formal viewpoint; parking in roadside pullouts only.

ACCESS UPPER: 2.3 miles south of Norris Jct. between Madison Jct. and Norris Jct. No formal viewpoint; parking in roadside pullouts only.

Lower Gibbon River Rapids   Mike Stevens

Gibbon River Rapids, located between Elk Park and Gibbon Meadows, is a two-part cascade (#8, #9) with the sections separated

Upper Gibbon River Rapids   Paul Rubinstein

Gibbon River Rapids ("Falls") and
Gibbon Falls ("First Canon Falls")

by about one-quarter mile. The rapids are directly alongside the Madison-Norris Road, but shielded by a natural line of trees. Even with a large turnout present, they are generally overlooked.

Formerly called "Gibbon Cascades" and "Mushroom Cascades," they appeared on park maps by 1880. By 1939, the names changed to Gibbon River Rapids. The interesting balanced pedestal rock in their midst is called Duck Rock.[21]

10 VIRGINIA CASCADE

LOCATION: 527914 4950947

FALL TYPE: Cascade

HEIGHT: 60 feet

STREAM: Gibbon River

MAP: Norris Junction, Wyo. - 1986

ACCESS: 2.7 miles east of Norris Junction between Norris Junction and Canyon Village. Visible only from Virginia Cascade Drive; entrance is 1.4 miles east of Norris Junction.

As early as 1880, park superintendent P.W. Norris appears to have named this cascade "Norris Falls" for himself. In 1886, the sloping beauty received its current name from Ed Lamartine, the foreman in charge of building the first road through the area. That same year Charles Gibson's new company, the Yellowstone Park Association, took over the hotels in the park; Lamartine chose the name for Virginia Gibson, wife of Charles. The name probably survived because geologist Arnold Hague had long liked the idea of naming Yellowstone Park features for states of the union. The feature today is one of only two park features that uses the name of a state (the other is Wyoming Creek).[22]

Early visitors who passed Virginia Cascade on the dusty stage road were entranced by the feature. "Virginia Cascades, seen from the lower end of the canyon," wrote G.L. Henderson in 1888, "reflects the light like a mirror, and is one of the most beautiful subjects for the artist in the whole Park."[23] Traveler Flora Chase Pierce passed the spot on August 8, 1897: "Here the Virginia Cascades fall in a gradual slant for 75 ft. I never saw anything like them."[24] These visitors saw the falls from its base, still the best vantage point.

Paul Rubinstein

11 LOWER FALLS OF THE YELLOWSTONE RIVER

LOCATION: 539977 4951546

FALL TYPE: Plunge

HEIGHT: 308 feet

STREAM: Yellowstone River

MAP: Canyon Village, Wyo. - 1986

ACCESS: Roughly 1.5 miles south of Canyon Village. Many viewpoints on both sides of the canyon; best view is at Artist Point, at the end of South Rim Drive; parking available.

David Rothenburger

This cataract, long believed to be the park's tallest at 308 feet, is also one of the great waterfalls of the North American continent. It has had more words written about it than any other park waterfall. Nearly half the historic visitor reactions to Yellowstone waterfalls we collected were written about Lower Falls and its upstream companion, Upper Falls.

A note in William Clark's journal of his famous 1803–07 expedition stated that the Yellowstone River had "a considerable fall" somewhere in the mountains. Clark then wrote "No" after it, an indication that even he did not believe what he had heard.[25]

But the waterfall was real. Native Americans had probably seen it for years. We may never know what Euro-American first looked upon it, but French fur trapper Baptiste Ducharme claimed to have seen Lower Falls in 1824, 1826, and 1839.[26] Explorers Jim Bridger and James Gemmell visited the falls in 1846. In 1851, Bridger drew a map for Father Jean DeSmet that showed "Falls 250 feet."[27]

Traveling prospectors of the 1860s brought stories back to Montana Territory of a huge waterfall on the Yellowstone River that appeared in frontier newspapers. One such article claimed the falls was "thousands of feet" high while another said it was 1,500 feet and called it "the most sublime spot on earth."[28]

The 1869 Folsom expedition gave the name to both of the great Yellowstone waterfalls from their positions on the river, and attempted to measure their heights. Their map carried the notation "Lower Falls 350 ft."[29] However, early visitors also referred to it as the "Great Fall" or "Grand Fall" of the Yellowstone.

A notch in the riverbed causes the green color of the water that extends partway down from the top of the falls. This allows the river to retain some of its green color instead of immediately breaking into spray. In 1872, Dr. A.C. Peale mentioned this green streak was present at that time.[30]

Howard O'Neill, in 1871, thought the fall was a thousand feet high:

> What bewildering admiration filled my soul as I gazed down upon this horribly beautiful cataract! Here the entire Yellowstone, with a contracted breadth of from fifty to seventy yards, falls through 'the wings of the winds,' in a clear perpendicular pitch of at least one thousand feet! But the depth from this western side of the falls appears immeasurable. A thousand fleeting shapes of spray and mist arise and glitter in the sunlight, giving birth to rainbow hues, which, in their tremulous changes, and aided but slightly by fancy, disclose arches of triumph, butterflies, birds, flowers, fairy figures, fireworks—in fact, every form and figure of beauty is embraced in this sublime natural panorama, which through all the bygone centuries has lavished its dazzling maze of beauty unseen and undreamt-of by civilized man.[31]

Many early visitors were inspired to write poetically about Lower Falls:

> . . . We almost felt we were trespassing on sacred ground.
> —EDWIN J. STANLEY, 1873.[32]

> As if preparing for its second leap, the river comes surging and tumbling in waves and eddies towards the brink. Advancing and prancing, and glancing, and dancing. Recoiling, turmoiling, and toiling, and boiling, until, almost at the edge, it unites into one glassy mass curved downward, soon separating into spray, and ending in a light vapor that floats down the valley, clothing the rocks with a soft green moss.
> —THOMAS E. SHERMAN, 1877.[33]

> . . . when nature is bent upon producing a masterpiece, where is the limit?
> —A PILGRIM, 1886.[34]

> . . . I felt that I had been permitted to enjoy visions of Paradise.
> —A PILGRIM, 1886.[35]

> The ragged edges of the precipice tear the water into a thousand streams—all united together, and yet apparently separate,—changing it to the appearance of molten silver.
> —DAVID FOLSOM, 1869.[36]

> No stereoscopic view, pencil sketch, or printed page can convey adequate conception; actual view alone ensures it, but once seen, vivid remembrance of them can only fade in death.
> —P. W. NORRIS, 1875.[37]

There is nothing in nature as beautiful as falling water, and here is its ultimate expression, its finest picture, its very climax.
—F. DUMONT SMITH, 1908.[38]

. . . From its foot, like incense before an altar of silver, rises the mist eternally.
—JOHN ATWOOD, 1898.[39]

The rainbows gleamed and vibrated in the clouds that arose from the falls and fell in great drops like summer showers as in atomized vapor, like the white robes of an angel fluttering in the wind.
—G.L. HENDERSON, 1887.[40]

. . . your head will swim and grow dizzy . . .
—DR. WAYLAND HOYT, 1878.[41]

Great White Falls, thunder forth thy song of triumph!
—MODE WINEMAN, 1908.[42]

All agreed that it was the most glorious spot on earth . . .
—SAMUEL HAUSER, 1870.[43]

12 UPPER FALLS

Paul Rubinstein

LOCATION: 539696 4950973

FALL TYPE: Plunge

HEIGHT: 109 feet

STREAM: Yellowstone River

MAP: Canyon Village, Wyo. - 1986

 ACCESS: Roughly 2.0 miles south of Canyon Village. Several viewpoints available; best view is at Uncle Tom's Trail parking area, overlook of Upper Falls.

Upper Falls, the upstream of the two most famous Yellowstone cataracts, is 109 feet high. Jim Bridger himself was familiar with this falls, as old-timer James Gemmell has stated that in 1846, he and Bridger visited it.[44]

After he visited the spot in 1864, prospector John C. Davis wrote what is probably the earliest recording of a person's impressions of the falls: "The full grandeur of the scene did not burst on me at once. Men who have engaged in a hand-to-hand struggle for a frontier existence lose sentiment after a few years; but when I realized the stupendous leap of the water, I could not help being impressed."[45]

N.P. Langford and Cornelius Hedges of the 1870 Washburn party saw Upper Falls from what became the lower vantage point to the north side of the falls, a spot no longer accessible. They made their way down

> . . . to this table rock, where we sat for a long time. As from this spot we looked up at the descending waters, we insensibly felt that the slightest protrusion in them would hurl us backwards into the gulf below. A thousand arrows of foam, apparently aimed at us, leaped from the verge, and passed rapidly down the sheet. But as the view grew upon us, and we comprehended the power, majesty, and beauty of the scene, we became insensible to danger and gave ourselves up to the full enjoyment of it.[46]

Hedges wrote two descriptions of Upper Falls, one in his diary and the other for a newspaper after he returned to Helena, Montana. For the newspaper, Hedges effervesced:

> Here we could look up into the foaming, furious jaws of the cataract, from whence would shoot out fierce, crested tongues, as if in wrath aimed to consume the beholder. The view at first is almost terrifying, and makes one's knees knock together in conscious impotence. But these watery arrows seemingly shot at the beholder, by a graceful curve bend beneath his feet to be quenched upon the stony buckler of the river's bed. Human ingenuity could not suggest a better point of view than is here presented to gather in all at once the beauty, majesty, and power of all the parts of a waterfall.[47]

The Upper Falls, occasionally called "Lesser Falls" in early park days, does not own the large number of early reactions that visitors recorded about Lower Falls, but here is one that is lovely:

> . . . we stand upon the platform at the falls, and raise our eyes to such a scene as no other spot on earth can give. Language is but a clumsy thing with which to paint the glories of this wonderplace. The richest pigments of artists of largest fame have failed; and while men have smiled at the flaming canvas, and said, 'It is impossible,' the baffled painter has grieved that his poor brush had failed to tell half the story of this exceeding loveliness.
>
> —ALMON GUNNISON, 1883.[48]

13 CRYSTAL FALLS

LOCATION: 539547 4951380

FALL TYPE: Three-step Plunge/Fan

HEIGHT: 129 feet (total)

STREAM: Cascade Creek

MAP: Crystal Falls, Wyoming - 1986

ACCESS: Roughly 1.8 miles south of Canyon Village. Several viewpoints available; most accessible viewpoint is at Uncle Tom's Trail parking area, overlook of Upper Falls.

Mike Stevens

You can see this striking, three-step waterfall of Cascade Creek from Uncle Tom's Point if you look north of Upper Falls. Cornelius Hedges of the Washburn expedition named it Crystal Falls in 1870. N.P. Langford of that party described it:

> Near the foot of the gorge the creek breaks from fearful rapids into a cascade of great beauty. The first fall of five feet is immediately succeeded by another of fifteen, into a pool as clear as amber, nestled beneath overarching rocks. Here it lingers as if half-reluctant to continue its course, and then gracefully emerges from the grotto, and, veiling the rocks down an abrupt descent of eighty-four feet, passes rapidly on to the Yellowstone. It received the name of "Crystal." [49]

The pool above the falls was noticed early and named Grotto Pool by park superintendent P.W. Norris, probably from Langford's description above. Captain John Barlow saw the pool in 1871: "One of these little falls drops into a cavern nearly concealed by overhanging cliffs, thence descending from a low ridge of rocks into a pool of great depth. A portion of the water passes through a crevice, or small tunnel, and darts out through the main fall of the cascade below, giving it a most singular appearance." [50]

Dr. A.C. Peale noticed that Crystal Falls was comprised of three distinct, tiered falls and measured it at 129 feet.[51]

But it was Superintendent Norris who really put Crystal Falls "on the map" by making it the subject of some of his poetry. Norris sometimes referred to the feature as "Triple Falls," from its three drops, and he wrote several paeans to it:

> Never more do I wish to leave it,
> My lovely last retreat,
> Evermore be this my music,
> And here my winding sheet.[52]

Norris was enamored of this place with its pinnacles, rainbows, deep mists, cascading waters, and the amber depths of Grotto Pool:

> Skipping rill from snowy fountains
> Dashing through embow'red walls,
> Fairy dell 'mid frowning mountains,
> Grotto pool and Crystal falls.[53]

In another stanza he gave us his alternative name for the falls:

> Where the halo's quivering shadows,
> O'er the Triple Falls,
> Tint the canyon, where wild waters
> Echo long its walls.[54]

By reading between the lines in Norris's book *Calumet of the Coteau* (1883), we can discern that the Crystal Falls area was the place he loved most in Yellowstone, a potential final resting place "if in this wild region it be mine to fall." Although Norris was buried in Michigan, his poetry and text embody that idea.

14 UNNAMED CASCADE BELOW RED ROCK POINT "Red Rock Cascade"

LOCATION: 540617 4951729

FALL TYPE: Cascade

HEIGHT: 200–250 feet

STREAM: Big Spring Creek

MAP: Unmapped

ACCESS: Roughly 1.6 miles south of Canyon Village. Visible from several points along canyon's south rim; most convenient viewpoint is at the bottom of Uncle Tom's Trail; moderate walking required to view.

Just below Lower Falls, this cascade of the Grand Canyon of the Yellowstone is seen annually by hundreds if not thousands of Yellowstone's visitors. However, it is another example of a waterfall completely overshadowed by other, more noticeable waterfalls around it. It careens steeply into the Grand Canyon of the Yellowstone from the north, about 300 yards downstream from the base of Lower Falls. The horsetail, ribbon-shaped falls takes on a rope-like appearance as its water level lowers in late summer.

Set amidst some of the most brilliant colors in the entire Grand Canyon of the Yellowstone, "Red Rock Cascade" takes on the appearance of a painting when viewed downriver from the bottom of the Uncle Tom's Trail.

Despite its prominence in a popular area of the park, this striking waterfall has never been named, although park superintendent P.W. Norris did name Big Spring Creek for its origin from a large "cold pure-water spring." We use the name "Red Rock Cascade" (originally suggested as "Red Rock Falls" by ranger David Rothenburger in 1997) for its location adjacent to the prominent landmark known as Red Rock. That tall pinnacle below Lower Falls, colored red by oxides of iron, is a well-known formation in the canyon. "Red Rock Cascade" cannot be observed from the Red Rock vantage point of Lower Falls, but instead must be viewed from the canyon's southern side.

David Rothenburger

15 CRECELIUS CASCADE

LOCATION: 568538 4924028

FALL TYPE: Two-tiered Cascade/Plunge

HEIGHT: 75 feet

STREAM: Unnamed Tributary of Eleanor Lake

MAP: Sylvan Lake, Wyoming - 1989

ACCESS: 7.7 miles west of the East Entrance and 18.3 miles east of Fishing Bridge Junction. Visible from the highway to the south on the eastern edge of Eleanor Lake.

Mike Stevens

A few hundred yards south of the East Entrance Road at the east end of Eleanor Lake is a delicate, double waterfall. Together, the two plunges are at least 75 feet high and visible from the main road. The feature was named in about 1901 by road engineer Hiram Chittenden for his construction foreman, S.F. Crecelius. Crecelius was directly responsible for this section of park road, built in 1901, which replaced a trail through Sylvan Pass.

Later, Crecelius Cascade became known as "Eleanor Cascade" and "Leonora Falls,"[55] perhaps for a character in Beethoven's "Fidelio" or Verdi's "Il Trovatore." Still later the name "Snow Fall" was used, but the name Crecelius has priority by virtue of age.[56]

16 UNNAMED FALLS AT SYLVAN PASS
"Talus Falls"

LOCATION: 569366 4923474

FALL TYPE: Horsetail/Cascade

HEIGHT: 100 feet

STREAM: Unnamed Tributary of Middle Creek

MAP: Unmapped

ACCESS: 7.0 miles west of the East Entrance and 19.0 miles east of Fishing Bridge Junction. Visible from the highway to the south at Sylvan Pass; seasonal only.

Mike Stevens

"Talus Falls" is seasonal, but it is seen by so many park visitors that we include it here. Located at the top of Sylvan Pass on the south side of the East Entrance Road, it is at least 100 feet high. It originates from an unnamed cliff at the top of Sylvan Pass and immediately disappears into talus at its base, hence its suggested name. In geology, "talus" is a sloping pile of rock fragments at the foot of a cliff.

The creek of "Talus Falls" is probably a tributary of Middle Creek, which most likely enters that stream subterraneously. Although prominent, this falls is short lived, lasting a few weeks in spring/summer until mid to late June.

17 UNNAMED FALLS EAST OF SYLVAN PASS "Sylvan Falls"

LOCATION: 574131 4924179

FALL TYPE: Plunge

HEIGHT: 20 feet

STREAM: Unnamed Tributary of Middle Creek

MAP: Unmapped

ACCESS: 3.8 miles west of the East Entrance and 20.9 miles east of Fishing Bridge Jct. Large roadside pullout on north side of the highway; obstructed view available from road.

Paul Rubinstein

This charming plunge lies on an unnamed stream, located on the north side of the main road about one mile east of Sylvan Pass. Although the falls faces south, it is in a narrow canyon and remains in shadows much of the time due to thick forests of spruce and fir. We initially thought it should be called "Shady Falls" for that reason, but then settled on "Sylvan Falls" because the trees are what shade it. It is also adjacent to Sylvan Pass, so the name seems doubly appropriate. A roadside pull-out at the bottom of this falls gives obstructed-view access to it. The best views require a short but difficult, steep scramble.

18 LEWIS FALLS

LOCATION: 529012 4901443

FALL TYPE: Cascade

HEIGHT: 30 feet

STREAM: Lewis River

MAP: Lewis Falls, Wyo. - 1986

ACCESS: 9.6 miles north of the South Entrance between West Thumb and the South Entrance. Easily viewed from the highway; roadside pullout available.

Paul Rubinstein

Lewis Falls is a splashing drop of the Lewis River about a mile downstream from Lewis Lake. The area was explored in 1872 by the Hayden Survey. Frank Bradley noted that their main party "encountered sharp rocks and a vertical fall of about 30 feet."[57]

Bradley gave the name for Meriwether Lewis of the Lewis and Clark Expedition (1803–1807), because he feared Lewis would otherwise be "without memorial" in the region he explored. Although the expedition never entered present Yellowstone National Park, it passed to the north by some 50 miles. Now, Lewis Lake, Lewis River Canyon, and the three Lewis falls all celebrate the explorer.

Because of its location above a highway bridge crossing of the Lewis River, Lewis Falls is one of the park's most photographed waterfalls. It is easily seen from one's car window when driving the South Entrance Road, and a pullout and parking area are nearby.

19 LEWIS CANYON FALLS (Upper)

LOCATION: 527758 4896913

FALL TYPE: Cascade

HEIGHT: 80 feet

STREAM: Lewis River

MAP: Lewis Canyon, Wyo. - 1989

ACCESS: 5.7 miles north of the South Entrance between West Thumb and the South Entrance. Visible from the edge of the highway; closest roadside pullouts are downstream.

A long sloping cascade of the Lewis River is visible from the present Grand Loop Road at the uppermost portion of Lewis River Canyon. Named as part of Lewis Canyon Falls, the cascade seems to have been so designated by historian Hiram Chittenden around 1895. Chittenden referred to upper and lower manifestations of Lewis Canyon Falls.[58] Although Chittenden gave both waterfalls the same name, this large cascade is a completely separate feature from its counterpart one-half mile downstream.

The falls consists of a 400-yard stretch of whitewater characterized by numerous riffles and pools during its step-down descent. Viewing this upper portion of Lewis Canyon Falls is not difficult. Motorists should use caution however as the number of pullouts on this section of the South Entrance Road is limited and footing at the canyon rim is somewhat precarious. A case in point is the tragic death of park visitor Andrew Joseph Haschke who, in 1974, fell into the canyon from very close to where this photograph was taken.

Paul Rubinstein

20 LEWIS CANYON FALLS (Lower)

LOCATION: **527688 4896094**

FALL TYPE: Segmented Plunge/Cascade

HEIGHT: 50 feet

STREAM: Lewis River

MAP: Lewis Canyon, Wyoming - 1989

ACCESS: 5.0 miles north of the South Entrance between West Thumb and the South Entrance. Not visible from the highway; requires a tricky descent into Lewis Canyon.

Mike Stevens

A half-mile downstream from the upper section of Lewis Canyon Falls, this double (segmented), sloping cascade is located about midway in the Lewis River Canyon. In 1872, Dr. Frank Bradley of the second Hayden Survey documented the falls.[59] Twenty years later, fishery researcher Barton Evermann's compatriots saw it while exploring the difficult area. He noted:

> *About halfway between the Upper Falls and the mouth of Crawfish Creek, they came upon a very beautiful fall of considerable size. The stream is divided by a small island into two parts, the larger portion of the water flowing around to the right of the island. This part was estimated to be at least 50 feet wide and to fall almost perpendicularly at least 30 feet, then descend about 20 feet more in a very steep rapid, in which the stream widens out very much. That part of the stream passing around to the left of the small rocky island is about 8 feet wide, and it comes down in a series of very steep cascades and two principal falls, each apparently vertical.[60]*

Today the segmented falls seems much wider, appearing to be 50 feet wide on each side of the island. Evermann's west side is the steeper of the two drops, but there are vertical drops on the east side as well. Although it is close to the South Entrance Road, lower Lewis Canyon Falls is not visible from the highway. Some fairly strenuous scrambling into Lewis Canyon is required in order to view the falls.

Mike Stevens

Many spectacular seasonal falls line Lewis Canyon in springtime.

21 MOOSE FALLS

LOCATION: 526237 4888580

FALL TYPE: Plunge

HEIGHT: 30 feet

STREAM: Crawfish Creek

MAP: Lewis Canyon,
Wyoming - 1989

ACCESS: 1.2 miles north of the South Entrance between West Thumb and the South Entrance. Roadside pullout on east side of the highway; easy walk required to view.

Paul Rubinstein

Moose Falls was named in 1885 by the Hague Survey in accordance with the philosophy of naming natural features after local fauna. A pullout on the south entrance road about a mile inside the park's south entrance offers easy access for visitors. You can view the falls from either side of the stream if you use the short trails provided.

In the past, this falls has been mistakenly referred to as "Crawfish Falls" on old postcards sold in the park. It even graced the cover of Yellowstone's first waterfall book, John Barber's *Ribbons of Water* in 1984.

Crawfish live in the warm, thermally heated waters of the creek. Though they are not large, it is noteworthy because crawfish are unusual at this latitude and elevation.

22 RUSTIC FALLS

LOCATION: 521834 4975501

FALL TYPE: Plunge/Horsetail/Fan

HEIGHT: 47 feet

STREAM: Glen Creek

MAP: Mammoth, Wyoming/
Montana - 1986

ACCESS: 4.7 miles south of Mammoth between Mammoth and Norris Junction. Small roadside pullout and viewpoint from highway available.

Mike Stevens

Named in 1879 by park superintendent P.W. Norris, Rustic Falls is a natural falls but rumors persist that it is man-made. These stories probably originated because Glen Creek's flow has been artificially augmented by means of an underground pipe from Indian Creek.

Members of the Hayden Survey saw the falls in 1871, and Joshua Crissman photographed it in 1872.[61] Captain John Barlow noted that "a clear cut, hundreds of feet in depth, through the mountain's base, allowed the passage of a small stream, which about midway rolled down a slightly inclined and rocky slope, then spread out into a pretty cascade."[62]

Tour guide G.L. Henderson loved Rustic Falls and the canyon of Glen Creek, and he appeared in numerous 1880s photos of the area taken by Frank Jay Haynes. Henderson wrote the following in 1888:

> *The falls of West Gardner are marvelously beautiful and the brilliant moss colored rocks on the opposite walls of the canyon enhance the beauty of the scene. Here we find 'sermons in stone and lectures in running brooks.' And the truth that man and man's work is nature's chief end in and glory.*[63]

William Henry Jackson, 1878

Rustic Falls before construction of Grand Loop Road

The falls has had other names. Haynes sold views of it in the 1880s under the names "West Gardiner Falls" and "Rural Falls."

Rustic Falls lies at the head of Golden Gate Canyon, where Golden Gate Bridge has been rebuilt three times since the original wooden one was erected in 1885. The canyon received its name from the golden lichens that color its walls. Artist Frederic Remington visited this spot in the 1890s and wrote that the canyon's colors were "beyond the pen or brush of any man."[64]

23 LOWER UNDINE FALLS

LOCATION: 528438 4976609

FALL TYPE: Plunge

HEIGHT: 35–40 feet

STREAM: Lava Creek

MAP: Unmapped

ACCESS: 3.8 miles east of Mammoth between Mammoth and Tower-Roosevelt Jct. Not visible from Undine Falls roadside overlook; 1-mile hike required to view.

Mike Stevens

The lesser-known plunge of Lava Creek, this feature is located about 100 yards below Undine Falls. In our eyes, it is less than 40 feet high, although some sources give it as 50. Located deep within Lava Creek Canyon, it is very difficult to reach. The only logical route to its base is by scrambling from the north side of the creek via the Lava Creek Trail. You can catch another pretty view of this prominent falls from the south rim of Mount Everts.

A stereoview of this falls under the designation "Gardner Falls" was published by the legendary photographer F. Jay Haynes in the late nineteenth century. That name did not survive, however.

Over time, the name Lower Undine Falls has become entrenched (although it is still unofficial), and has been used by Mammoth residents as a way of differentiating between it and Undine Falls above it.

Lower Undine Falls should not be approached from the Undine Falls pullout under any circumstances. The sheer cliffs and terrible footing are extremely dangerous as illustrated by a fatal fall of a park visitor here in 1980.

William Henry Jackson, 1878

Lower Undine Falls

24 UNDINE FALLS

LOCATION: 528566 4976585

FALL TYPE: Three-tiered Plunge/Fan

HEIGHT: 60 feet

STREAM: Lava Creek

MAP: Mammoth, Wyoming/ Montana - 1986

ACCESS: 4.0 miles east of Mammoth between Mammoth and Tower-Roosevelt Jct. Roadside overlook on north side of the highway; parking available.

Mike Stevens

This three-step waterfall appeared on the cover of *National Geographic* magazine in July, 1977. The multi-step falls consists of three plunges that you can see from an overlook on the Mammoth-Cooke City Road.

Originally called "East Gardner Falls," "Cascade Falls of the East Gardiner," or "Gardiner River Falls," Undine received its present name in 1885 from geologist Arnold Hague. Undine (Webster pronounces it UN deen) was named for wise, usually female water spirits from German mythology who lived around waterfalls and who could gain souls by marrying mortal men.

A number of early Yellowstone explorers such as Captain John Barlow, Captain William Ludlow, and Dr. A.C. Peale saw Undine Falls. Ludlow's description mentioned all three drops. Park superintendent P.W. Norris claimed to have discovered a passageway behind the falls in 1879. Captain W.A. Jones was there in the summer of 1873 and noted:

> We made our nooning near a lovely fall of the east fork of Gardiner's
> [sic] River, after traversing a beautiful country of high, rolling hills . . .
> A beautiful effect is produced about half-way down the face of the fall,
> where a horizontal dish-like ledge juts out from the wall. Some of the

falling water rushes down and into the dish of the ledge, so that its impetus throws it up again at several points in low, heavy fountain-like jets, while another portion jumps clear over and beyond the ledge, in a thin transparent sheet whose convex surface looks exceedingly like a glass cover preserving the little fountains beneath from defilement.[65]

1908 visitor F. Dumont Smith captured the spirit of the area: "Just below, the little stream goes wandering and whispering to itself, and you know that somewhere down there Undine has returned, and if you were not so tired you could find her."[66] Smith's use of "Undine" in singular form probably refers to the character in the 1814 French romance by De la Motte Fouque.

25 WRAITH FALLS

LOCATION: 529889 4975806

FALL TYPE: Cascade

HEIGHT: 100 feet

STREAM: Lupine Creek

MAP: Blacktail Deer Creek, Wyo. - 1986

ACCESS: 5.7 miles east of Mammoth between Mammoth and Tower-Roosevelt Jct. Not visible from highway; 0.5-mile walk from Wraith Falls Trailhead required to view.

Mike Stevens

Wraith Falls, a gently sloping cascade, was named in 1885 by members of the Hague parties of the USGS. Although there is no documentation of the reason for this name, the survey members were apparently reminded of a ghost or spectre in the gossamer rivulets of white water here.[67] In fact, during the spring runoff when the falls is full, it does indeed have the classic shape of an apparition.

An easy, half-mile trail leads to this falls, and it takes hikers to an overlook that was moved and revamped in the early 1990s. Signs mark the trailhead on the Mammoth-Tower Road a mile east of the Lava Creek Picnic Area. Keen-eyed visitors can even spot this falls in the distance from the upper terraces at Mammoth.

Wraith Falls is a perfect example of the misuse of the word "falls." It is not a true waterfall, but when viewed from the front takes on this illusion. From the cliffs above, it does not even resemble a cascade but instead a long, flat rapid.

26 TOWER FALL

LOCATION: 548443 4971117

FALL TYPE: Plunge

HEIGHT: 132 feet

STREAM: Tower Creek

MAP: Tower Junction, Wyoming/
Montana - 1986

ACCESS: 2.2 miles south of
Tower-Roosevelt Junction
between Tower-Roosevelt
Junction and Canyon
Village. Viewpoint is roughly
100 yards from parking area.

John Landrigan

This "chastely-beautiful" waterfall was called "Little Falls" by fur trappers. Jim Bridger himself gave that information to Father Jean DeSmet who showed it on an 1851 map.[68]

Tower Fall was named in 1870 by a member of the Washburn party, probably Samuel Hauser, who wrote in his diary: "Campt near the most beautiful falls—I ever saw—I named them 'Tower falls'—from the towers and pinnacles that surround them."[69]

Prospector A. Bart Henderson had seen it in 1867, noting as did Hauser that it was "the most beautiful falls I ever saw." Robert Strahorn in 1880 called it "one of the most beautiful falls to be found in any country," and in 1908, Mode Wineman averred that it was "a thing of hidden beauty in the wilderness." N.P. Langford called it "one of the most beautiful cataracts in the world."[70]

Lt. Gustavus Doane accompanied the 1870 party, and his reaction is probably the best known of early ones: "Nothing can be more chastely beautiful than this lovely cascade, hidden away in the dim light of overshadowing rocks and woods, its very voice hushed to a low murmur unheard at the distance of a few hundred yards. Thousands might pass by within a half-mile and not dream of its existence, but once seen, it passes to the list of most pleasant memories."[71]

According to Langford, the party argued around its campfire as to whether the name of the falls should be "Minaret" or "Tower." While "Minaret" initially won the vote, subsequent accusations that the proposer had a girlfriend named "Minnie Rhett" resulted in a new vote that gave the nod to Tower.[72]

We include some historical comments on Tower Fall here, complete with their comparisons to other waterfalls:

> *Immediately about the head of the falls the rocks were worn into curious and fantastic shapes, looking, in daylight, like spires or steeples, rising from thirty to sixty feet above the falls; but, in the moonlight, reminding one of the portal of an old castle, or a number of the fabled genii standing ready to hurl adventurous mortals into the gorge below, which was enveloped by the shadows of the night in impenetrable darkness.*
> —WALTER TRUMBULL, 1870.[73]

> *From between two of these turrets the stream makes its final leap . . . and then, as if satisfied with itself, flows peacefully into the Yellowstone. We attempted to compare it with the famous Minnehaha, but those who had seen both said there was no comparison. It was not as terrible in its sublimity as Niagara, but beautiful and glorious. You felt none of the shrinking back so common at the Great [Lower] Fall, but rather, as you stood below and gazed upon its waters broken into white spray, you felt as though you wanted to dash into it, and catch it as it fell.*
> —HENRY WASHBURN, 1870.[74]

Oil painting by Thomas Moran, 1872

"Tower Fall and Sulpher Mountain"

> *. . . one of the greatest beauties of the valley . . . on either side the somber brecciated columns stand like gloomy sentinels.*
> —DR. F.V. HAYDEN, 1871.[75]

> *Great towers, shapely as cathedral spires, rise on either side, with slender fingers, like the minarets of a mosque, strangely colored, forming royal setting for the water, which, from two hundred feet above, falls into the boiling chasm. The surroundings are much like those of Minnehaha Falls, only here is greater majesty.*
> —ALMON GUNNISON, 1883.[76]

A boulder that balanced precariously on the lip of Tower Fall (at least since William Henry Jackson photographed it in 1871) finally fell from its perch in 1986.

27 BOULDER FALLS

LOCATION: 548430 4971125

FALL TYPE: Plunge

HEIGHT: 20 feet

STREAM: Tower Creek

MAP: Unmapped

ACCESS: 2.1 miles south of Tower-Roosevelt Junction between Tower-Roosevelt Junction and Canyon Village. Not visible from highway or overlook; area at the brink of the falls is closed to human travel.

David Rothenburger

Boulder Falls, an obscure waterfall of Tower Creek, is located about 100 feet above its more famous sister, Tower Fall. The name is a very old one, apparently given by photographer Henry Bird Calfee at the time he photographed it. About 1880, Calfee distributed copies of his stereoview number 237 (below), labeled "Boulder Falls, Tower Creek."

We duplicated an early Haynes photo of this falls by climbing the hill above the Tower Hamilton Store to find Haynes' original vantage point.

Reaching Boulder Falls from upstream is illegal and the area is closed to human travel. Hiking through the area of rock spires known as Devil's Den is quite dangerous and closed to the public. Footing is unstable, damage to friable rock formations is probable, and the possibility of falling over Tower Fall is very real.

No. 237. Boulder Falls, Tower Creek.

Upper half of Tower Fall

28 LOST CREEK FALLS

LOCATION: 545840 4972817

FALL TYPE: Plunge

HEIGHT: 40 feet

STREAM: Lost Creek

MAP: Tower Junction,
Wyo./Mont. - 1986

ACCESS: 0.3 mile south-
west of Roosevelt Lodge
at Tower-Roosevelt Jct.
Short trail walk required
to view.

Paul Rubinstein

Located on Lost Creek just one-quarter mile above Roosevelt Lodge, Lost Creek Falls is an easy walk for Roosevelt visitors. Hiram Chittenden's 1903 book announced: "Lost Creek Falls . . . is well worthy of a visit. It reminds one somewhat of the falls of Minnehaha. The formation of the walls is very unusual, and the water pours over the brink in a light spray which forms with the surrounding verdure, a scene of quiet beauty rarely found in so wild and rough a country."[77]

This falls is especially affected by loss of water in autumn. It offers an inviting treat for those willing to take the short walk to view the sheer, dark-colored wall over which the water drops. The easy, well-maintained trail ends about 100 yards short of the falls but provides a fine view. Travel beyond the trail is unsteady due to loose footing and steep slopes.

Lost Creek was named in 1878 by geologist W.H. Holmes, who wrote: "I have called [it] Lost Creek, because it apparently sinks from sight in the lower part of its course."[78] The stream sinks into meadows before it reaches the Yellowstone River.

29 UNNAMED CASCADE IN ICE BOX CANYON

ACCESS: *7.9 miles southwest of the Northeast Entrance and 19.9 miles east/northeast of Tower-Roosevelt Junction. There are no accessible views of this falls; a dangerous route along the rim is required to view — but not recommended.*

Though short, Ice Box Canyon is quite a setting. The waters of Soda Butte Creek flow mildly through flat country both above and below the canyon, yet in it carve a steep, narrow gorge for less than half a mile. Both ends of this unique chasm contain waterfalls with a long, 60-yard cascade between them. Ice Box Canyon is over 50 feet deep and 15 to 30 feet wide. It is so deep and narrow that the ice of winter clings to its sides long after the surrounding snow has melted, thus the name.

Geologically, Soda Butte Creek has scoured its bed of loose rock so the creekbed is very slippery and extremely difficult to stand in, let alone walk on, especially in the swift waters rushing through the canyon. Aquatic surveys here mention many deep holes. They are correct!

In the writing of this book, Ice Box Canyon proved to be a formidable obstacle. In late July 1996, Mike Stevens, while sloshing up the middle of the river, had to end a promising scouting mission when the shallowest place he could find was just below his neck. He then tried surveying from the canyon rim. Unfortunately, the ground near these sheer ledges was so steep and the footing so hazardous that he thought better of it. So although it is possible to get directly adjacent to the long, 60-yard cascade in the center of Ice Box Canyon and even listen to its roar, we still have never seen it.

30 ICE BOX FALLS

LOCATION: 572147 4975376

FALL TYPE: Cascade

HEIGHT: 18 feet

STREAM: Soda Butte Creek

MAP: Map of Soda Butte Creek,
USFWS - 1982

ACCESS: 7.6 miles southwest
of the Northeast Entrance and
20.2 miles east/northeast of
Tower-Roosevelt Junction.
Roadside pullout in vicinity, but no
viewpoints without some walking
along the rim of Ice Box Canyon.

Joanne Sides

Ice Box Falls begins at the upper-most end of Ice Box Canyon. It is plainly visible from the Northeast Entrance Road for a split-second if one is in the passenger seat of a car traveling east toward Cooke City. There are actually two falls where the creek is pinched between large boulders. This squeezing of water gives the falls a chute-like appearance. It was first documented in the 1915 publication, "The Fishes of Yellowstone National Park."[79] Years later, the USFWS 1981 *Annual Project Report* noted them as "2 series of cascade/falls." Its name, Ice Box Falls, has been in local usage for some time.

We used the working name "the chutes" because of the falls' distinctive structure. This falls actually has chutes in two places. The upper chute is on the stream's west side. Almost immediately the water rockets through a second chute downstream. Unfortunately, we don't believe there is currently any spot where one can view both chutes at once. As the park upgrades its road system, we hope they will construct new turnouts in this area so folks can better view this lovely double waterfall.

31 UNNAMED FALLS IN LOWER ICE BOX CANYON

ACCESS: *8.2 miles southwest of the Northeast Entrance and 19.6 miles east/north-east of Tower-Roosevelt Junction. There are no accessible views of this falls; a difficult bushwhack into a creek is required to view—but not recommended.*

At the lower end of Ice Box Canyon lies a well-concealed and treacherous waterfall. It is deeply hidden in thick forest and a narrow canyon. Although only yards from the highway, it may be one of the most difficult in the entire park to view. High water in the late season makes any in-the-water navigation here unthinkable until late August. Furthermore, the immediate geography makes viewing this falls from above impossible.

The falls itself is a sharp plunge, 15 feet in height. The canyon walls are vertical as well; therefore any approach to this unnamed waterfall must be made by wading in the center of Soda Butte Creek. The distance is not far, but the footing is unsteady. The authors do not recommend this hike for anyone until after September 1.

32 UNNAMED FALLS ON BARRONETTE PEAK "Y Falls"

ACCESS: *3.7 miles southwest of the Northeast Entrance and 22.5 miles east/ northeast of Tower-Roosevelt Junction. Visible to the west on the slopes of Barronette Peak along with numerous other seasonal waterfalls.*

No book on Yellowstone's waterfalls would be complete without a mention of Barronette Peak. This 10,404-foot mountain in the park's northeast corner is a geologic wonder. During spring runoff, its sides become littered with waterfalls. No less than 100 falls and cascades stream down its sheer face.

These seasonal falls are easily seen from the Northeast Entrance Road as it passes this spectacular scene. Even in late summer, long after the waterfalls have ceased flowing for the season, afternoon thunderstorms can rejuvenate them. During the brief, heavy downpours, the floodgates open and for a few hours Barronette Peak comes to life once again. This phenomenon is not limited to Barronette Peak. Many of the park's jagged northeasterly peaks share this geology, including Abiathar and Cutoff Peaks as well as Amphitheater Mountain.

"Y Falls" can be seen at lower right in this photograph; Photo by Paul Rubinstein

PART II: The Backcountry

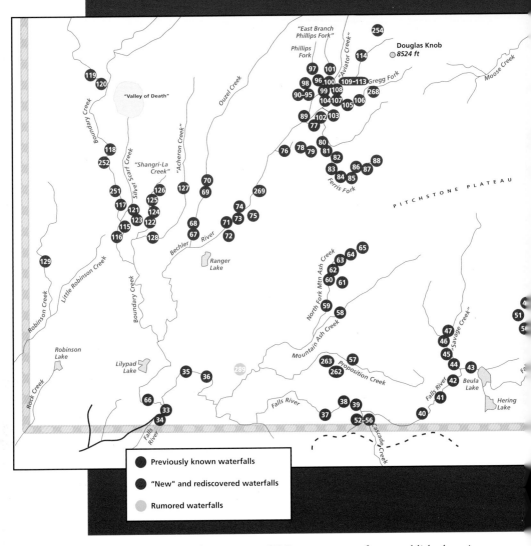

"East Branch Phillips Fork"

Phillips Fork

Douglas Knob
8524 ft

254

114

Moose Creek

97 101

"Aviator Creek"

Gregg Fork

98 96 100 109–113

90–95 99 108 268

104 107 105 106

119
120

"Valley of Death"

Ouzel Creek

89 102 103
77

Boundary Creek

"Acheron Creek"

Silver Scarf Creek

"Shangri-La Creek"

76 78 79 80 81

82

83 84 85 86 87 88

PITCHSTONE PLATEAU

Ferris Fork

118
252

251

126 127

70
69

269

117

121 125

124

123 122

116 115 128

68 67

74 73 75

71 72

Bechler River

Ranger Lake

North Fork Mtn Ash Creek

65
63 64
62
60 61

129

Little Robinson Creek

Boundary Creek

59 58

Mountain Ash Creek

Savage Creek

47
46
45
44 43

4

51

5

Robinson Creek

Robinson Lake

Rock Creek

Lilypad Lake

35 36

289

263 57
262

Proposition Creek

Beula Lake

42

41

Falls River

Hering Lake

66

33
34

Falls River

38 39

37 52–56

40

Falls River

Cascade Creek

● Previously known waterfalls

● "New" and rediscovered waterfalls

● Rumored waterfalls

The backcountry is that portion of Yellowstone away from established, main roads. Most of the features in "Part II: The Backcountry" require hiking on or off-trail, generally at a distance of more than a half-mile.

We consider the Falls River one of the most important rivers in Yellowstone. Within park boundaries, it contains no less than 14 different waterfalls and cascades. This major river originates from large springs at the foot of the Pitchstone Plateau and appears to have been named before 1839 by fur trappers. Trapper Osborne Russell reported in his 1838 journal: " . . . we fell onto the middle branch of Henry's fork which is called by hunters 'The falling fork' from the numerous Cascades it forms whilst meandering thro. the forest previous to its junction with the main river."[80]

Members of the Hayden Survey of 1872 accepted the name-form Falls River.[81] In Idaho, it has been sometimes called "Fall River." This disparity in names ultimately led to a 1997 decision by the USBGN which declared the official name-form for this river to be "Fall River" in an unfortunate win for the state of Idaho. Wyoming, the Hayden Surveys, and all the rest of history have correctly labeled the river as "Falls River," but Idaho's lobbying effort for its local usage won out, with the USBGN making, in our opinion, a bad decision. In this book, we retain the historic and, we believe, correct name-form "Falls River."

33–34 CAVE FALLS

Paul Rubinstein

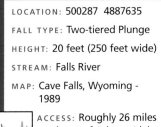

LOCATION: 500287 4887635

FALL TYPE: Two-tiered Plunge

HEIGHT: 20 feet (250 feet wide)

STREAM: Falls River

MAP: Cave Falls, Wyoming - 1989

ACCESS: Roughly 26 miles northeast of Ashton, Idaho, on Cave Falls Road. Parking and overlook available.

This expansive waterfall **(#33)** of the Falls River in the southwest corner of the park is only 20 feet high, but its spectacularity rests in the fact that, at 250 feet wide, it is probably the park's widest waterfall. Its immediate upper step is about three feet high and a lower step (marked on the 1989 Cave Falls 7½-minute quadrangle as "falls") about 100 yards downstream is around five feet high **(#34)**

Explorer W.C. Gregg and topographer C.H. Birdseye named the fall in 1920–21 for the existence of a 50-by-50-foot cave just below the falls on the river's north bank. Gregg wrote: "The cave is one of those extravagant gifts of the Creator, thrown in on top of more than we could ask for.[82]

The most thorough geologic account of this cave came from Joseph P. Iddings of the Hague Survey. He wrote: "The middle one is a beautiful fall, 15 or 20 feet high and about 200 feet wide, with a cascade in low steps above it. At the west end of this fall there is a low arched cave, formed by a sheet of dense, gray, glassy rhyolite, with small phenocrysts, overlying a mass of brecciated glassy rhyolite which is more easily eroded."[83]

Cave Falls is accessible by road from Ashton, Idaho, and is popular with local Idaho residents. It is the starting point for many hikes in the Bechler region.

35 UNNAMED RAPIDS ON THE LOWER FALLS RIVER "Forders' Cascade"

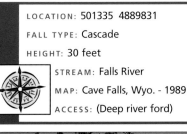

LOCATION: 501335 4889831

FALL TYPE: Cascade

HEIGHT: 30 feet

STREAM: Falls River

MAP: Cave Falls, Wyo. - 1989

ACCESS: (Deep river ford)

"Forders' Cascade" is found one and one-half miles upstream from Cave Falls on the Falls River. Marked as "rapids" on the 1989 Cave Falls 7½-minute quadrangle, it is actually a gently sloping, 30-foot cascade of whitewater that splits and eddies its way between forested banks. Although not a vertical drop, it is more impressive than its size would indicate due to the large volume of water in the river this far downstream. The name was chosen because in order to view the cascade, the hiker must ford at least one significant watercourse, either Falls River or Bechler River.

Mike Stevens

36 UNNAMED FALLS ON THE LOWER FALLS RIVER "White Angel Falls"

LOCATION: 502440 4889749

FALL TYPE: Cascade

HEIGHT: 14–16 feet

STREAM: Falls River

MAP: Cave Falls,
Wyoming - 1989

ACCESS: (Deep river ford)

Another mapped waterfall on the Falls River lies roughly two miles above Cave Falls and one-half mile above "Forders' Cascade." We learned of its existence from the notation "falls" on the 1989 Cave Falls 7½-minute quadrangle. It may also be the falls indicated on a 1904 Northern Pacific Railroad map of the park.

The feature itself is not high, but it is still impressive. Its appearance is similar to that of Cave Falls, and in our opinion much more scenic than Bechler Falls. Viewing the falls in clear mid-afternoon sun, it was a blaze of white. It almost hurt to look at it. The shine was particularly intense due to the water's agitation throughout its plunge. The falls' shape was less uniform than Cave Falls, which somehow suggested the idea of an angel's wing—that and the brightness resulted in the name "White Angel Falls."

Mike Stevens

Who Was Jack?

For us, another fascinating aspect of "White Angel Falls" was the existence of a sign posted 10 feet above the ground on a tree overlooking the falls. It read, "JACK'S FALLS." The sign was four inches high, machine cut and beveled, with the words carved into brown-stained wood and painted in white. It appeared to be not more than a year or two old. In a search for clues as to the history of the sign and the name "Jack's Falls," we first consulted the Bechler subdistrict ranger, but she professed to know nothing about it. Then we contacted longtime Bechler ranger Dunbar Susong, and although he had seen this falls, he did not remember any sign. Faced with the prospect of solving this riddle on our own, we next turned to park headquarters at Mammoth. Because the sign was so official looking, we theorized that perhaps it was manufactured in the park's sign shop. But during an inquiry with chief signmaker Virgil Hall, he informed us that he did not make the mysterious sign. He stated it was not up to park standards in either form or construction. He believed it should be taken down and brought to him, because the Park Service is anxious to remove any such unofficial markers. So the origin of the sign remains a mystery, probably an attempt by someone to name the falls after himself or a friend.

37 RAINBOW FALLS

LOCATION: 509704 4887448

FALL TYPE: Segmented Plunge

HEIGHT: 55 feet

STREAM: Falls River

MAP: Cave Falls, Wyoming - 1989

ACCESS: Moderate to difficult off-trail hike.

Mike Stevens

This book contains the first correct published photo of Rainbow Falls on the Falls River since Jack Haynes published one in 1922.[84]

This strangely shaped waterfall, about 55 feet in height, was apparently confused by historian Hiram Chittenden with Terraced Falls, at least with regard to its height. Chittenden listed the height of this falls as "140 feet (total of three falls)."[85] Probably Chittenden confused this entry with one for Terraced Falls (only a mile upstream and much more prominent) made by Dr. Hayden, for there are not "three falls" here nor is Rainbow Falls "140 feet high."

Rainbow Falls was named in 1885 by members of the Hague parties of the USGS,[86] shown on the 1886 map, and then essentially forgotten by Yellowstone writers until rediscovered in 1921 by W.C. Gregg and Jack Haynes. Interestingly, in his *Outlook* article, "The Cascade Corner of Yellowstone Park," Gregg published an uncaptioned photo of Rainbow Falls, probably because he did not realize it was already named Rainbow Falls. In fact, Gregg stated: "I don't want to suggest a naming contest. I would take to my bed if an avalanche of 'Rainbow Falls' and 'Bridal Veil Falls' came in."[87]

Rainbow Falls is a divided falls with one-half stepping down about five feet at the brink before plunging, while the other half falls the full 55 feet in one uninterrupted plunge.

The Mystery of Rainbow Falls

In 1983, long before he was involved in any waterfall project, Mike Stevens made his first trip to Rainbow Falls as part of a day-hike to Union Falls. The trip was difficult and hurried, but traveling alone, he did manage to reach a noisy waterfall, which he assumed to be Rainbow Falls.

Six years later, he noticed that John Barber's book *Ribbons of Water* contained a photograph of Rainbow Falls. Stevens thought he vaguely recognized the published photo as being one he had seen in 1983 and accepted that it was correct. He maintained only a dim memory of his moments there.

In 1994, during some research into old documents, Lee Whittlesey was reading a 1920s article on the Bechler region when he came across a black-and-white photo of an unidentified waterfall. Stumped, he asked Paul Rubinstein if he could identify it. Rubinstein had never seen it before and had no idea what it could be. Soon we all went on to other things and this strange photo was forgotten.

After we started research for this book, Rubinstein started to catalog all of Stevens' waterfall slides. He found two slides from 1983 that he did not recognize and asked Stevens where they were taken. Stevens could not remember, but he sensed that the two slides looked familiar in some strange way. Then Rubinstein realized that they were of the same falls as Whittlesey's uncaptioned 1920s black-and-white photo. We labeled the slides "Mystery Falls" and vowed to find the feature.

About this time the three of us began to theorize that something was not right about Rainbow Falls. Stevens had supposedly been there in 1983, yet we had found no pictures of it in his collection. Whittlesey thought he had walked past there in the 1970s, but had no real memory of the falls. Barber's book purported to show the falls, but we knew of no one else who had been there and so could not confirm that the photo was accurate.

In 1995, Stevens traveled back to Rainbow Falls to set the record straight. Once there he thoroughly surveyed the area and, using GPS readings, confirmed its location. Stevens then realized that his unlabeled 1983 slides and Whittlesey's uncaptioned 1920s photo were both of Rainbow Falls.

What had confused us all those years was a series of unfortunate coincidences. Stevens had failed to label his 1983 slides and could not remember what he saw at that time. The book *Ribbons of Water* showed an unnamed cascade 100 yards upstream and incorrectly identified it as Rainbow Falls. Whittlesey's 1920s article had captions for most other waterfalls in the Bechler area, but not for Rainbow. Finally, Whittlesey's book *Wonderland Nomenclature* showed an incorrect height for Rainbow Falls ("140 feet" instead of "55 feet") based upon a mistake by Hiram Chittenden in 1895.

Thus, a seemingly simple waterfall on the map confused us for years.

38 TERRACED FALLS

LOCATION: 510827 4888057

FALL TYPE: Six-tiered Plunge

HEIGHT: 140 feet

STREAM: Falls River

MAP: Grassy Lake Reservoir, Wyoming - 1989

ACCESS: Easy to moderate on-trail hike.

Mike Stevens

Terraced Falls, perhaps the most striking waterfall of the entire Falls River, is composed of six falls totaling 140 feet. Members of the 1872 Hayden Survey wrote of five falls here, but geologist Walter Weed noted six in 1886 with heights of 35, 25, 50, 5, 10, and 5 feet, respectively. Geologists Weed, J.P. Iddings, and S.L. Penfield all visited the place in 1886, and it was probably one of these Hague Survey members who gave the name to the falls in 1885–86. Although an attempt was made in the 1920s to rename it "Totem Falls," the USBGN decided to keep the original name.[88]

Various observers are not united in their estimates of the height of Terraced Falls. Rudolph Hering wrote: "The largest fall, 145 feet in height, is surrounded by a grotesque group of columns of rock."[89] Frank Bradley stated: "These show a total descent of 141 feet, consisting of three larger falls above, the third being 47 feet high, with three small ones at the bottom. The upper two are somewhat of a horseshoe form, while the third and highest has a nearly straight edge."[90] The Norris map of 1880 showed it as "Great Falls, 140 feet," while Jack Haynes gave the height in 1922 as 65 feet, perhaps using only the tallest two falls.[91] A more recent hiking guide says that Terraced Falls is "a series of five falls totaling about 150 feet."[92]

Terraced Falls is easily accessible by trail from the Ashton-Flagg Ranch Road along the park's south boundary. In two miles the trail passes several other features described in this book and the authors recommend it highly for anyone who wants an introductory taste of the Yellowstone backcountry.

39 CASCADE ACRES

LOCATION: 511472 4887774

FALL TYPE: Segmented Cascade

HEIGHT: 50 feet (total)

STREAM: Falls River

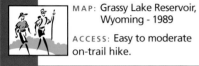

MAP: Grassy Lake Reservoir, Wyoming - 1989

ACCESS: Easy to moderate on-trail hike.

Paul Rubinstein

These bewitching cascades are located on the Falls River east of Terraced Falls. The characteristic name was given in 1921 by explorer W.C. Gregg and topographer C.H. Birdseye, who originally wanted "Acres of Cascades" to be the name.[93] The name is doubly appropriate because Cascade Creek, one of the park's loveliest streams, joins the Falls River just above Cascade Acres.

From the Terraced Falls Trail, this cascade is easily viewed at a vantage point a quarter-mile upstream from Terraced Falls.

There is another set of unnamed cascades shown on the 1989 Grassy Lake 7½-minute quadrangle about one-quarter mile above Cascade Acres. They are equally as impressive in appearance as Cascade Acres but more difficult to reach.

40 UNNAMED FALLS ON THE UPPER FALLS RIVER "Forgotten Falls"

Paul Rubinstein

LOCATION: 514771 4887011

FALL TYPE: Plunge

HEIGHT: 20 feet

STREAM: Falls River

MAP: Map of Falls River Basin, USFWS - 1979

ACCESS: Moderate to difficult off-trail hike.

"Forgotten Falls," a plunge on the Falls River north of Grassy Lake Reservoir, is hidden in a small area of dense pines and firs where the land appears too flat to contain any type of waterfall. There does not appear to be any relief at all in its immediate vicinity, but a low rumbling is audible long before one can see its vertical drop.

Our suggested name stems from the history of "Forgotten Falls." It is likely to have been one of six waterfalls mentioned by the 1872 Hayden Survey. But it seems to have been forgotten after that, probably due to its small size when compared to other falls downstream. It was not documented again until a USFWS survey recorded it in September 1975 and included it on their hand-drawn map.

The falls is pleasing to the eye, large, with twisted tree-trunks criss-crossing its face, giving it a far more impressive appearance than its 20-foot height would indicate. The best views are from the south side about 30 yards below the falls. Immediate approaches are tricky due to hidden swamps and marshes as well as muddy slopes along the riverbank.

41 – 42

UNNAMED CASCADE ON THE UPPER FALLS RIVER
"Mist Cascade"

LOCATION: 515582 4887452

FALL TYPE: Cascade

HEIGHT: 40 feet

STREAM: Falls River

MAP: Unmapped

ACCESS: Moderate to difficult off-trail hike.

Paul Rubinstein

Far up the Falls River, just west of its source at Beula Lake, is "Mist Cascade" (#41). It is a long, gently sloping cascade, similar in physical appearance to Wraith Falls.

Our suggested name has a double meaning. Not only does the water have a tendency to mist against the 25-foot cliffs lining the cascade's south side, but its presence seems to have been "missed" by a USFWS survey in 1975. We found it completely by accident. In our 1995 search for "Forgotten Falls," we started our Falls River survey too far upstream and instead stumbled onto this lovely little gem.

It is tucked into a scenic spot where the river begins a long, gentle turn from a southerly to a westerly course. The best views of this rarely visited feature are from its southeast side along the cliff edges. The approach to "Mist Cascade" is relatively easy because of thin lodgepole forest surrounding the area with only moderate downfall. The USFWS indicated yet another waterfall (height 3m) on their hand-drawn map, approximately three-quarters of a mile upstream from here (#42). Start any attempt to reach the various falls in this area from the Ashton-Flagg Ranch Road between the Grassy Lake and Beula Lake trailheads.

43 UNNAMED FALLS ON FALLS RIVER
"Bradley Falls"

Paul Rubinstein

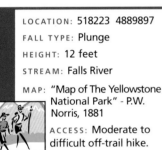

LOCATION: 518223 4889897

FALL TYPE: Plunge

HEIGHT: 12 feet

STREAM: Falls River

MAP: "Map of The Yellowstone National Park" - P.W. Norris, 1881

ACCESS: Moderate to difficult off-trail hike.

Several hundred yards downstream from where the Falls River leaves Beula Lake is a 12-foot vertical plunge that we call "Bradley Falls." We include it not for its height, but rather its history. It was first recorded by Dr. Frank Bradley during the second Hayden Survey. While describing Beula Lake, he noted, "From the west end of the more northern lake, about 30 feet of water flow out rapidly, soon jumping over a fall of 12 feet."[94] This is the only written record of this serene little waterfall. He goes on to mention other falls downstream on the Falls River including two small unnamed falls, Cascade Acres, our "Mist Cascade" and "Forgotten Falls." In approximating their heights, he says, "Five other falls succeed of 6, 12, 40, 20 and 30 feet, before we reach the Great Falls (Terraced Falls)."

During Yellowstone's first decade as a national park, this feature appeared on most park maps. Yet after 1881 it was not shown. The USFWS rediscovered this falls in 1979 when they included it on their sketch map of the Falls River Basin. It failed however to reappear on any officially published maps. "Bradley Falls" is another of the many Yellowstone features that has been lost over time.

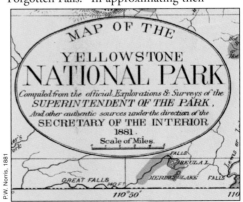

P.W. Norris, 1881

"Bradley Falls" (at outlet of Beula Lake), Moose Falls (on right as "Falls), and Terraced Falls (on left as "Great Falls").

The Pitchstone Plateau

> *The Continental Divide winds among the Park's southern plateaus in the manner of a serpent. From these circumstances, Yellowstone Park has become truly the wondrous land of water.... Nowhere else does water so well display its varied charms. From the Divide's snowy, timber-rimmed pockets, icy rivulets flow into sylvan pools, thence to rushing rivers with thundering waterfalls.*
> — MERRILL D. BEAL, *The Story of Man in Yellowstone*[95]

What Beal said is true to varying degrees for each of the southern plateaus of Yellowstone; it is simply more so for the Pitchstone Plateau. The existence of this marvelous work of nature is a boon to the creation of waterfalls. The Pitchstone is the recipient of 50 feet of annual snowfall. Yet, if you take a summer hike over it, you would certainly notice an area that seems particularly arid.

In 1878, members of the third Hayden Survey named this one-hundred-square-mile plateau for a kind of obsidian, one of the more common volcanic rocks of Yellowstone Park. The Pitchstone is much like a moonscape with little water and vast untimbered areas of young volcanic rocks. It is the surface of the youngest lava flow from the Yellowstone caldera (70,000–80,000 years), so it is still quite abrupt at its edge and very porous.

Many of the plateau's streams are mapped incorrectly as to the location of their headwaters. Current topographic maps often show creeks that are formed high up on the plateau before flowing directly over the edge. In reality, it is much more common that the waters emerge along the base of the plateau. This happens when water that normally might be expected to run off instead soaks into the porous rock.

In the course of our research we surveyed most of the circumference of the Pitchstone Plateau, and found two types of stream originations. Most common are "Type A" streams. These begin where countless springs and seeps in a small, local area emerge and combine to begin a creek. The flow generally starts small, but additional springs increase its flow in a relatively short distance. Less common but still present are "Type B" streams. These are creeks where the water literally gushes straight out of the plateau's base, sometimes even directly out of solid rock. A number of these creeks emerge so forcefully that one gets the impression of a river beginning all at once and, in many cases, the watercourses originate as falls or cascades. Though it is the cradle of a large number of our presented waterfalls, the Pitchstone Plateau seems likely to be the home of many more yet to be found.

44–47   UNNAMED FALLS AND CASCADES NORTHWEST OF BEULA LAKE "Savage Creek Cascades"

"Savage Creek" Fall #1

"Savage Creek" Fall #2

Photos by Paul Rubinstein

LOCATION/FALL TYPE/HEIGHT:

FALL 1: 516851 4890778; Segmented Cascade; 70 feet

FALL 2: 516759 4890865; Six-step Plunge; 70 feet

FALL 3: 516646 4891072 Cascade; 25 feet;

FALL 4: 516669 4891244; Plunge; 20 feet

STREAM: "Savage Creek"

MAP: Unmapped

ACCESS: Moderate to difficult off-trail hike.

Less than a mile northwest of Beula Lake on the southern slopes of the Pitchstone Plateau lies the mouth of a major unnamed creek. The stream's flow is so full that it nearly doubles the size of the Falls River upon emptying into it. We call it "Savage Creek."

More than a dozen falls and cascades exist in this creek's drainage if one chooses to count them individually. For simplification, we choose to present the four most important features. Moving upstream, the first feature **(#44)** encountered is a 70-foot segmented cascade that twists and splits down through an open, treeless canyon. The fires of 1988 burned severely here. The removal of nearly all ground cover allows visitors to view this cascade from some distance.

Just upstream is another feature of almost equal size **(#45)**. Its descent however is not a cascade, but rather a 70-foot, six-step waterfall. Like a great stairway, it sinks evenly down a remarkably similar canyon to its successor below. Scorched trees and an exposed hillside make this falls visible from as far away as the bluff above Beula Lake's western shore, some three miles to the southeast. This is perhaps the most violent feature on the stream.

Again moving up "Savage Creek," one almost immediately encounters the third cascade (**#46**). This feature is the most complex of the series. It is comprised of two steep cascades intersecting at precisely the point where a natural hillside spring feeds into them. The result is a convergence of waters in the shape of the letter "W." Facing this W-shaped cataract, the viewer sees a 25-foot cascade on the right (from the waters of "Savage Creek" itself), a 100-foot cascade on the left (from a substantial tributary of almost equal flow), and the dainty waters of the artesian spring directly between them.

One hundred yards above the "W" the creek pours over its most traditional waterfall (**#47**), a 20-foot vertical plunge pinched between large boulders. Nowhere on the stream is its powerful and violent nature better felt than by standing directly alongside the base of this fall.

Above this fourth feature the stream is dotted with smaller waterfalls and cascades, however, the terrain changes markedly. At the perimeter of the immediate fire-burn, the forest on the upper reaches of "Savage Creek" returns to a lush green environment.

The reasons for our name "Savage Creek" are two-fold. First, it is for the obvious "savage" nature of the large creek during the majority of its descent. Second, it was three park employees, Lee Ramella, Paul Rubinstein, and Mike Stevens, who initially documented this stream's complex and turbulent character in July, 1998. All Yellowstone Park employees have been informally known over the years as "savages," a term which originated during the stagecoach era when it applied to stagecoach drivers. A 1920 explanation: "They used to hell-for-leather round those narrow mountain curves in order to hear the doods [sic] and tourist ladies screech. So we got to calling them savages because they were such a raw bunch."[96]

48–51 FOUR SPRINGS

LOCATION/FALL TYPE/HEIGHT:

FALL 1: 521282 4892421;
Segmented Cascade; 60 feet

FALL 2: 521230 4892328;
Segmented Cascade; 75 feet

FALL 3: 521117 4892246;
Cascade; 100 feet

FALL 4: 521006 4892199;
Segmented Cascade; 180 feet

STREAM: Falls River

MAP: Map of "Yellowstone National Park" - F. V. Hayden, 1876

ACCESS: Moderate to difficult off-trail hike.

Four Springs Fall #2   Mike Stevens

Several miles northeast of Beula Lake is the ultimate source of the Falls River. Unlike most rivers, which begin as small brooks or seeps, this major Yellowstone watercourse begins its life as a full-fledged river that literally gushes out of the side of the Pitchstone Plateau as a series of immense springs. How appropriate that a river so long known by the name Falls River actually begins its very existence in such a complex intermingling of falls. This incredible feat of nature creates four roughly parallel cascades of 50 to 180 feet in height (#48-#51)

In an effort to determine the source of the Falls River, the second Hayden Survey reached this spot in 1872. They documented the area on their map as Four Springs. In Dr. Frank Bradley's words: "The extreme source of this river is in the great watershed of the northern mountain [The Pitchstone Plateau], from whose southern face

Four Springs and, at right, Lewis Falls, Lewis Canyon Falls, and Moose Falls

it bursts in four immense springs, which leap from its steep rocky sides as full-grown streams, and rush in beautiful cascades, from 75 to 100 feet high, down a slope of about 40 degrees to form two large branches, which a mile below, unite in a stream carrying about 20 feet of water."[97]

Park employees Mike Stevens, Tom Murphy, and Aaron Vigneault revisited these springs in July, 1998. They made roughly the same observations as the Hayden Survey, although the three reported no less than seven cascades of some degree. Four were at least 60 feet in height. As the trio worked from east to west, they found more and higher cascades. The last was the tallest—they estimated between 180–200 feet. At its bottom, the water was already at least 20 feet wide, knee deep, and moving very rapidly. Vigneault discovered that its flow gushed out of solid rock from a single hole (about 10–12 inches in diameter) under tremendous pressure. During a 1976 survey of the area, Park geologist Rick Hutchinson named this tallest cascade "Beargrass Cold Springs."

Four Springs Fall #4, the tallest and most westerly.   Mike Stevens

"Never was a stream more fittingly named," wrote John Muir of Yosemite's Cascade Creek, and Yellowstone's is no different. This beautiful stream is actually one of four in Yellowstone that bears the name Cascade Creek. It flows northwest from Tillery Lake in the Teton National Forest to the Falls River just inside the park's south boundary. It seems to have been named in 1878 by members of the third Hayden Survey, probably by topographer Henry Gannett in whose report the name appeared. The creek has a long series of cascades on it, with five of them within park boundaries.

In 1988, ranger Dunbar Susong laid out and started the construction of a maintained trail along Cascade Creek (known today as the Terraced Falls Trail). The route to Terraced Falls prior to that time was a route of least resistance over many fallen trees with heavy undesirable impact on the landscape due to equestrian use. Susong restricted the new trail to foot travel to prevent the excessive damage horses would undoubtedly cause on the sidehill traverses and at the Terraced Falls overlook. Because the trail parallels what is surely, inch-for-inch, one of the most scenic streams in the park, we believe it is an ideal place for the novice Yellowstone hiker.

52 UNNAMED CASCADES ON CASCADE CREEK "Pothole Cascades"

Paul Rubinstein

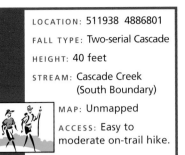

LOCATION: 511938 4886801

FALL TYPE: Two-serial Cascade

HEIGHT: 40 feet

STREAM: Cascade Creek
(South Boundary)

MAP: Unmapped

ACCESS: Easy to
moderate on-trail hike.

"Pothole Cascades," the finest feature of Cascade Creek inside the park boundary, is also the tallest. At 40 feet, the wide, two-step cascade is the most impressive falls on the stream. It is located just east of the Terraced Falls Trail, one-quarter mile below the trail fork that leads to the Falls River ford. Hikers often miss it because, although quite audible, it cannot be seen from the trail. The upper step slopes gently for about 10 feet, followed by a much steeper 30-foot lower drop. This second descent has an intriguing geologic curiosity at its base: a formation known as a pothole. Gouged into the shallow streambed is a six-foot deep circular hole. Although somewhat small, in the lower water of mid-summer this natural bathtub is an enjoyable place in which to swim. In 1998, park employee Mike Yochim suggested the name "Pothole Cascades" as a way of noting this unique feature.

53–56   UNNAMED CASCADES ON CASCADE CREEK "Diamond Cascade," "Humpback Cascade," and "Cleft Cascades"

The second of five cascades on the short one-mile stretch of Cascade Creek is a pleasant 15-foot drop (#53). Paul Rubinstein calls it "Diamond Cascade" for its four distinct and separate sections that all seem to intermingle as they fall, creating a diamond-shaped appearance.

Just downstream is the third feature of the stream, a small 15-foot, sliding cascade (#54). We call it "Humpback Cascade" for its curved shape with a protruding center.

Almost immediately below it are the fourth and fifth cascades (#55, #56) on Cascade Creek, located 50 yards above the mouth of the stream. "Cleft Cascades," as we call them, have two sections. The upper is a narrow, twisting, 20-foot chute, while the lower is more open and fans out before falling into a calm, shallow pool.

"Cleft Cascades" (lower)

Paul Rubinstein

57 UNNAMED FALLS ON PROPOSITION CREEK "Siren Falls"

Jed Winkelman

LOCATION: 511404 4890142

FALL TYPE: Cascade

HEIGHT: 20 feet

STREAM: Proposition Creek

MAP: Map of Mountain Ash Creek & Tributaries, USFWS - 1979

ACCESS: Moderate to difficult off-trail hike.

This falls stands isolated in a small canyon on the upper reaches of Proposition Creek. It is approximately two miles north/northeast of the crossing of Mountain Ash Creek Trail and the Falls River, and about a mile upstream from where the same trail crosses Proposition Creek.

In a letter from the USFWS's David Lentz to author Lee Whittlesey dated Nov. 6, 1979, Lentz described the area:

> *On our fish barrier map of Proposition Creek, the falls farthest upstream is a cascading falls with a vertical drop of about 20 feet and a horizontal length of about 50 feet. Just downstream is a second cascade with a vertical height of about 10 feet. Both of these appear to be barriers to upstream fish movement. There are also several smaller cascades upstream from the Marysville Road crossing to the 20-foot cascades.*

Mike Stevens began referring to it as "Siren Falls" after his initial visit there. With only a rough idea as to its location, he set out on a course that was complicated by heavy timber and no reference points. With limited visibility, he was drawn directly to the falls by its siren-like call. The mythological siren was a nymph who sang so alluringly that she drew sailors to their deaths when their ships reached the rocky coast.

58 UNION FALLS

LOCATION: 510393 4893049

FALL TYPE: Plunge Fan

HEIGHT: 250 feet

STREAM: Mountain Ash Creek

 MAP: Grassy Lake Reservoir, Wyoming - 1989

ACCESS: Moderate to difficult on-trail hike.

This breathtaking falls is one of Yellowstone's tallest at 250 feet and is also one of the most frequently named candidates for the title of "most beautiful" of Yellowstone's waterfalls. Formed by the union of Mountain Ash Creek and an unnamed branch, it was named during the period 1884–86 by members of the Hague parties of the USGS. Geologist J.P. Iddings wrote: "The water descends over rocks to 50 ft. below the crest where the branch stream joins the falls. Hence 'Union Falls.'"[98]

Union Falls was featured on a commercial poster in the 1970s, the cover of Charles Maynard's 1996 book *Waterfalls of Yellowstone,* and the cover of a magazine, *Engineer and Engineering Weekly* for April, 1928. It is so spectacular that a lengthy spur trail was built to access its overlook.

In the 1920s, the name "Teepee Falls" was suggested, but the USBGN decided to keep the name Union.[99]

How does one describe Union Falls? It is a massive, imposing, and gorgeous waterfall. It is geologically unique in appearance with its twin streams falling mightily over its sheer face of rock. It ranks as one of the most popular employee day-hikes in the entire park. Writer and researcher Lee Silliman described it in "Dancing Waters," his 1998 photo exhibit:

> Union Falls is an astounding coincidence. Two tributaries of Mountain Ash Creek have set their confluence amidst a precipitous, 250-foot high igneous face of the Pitchstone Plateau. But here beauty shunts geology aside. Like an effervescent fountain, these commingled waters skip and dance in translucent play with a grace unrivaled by any waterfall in the park. While the Lower Falls of the Yellowstone stuns with mightiness of volume and scale, Union Falls pleases with delicate sublimity.

For those interested in making the trek to Union falls—the tallest, officially named, true waterfall in all of the Yellowstone backcountry—there are several choices. Trailheads at Grassy Lake, Fish Lake, and Cave Falls all lead to the falls. The shortest is the Grassy Lake trailhead with a round-trip of 15 miles. This route is the most strenuous with at least one large ridge to climb on the return trip. Consult any park trail guide for more information on this extremely worthwhile and memorable hike.

Union Falls; Photo by Mike Stevens

59 UNNAMED FALLS ON THE NORTH FORK OF MOUNTAIN ASH CREEK "Early Morning Falls"

Josh Steele

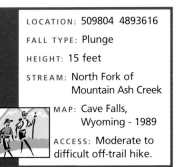

LOCATION: 509804 4893616

FALL TYPE: Plunge

HEIGHT: 15 feet

STREAM: North Fork of
Mountain Ash Creek

MAP: Cave Falls,
Wyoming - 1989

ACCESS: Moderate to
difficult off-trail hike.

"Early Morning Falls" is the name we propose for this plunge on the North Fork of Mountain Ash Creek, just upstream from the area known as Scout Pool and about a mile downstream from Morning Falls. A mapped falls, it is a true vertical plunge, but often partially obscured by fallen trees in the stream.

We include it here because of the confusing history concerning its much larger upstream counterpart, Morning Falls. Several park hiking and trail guides not only mention Morning Falls, but also give directions for how to find it. The problem is that some of these guides underestimate the distance from Scout Pool to Morning Falls. Consequently, some would-be adventurers who bushwhack up this large creek turn back after viewing this small waterfall, thinking they have seen Morning Falls, and return home disappointed.

60 MORNING FALLS

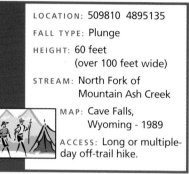

LOCATION: 509810 4895135

FALL TYPE: Plunge

HEIGHT: 60 feet
(over 100 feet wide)

STREAM: North Fork of
Mountain Ash Creek

MAP: Cave Falls,
Wyoming - 1989

ACCESS: Long or multiple-
day off-trail hike.

A relatively recent waterfall discovery of the Yellowstone backcountry is this stunning, 60-foot falls located on the North Fork of Mountain Ash Creek about two miles northwest of Union Falls. Its stature is further enhanced by its 100-foot width. The name was suggested in 1976 by guidebook writer Tom Carter because the falls faces southeast while the rest of the stream faces southwest; hence the falls catches the first rays of the morning sun.[100] Carter told the authors that "at the falls, the stream flows in a southerly direction, but the waterfall's cliff face is not perpendicular to the flow." This geology is what gives Morning Falls its unusual southeasterly face.

Its history is not well-known. There is no reference to this falls or any other on this stream by the Hague Surveys, who discovered nearby Union Falls. Likewise, there is no mention of it by W.C. Gregg during any of his Bechler Region explorations. It was seen by the USFWS in the 1970s when they surveyed the entire stream, but they were definitely not the discoverers. So who was here first? It will probably never be known. The earliest record we have found of anyone seeing this waterfall is in the late 1960s.

In the summer of 1969, ranger Butch Bach and a friend Rod Busby had just completed a hike to Union Falls. They were driving on the Ashton-Flagg Ranch Road (known then as the Reclamation

Mike Stevens

Road) when they picked up a hitchhiker. After hearing of their hike that day, the hitchhiker asked if they had seen the other large fall in the area. No, they replied. He told them that it had only been discovered that year, describing it as 100 feet high and 100 feet wide. He estimated that only a few people had ever seen it. The next week Bach and Busby returned to the area and bushwhacked to the new waterfall. Bach says that even though they had hoped to be one of the first there, they found a somewhat worn trail to the falls. Although the possibility does exist that what they found was a well-worn game trail, it is more likely that Morning Falls has been known far longer than any historical record will ever show.

In the past, some rangers of the region have informally referred to Morning Falls as "North Fork Falls" and "Susong Falls" (for ranger Dunbar Susong).

61 UNNAMED FALLS EAST OF MORNING FALLS "Riverwalk Falls"

LOCATION: 510219 4895182

FALL TYPE: Double-tiered Cascade

HEIGHT: 40 feet

STREAM: Unnamed Tributary of the North Fork of Mountain Ash Creek

MAP: Unmapped

ACCESS: Long or multiple-day off-trail hike.

Mike Stevens

Close to Morning Falls yet another beautiful waterfall goes unnoticed by most who venture this far into the Bechler wilderness. It is less than a half-mile up the unnamed tributary that flows into the North Fork from the east at the base of Morning Falls. This small creek was surveyed and photographed by park employees Mike Stevens, Tom Murphy, and Aaron Vigneault in August 1998.

It is a three-step falls. The main, vertical drop descends about 25 feet, followed by an 8–10 foot drop a few yards downstream and then another, slightly shorter and more disorganized drop below at about the same distance for a total of 40 feet. Farther downstream are two more separate falls, each of 15 feet.

Employee Aaron Vigneault suggested the name "Sidewalk" and then "Riverwalk Falls," because it is a difficult approach unless one walks directly in the creek. The broad, flat streambed is reminiscent of an urban sidewalk and provides an easier approach. Since the micro-topography of "Riverwalk Falls" makes it impossible to adequately photograph all its tiers at once, only the upper part is shown.

62–65
UNNAMED SERIES OF CASCADES ON THE NORTH FORK OF MOUNTAIN ASH CREEK "Dawn Cascades"

LOCATION/FALL TYPE/HEIGHT:
FALL 1: 510006 4895480;
Multi-step Cascade; 60 feet

FALL 2: 510115 4895778;
Multi-step Cascade; 40 feet

FALL 3: 510472 4896004;
Serial Cascade; 80 feet

FALL 4: **511050 4896163**;
Cascade; 75 feet

STREAM: North Fork of
Mountain Ash Creek

MAP: Grassy Lake Reservoir,
Wyoming - 1989

ACCESS: Long or multiple
day off-trail hike.

The first of the four "Dawn Cascades" above Morning Falls.

Paul Rubinstein

During our search for waterfalls we hiked along numerous beautiful streams. Near the top of our list of experiences is this portion of the North Fork above Morning Falls.

Our information comes from four separate surveys: Paul Rubinstein with park employees Marc Phillips and Jennifer Huggins in 1993; Mike Stevens with park employee Tom Mazzarisi in 1995 and again in 1998 with employees Tom Murphy and Aaron Vigneault; and thermal researcher Rocco Paperiello with researchers Mike and Cynthia Keller also in 1998.

Just above Morning Falls a lovely cascade **(#62)** falls about 60 feet in a series of steps that often carry only part of the stream's breadth. The creek here has holes that showcase its remarkably clear, roiling water. The surrounding area is varied, but contains enough open space to offer abundant views of the stream.

Within a quarter mile of the brink of Morning Falls, a second beautiful cascade **(#63)** is similar to the first except that it is just over 40 feet in its drop.

Continuing upstream, beyond a few bends in the scenic river, one comes to a third cascade **(#64)**. It descends as a 40-foot sloping cascade that briefly levels and then repeats itself. The 80–100 foot descent is more like a ramp than the previous cascades. One can only view both segments from the sunny, northeast side. This particular feature was considered important enough to be mapped by the USGS in 1989 on the 7½-minute Grassy Lake Quadrangle (shown as "cascades").

Finally, another fraction of a mile brings us to the fourth cascade **(#65)**, and again it seems the water itself competes to be the main attraction in spite of the

The third and largest of the "Dawn Cascades"

cascade's presence. This gently sloping 75-foot section is characterized by many shades of green algae in its banks. The name "Emerald Cascade" has been used by park employee Cynthia Keller to describe this uppermost feature on the stream. Though the water flow is still fairly hearty here, travel beyond this point quickly leads to the spring-fed origins of the creek. Because these four cascades begin just above Morning Falls, and because they are in relatively open country that is exposed to first light, we refer to them collectively as the "Dawn Cascades."

66 BECHLER FALLS

ike Stevens

LOCATION: 499126 4888265

FALL TYPE: Cascade

HEIGHT: 15 feet

STREAM: Bechler River

MAP: Bechler Falls, Wyoming - Idaho - 1989

ACCESS: Easy to moderate on-trail hike.

Bechler Falls is more of a rapids than a vertical falls. It was named by topographer C.H. Birdseye and/or W.C. Gregg around 1921 from its location on the Bechler River.[101] An easy, one-mile walk from the Cave Falls parking area leads to this cascade. Bechler River was named in 1872 by the Hayden Survey for Gustavus Bechler, the topographer who produced a number of maps for the survey.

67 UNNAMED FALLS ON LOWER OUZEL CREEK "Weeping Falls"

Paul Rubinstein

LOCATION: 502064 4897665

FALL TYPE: Plunge

HEIGHT: 20 feet

STREAM: Ouzel Creek

MAP: Unmapped

ACCESS: Moderate to difficult off-trail hike.

A pretty plunge of Ouzel Creek is hidden in dense forest a short distance below Ouzel Falls. Paul Rubinstein proposed the name in 1995 because a significant amount of water joins the stream from a "weeping wall" just below the falls. The wall supports a luxuriant plant growth, which in turn, seems to alter its outflow into a kind of intense oozing or "weeping." The surroundings are lush and verdant.

This falls was seen and photographed in 1974 by Lee Whittlesey. This seems to be one of the few waterfalls the USFWS missed while surveying a stream. Their study of Ouzel Creek failed to mention this beautiful but well-concealed gem.

68 OUZEL FALLS

LOCATION: 502041 4897894

FALL TYPE: Horsetail/Fan/
Plunge

HEIGHT: 230 feet

STREAM: Ouzel Creek

MAP: Cave Falls,
Wyoming - 1989

ACCESS: Moderate to
difficult off-trail hike.

Paul Rubinstein

Touted as one of Yellowstone's tallest waterfalls, this wispy yet elegant waterfall of Ouzel Creek is 230 feet high. It was named in 1885 by the Hague Survey for the water ouzel or American dipper (*Cinclus mexicanus*), a small, slate-gray bird that feeds along the bottoms of streams. Ouzel Falls is best observed in the early season as it loses a great deal of its water towards the latter part of August. By late autumn it is little more than a few thin strands of white against the rhyolite cliffs.

Hikers can easily spot Ouzel Falls from the Bechler River Trail. The white spray is clearly visible from several miles away in the open grasslands of Bechler Meadows. To reach the base of the falls, one must leave the trail and bushwhack approximately a half-mile. This seemingly short off-trail trip is not for the novice hiker. It requires a ford of the Bechler River and circumnavigation of several deep swamps. Those hazards are then followed by dense forest with tricky slopes.

69-70   UNNAMED FALLS ON UPPER OUZEL CREEK
"Emerald Pool Falls" and "Chasm Falls"

Photos by Mike Stevens

"Emerald Pool Falls"   *"Chasm Falls"*

#69 "EMERALD POOL FALLS"

LOCATION: 502898 4901906

FALL TYPE: Plunge

HEIGHT: 15 feet

STREAM: Ouzel Creek

MAP: Trischman Knob, Wyoming - 1986

ACCESS: Extremely strenuous off-trail hike.

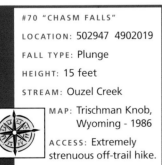

#70 "CHASM FALLS"

LOCATION: 502947 4902019

FALL TYPE: Plunge

HEIGHT: 15 feet

STREAM: Ouzel Creek

MAP: Trischman Knob, Wyoming - 1986

ACCESS: Extremely strenuous off-trail hike.

These two jewels of the backcountry lie about 250 yards apart, approximately two miles upstream from Ouzel Falls. What sets them apart from Yellowstone's other waterfalls is the color of their water. Both "Emerald Pool Falls" (#69) and "Chasm Falls" (#70) plunge 15 feet into intense emerald-green pools. These two falls had been long known to us from the 7½-minute quadrangle maps, yet we knew of no one who had been there on foot. The locations are remote enough to have made that reasonable in retrospect.

Park employee Lee Ramella suggested the name "Emerald Pool Falls" for the downstream of the two, to honor its striking color. He was so enamored that he scrambled down to the brink of the falls from the canyon rim to measure the height of the falls.

"Chasm Falls" is in an unusual setting. It appears to be in a depression, surrounded on all sides by the walls that form the edge of the stream. The falls plunges into a hole with vertical sides carved from the rock. Whatever canyons may be formed by waterfalls elsewhere in Yellowstone, none has the effect that this chasm does in framing the falls and its pool. It is as if a hole has been cut in the hard rock with a giant cookie cutter.

The chasm does not allow photography from the falls' base, but one can go to a point nearly opposite the falls as seen here. Still it may be even better to shoot from somewhere downstream since the gorge is long and narrow.

The jewel-colored water in the pools below each of these two falls is so inviting that it is almost impossible to resist. It is made all the more so by the arid surroundings and strenuous approach.

71–72 COLONNADE FALLS

LOCATION: 504260 4898199

FALL TYPE: Two-tiered Plunge

HEIGHT: 35 feet (upper)
67 feet (lower)

STREAM: Bechler River

MAP: Cave Falls, Wyoming - 1989

ACCESS: Moderate to difficult on-trail hike.

Paul Rubinstein

Members of the Hague Survey named this double plunge **(#71)** of the Bechler River in 1885. A colonnade is a series or row of columns placed at regular intervals, or a double row or avenue (as of trees). The reason for the name is undocumented, but it probably referred either to the nearby columnar basalt layers that resemble columns or to the fact that there were two waterfalls, or perhaps to both.[102]

The Bechler River Trail runs along the southeast side of Colonnade Falls, but there is a noticeable lack of unobstructed overlooks from this main trail. The magnificent two-step display is best viewed from a short spur trail located just downstream of the lower falls. Here the hiker is treated to a superb vista. Directly below the viewer's feet is another unnamed, 25-foot plunge-type waterfall **(#72)** on a small tributary to the Bechler River.

One of the most interesting views of Colonnade Falls is from above. Aerial photographs of this waterfall have appeared in several Yellowstone publications, and a short fly-over sequence of both Colonnade Falls and Iris Falls appeared in the 1994 IMAX film, *Yellowstone.*

73-74 IRIS FALLS

LOCATION: 504588 4898493

FALL TYPE: Plunge

HEIGHT: 45 feet

STREAM: Bechler River

MAP: Cave Falls,
Wyoming - 1989

ACCESS: Moderate to
difficult on-trail hikes.

Paul Rubinstein

Iris Falls (#73) was named
either for its irised spray that
often creates a rainbow or
for Iris, a Greek and Roman
female goddess of the rainbow. Regardless, rainbows
seem to have been forefront
in the thinking of the Hague
Survey members who named
it in 1885.[103] W.C. Gregg,
who explored the area in 1920,
wrote that Iris Falls was "a
notable spectacle," which had
probably been seen by but
few people.[104]

There are two excellent
places in which to observe
and photograph this classic
waterfall. Both a facing view
and a brink shot are located along the Bechler River Trail. It is only about a quarter-
mile upstream from the two plunges of Colonnade Falls. They could almost be
considered as one large, three-step waterfall.

A sharp-eyed observer will see yet another unnamed waterfall (#74), 15–30 feet
high, several hundred yards above Iris Falls. It is towards the upper end of Treasure
Island (the large forested island in the middle of the Bechler River) on a tributary
stream entering the Bechler River from the west.

75 UNNAMED FALLS IN BECHLER CANYON "Treasure Island Falls"

LOCATION: 505151 4898447

FALL TYPE: Multi-segmented Plunges

HEIGHT: 5–25 feet

STREAM: Unnamed Tributary of the Bechler River

MAP: Unmapped

ACCESS: Moderate to difficult off-trail hike.

Rocco Paperiello

At least six individual falls flow from the east canyon wall on the south end of Treasure Island, forming an unnamed stream that flows only a short distance to the Bechler River. Visible from the main trail, the waterfalls are largely vertical, of varying heights, and similar to our "Instant Falls" on the Lamar River, except that there are more of them.

"Treasure Island Falls" takes its suggested name from nearby Treasure Island, named in 1920–21 by explorer W.C. Gregg, probably for the Robert Louis Stevenson book. The name, which evokes visions of an idyllic, unexplored utopia where pirates might bury treasure, is appropriate for the Cascade Corner region of the park.

76 ALBRIGHT FALLS

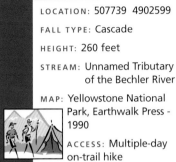

LOCATION: 507739 4902599

FALL TYPE: Cascade

HEIGHT: 260 feet

STREAM: Unnamed Tributary
of the Bechler River

MAP: Yellowstone National
Park, Earthwalk Press -
1990

ACCESS: Multiple-day
on-trail hike

Albright Falls, a long, sloping cascade, was named
in 1986 by park superintendent Bob Barbee following
the death of Horace Marden Albright. Albright helped
to found the National Park Service in 1916, served as
Yellowstone's superintendent from 1919 to 1929, and
was an advisor and mentor to the Park Service for the
rest of his life. His efforts to preserve the Bechler area
from the dams of Idaho developers were heroic and
saved the Cascade Corner from inundation.

The selection of this falls to honor Albright came
at the suggestion of longtime Bechler ranger Dunbar

Paul Rubinstein

Susong, who searched at length for a suitable choice. Also considered in the search were Morning Falls and our "Birdseye Falls."[105] On the naming of the waterfall for Albright, Park superintendent Bob Barbee wrote in 1986: "A few weeks before his death on March 28 of this year I discussed with Mr. Albright the idea of naming this unnamed [sic] waterfall in southwestern Yellowstone in his honor. While naturally somewhat reticent, he was positive about the idea."[106]

The cascade was first reported in 1921 by W.C. Gregg, who noted that "we who saw it ran out of adjectives."[107] In 1921, the General Federation of Women's Clubs proposed the name "Anthony Falls" for this feature in an attempt to honor Susan B. Anthony. However the USBGN failed to approve that name. In fact, Jack Haynes photo 21081, originally titled "Anthony Falls" later appeared as "unnamed 235 ft. cascade."[108] The falls was also called "Batchelder Column Cascade" for many years, because of its location near the rock formation of that name.

Albright Falls can be readily seen from the Bechler River Trail. Unfortunately, trees obscure it somewhat from nearly every angle.

Cascade Gregg

In 1920–21, William C. Gregg (1862–1946) of Hackensack, New Jersey, made the most comprehensive explorations and studies of the Bechler area and took some of the first photos of its many features. Traveling with photographer Jack Haynes and topographer C.H. Birdseye, his waterfall discoveries changed Yellowstone as we know it. His magazine articles in *Saturday Evening Post* and *Outlook* were responsible to a large degree for saving the area's features from inundation by a proposed dam in Bechler Meadows.[109]

Gregg revisited the Bechler country in 1923, 1926, and 1928. He has been called a "staunch conservationist and champion of national park ideals," and as a result of his explorations and the resulting protection of the Cascade Corner area of Yellowstone, he became affectionately known as "Cascade Gregg."

Gregg also named several Bechler area features, among them Cascade Corner, Cascade Acres, Ranger Lake, Cave Falls, Three River Junction, and Treasure Island.

Ferris Fork and Tributaries

77 RAGGED FALLS

LOCATION: 508820 4903697

FALL TYPE: Segmented Cascade

HEIGHT: 45 feet

STREAM: Ferris Fork of the
Bechler River

MAP: Trischman Knob,
Wyoming - 1986

ACCESS: Multiple-day
on-trail hike.

Paul Rubinstein

Ragged Falls is located on the Ferris Fork about 200 yards above Three River Junction. This cascading waterfall was characteristically named for its ragged appearance in 1921 by park photographer Jack Haynes.[110] W.C. Gregg, whom Haynes had accompanied on his 1921 expedition, originally wanted to call it "Rugged Falls," but Ragged prevailed. Its twisting, jumbled waters fall in a haphazard pattern that undoubtedly inspired both names.

This falls is easily seen from the Bechler River Trail, which passes next to its brink. The superior vantage point, however, is from the opposite (eastern) side of the stream. Seen from straight on, the falls opens up nicely, truly showing off its varied shapes and chaotic nature. Ragged Falls is the first of five named waterfalls on the Ferris Fork, although it is the only one found along a maintained trail.

78-79

UNNAMED FALLS SOUTHEAST OF THREE RIVER JUNCTION
"Bride Falls" and "Groom Falls"

David Rothenburger

LOCATION: 508928 4903289

FALL TYPE: Segmented Cascades

HEIGHT: 20 feet each

STREAM: Unnamed Tributary of the Ferris Fork of Bechler River

MAP: Unmapped

ACCESS: Multiple-day off-trail hike

"Bride Falls" (**#78**), at right, and "Groom Falls" (**#79**), at left, are two separate waterfalls on the first tributary of the Ferris Fork above Ragged Falls. This unnamed stream enters the Ferris Fork from the south. Approximately three-quarters of a mile above its mouth, it splits around a small island. During the separation, the twin branches plunge side-by-side, thus creating matching waterfalls. Ranger David Rothenburger proposed the names during a 1997 visit to the area, because he imagined the more westerly of the two falls was shaped like a wedding dress while the easterly falls was more masculine in stature.

80 TENDOY FALLS

LOCATION: 509739 4903225

FALL TYPE: Plunge

HEIGHT: 33 feet

STREAM: Ferris Fork of the Bechler River

MAP: Trischman Knob, Wyoming - 1986

ACCESS: Multiple-day off-trail hike.

Mike Stevens

Tendoy Falls was named in 1921 by W.C. Gregg and Jack Haynes for Tendoy, a chief of the Lemhi Shoshones (1834?–1907), who lived near Yellowstone National Park in eastern Idaho. His name most likely means "the climber" or "he climbs rocks," although another source gives it as "he likes broth."[111] William D. Pickett, a hunter who knew Tendoy, described him as "a high-class man, frank, intelligent and witty, with a natural dignity that was very impressive."[112]

The falls is about a mile above Ragged Falls. It is set between gray, 40-foot cliffs that line both sides of the creek for some distance downstream. The superior vista of this falls is from the ledge on the western side. A spur trail leads away from the Bechler River Trail and continues up the Ferris Fork about halfway to Tendoy Falls. The path ends in the middle of a small but noteworthy thermal area that includes several beautiful hot springs and one natural hot tub informally called the "Ferris Fork Pool." Beyond this pool the hiker must carefully maneuver between the various springs and runoff channels for close to half a mile before reaching Tendoy Falls.

81 GWINNA FALLS

LOCATION: 509615 4902969

FALL TYPE: Plunge

HEIGHT: 15 feet

STREAM: Ferris Fork
of the Bechler River

MAP: Trischman Knob,
Wyoming - 1986

ACCESS: Multiple-day
off-trail hike.

Located a half-mile above Tendoy Falls, this waterfall was first named "Nokomis Fall" in 1921 by explorer W.C. Gregg. Nokomis was the grandmother and nurse of Hiawatha in Longfellow's poem of that name. The USBGN changed the name to Gwinna, the Shoshone Indian word for "eagle."[113] The falls appears under this name on virtually all Yellowstone Park maps to this day. Although several maps and publications list its height at 20 feet, the correct height of Gwinna Falls, as mapped by its original discovers Gregg and Birdseye, is 15 feet.

A small step-down falls, it is partially obscured on the western side of the stream by lodgepole pines. In addition, the creek makes a slight turn towards the northeast at the lip of the falls, giving it an odd angle for good viewing. However, it can be seen and photographed from the eastern bank of the Ferris Fork with no obstructions. Late morning is the most likely time of day in which to catch Gwinna Falls in bright sunlight.

Paul Rubinstein

82   SLUICEWAY FALLS

LOCATION: 509697 4902655

FALL TYPE: Plunge

HEIGHT: 10 feet

STREAM: Ferris Fork of the Bechler River

MAP: Trischman Knob, Wyoming - 1986

ACCESS: Multiple-day off-trail hike.

Mike Stevens

Writers have always reported that Sluiceway Falls was discovered and named in 1921 by explorer W.C. Gregg. There is no record of what inspired the name, but it is suspected to be the physical appearance of the falls. (A sluiceway is an artificial channel for water often used by prospectors in mining days.) Park maps place the falls halfway between Gwinna Falls and Wahhi Falls.

As with Quiver Cascade, we were faced with a puzzling question about Sluiceway Falls: its height. Although previous documentation and park maps show the falls as 35 feet, there are actually no features of that size between Gwinna Falls and Wahhi Falls on the Ferris Fork. However, there are several much smaller waterfalls in the area. Why have all maps and references to Sluiceway Falls listed it at 35 feet?

We pondered this disparity and first reasoned that Sluiceway Falls was probably not one, but rather a sequence of three separate waterfalls within one-quarter mile of each other, totaling 35 feet. That would account not only for the size discrepancy, but also for an inconsistency in the only two previously published photos of this waterfall. Jack Haynes's 1921 photo 21068, labeled "Sluiceway Falls," shows a waterfall of not more than 10–15 feet in height. John Barber's 1984 photo labeled "Sluiceway Falls" shows a different feature than Haynes, also of around 10 feet.

Later however, when we saw C.H. Birdseye's 1922 map of Cascade Corner, the true answer came to light. On it, Sluiceway Falls is listed as only 10 feet in height. Why all subsequent documentation has mistakenly shown this falls to be 35 feet is not known. What is apparent is that Gregg's party did indeed name only one feature, and Jack Haynes photographed it. It appears that Sluiceway Falls was indeed singled out for its unusual physical appearance.

83-84 WAHHI FALLS

Wahhi Falls (upper)

Wahhi Falls (lower)

LOCATION UPPER (#83): 509850 4902232

LOCATION LOWER (#84): 509812 4902374

FALL TYPE: Two-serial Plunge

HEIGHT: 28 & 18 feet

STREAM: Ferris Fork of the Bechler River

MAP: Trischman Knob, Wyoming - 1986

ACCESS: Multiple-day off-trail hike.

This two-step waterfall **(#83, #84)** of the Ferris Fork has heights of 28 feet (upper) and 18 feet (lower). In fact, the original suggestion for its name (by W.C. Gregg in 1921) was "Two Step Falls." In March 1922, however, the USBGN approved the name Wahhi Falls from a Shoshone Indian term (*wahat hwa*) meaning "two step" or "double."[114] The falls themselves are both plunges.

The upper drop is the far more scenic of the two. Its setting between high slopes and its classic shape make it one of the most photogenic falls in the area. A large cave at its base further enhances its beauty. Upper Wahhi Falls is perhaps the finest waterfall on the entire Ferris Fork.

Some confusion has existed over the lower falls. Obscured from nearly all angles, hikers often miss it as they travel upstream from Sluiceway Falls. In fact, the authors missed the lower falls no less than three times before finally viewing it in 1997. Jack Haynes's 1921 photograph of this falls does show both drops. Reaching Haynes's original vantage point however is extremely difficult, involving deep fords and rock scrambling. Lower Wahhi Falls can only be seen clearly from the east side of the Ferris Fork.

85–88

UNNAMED CASCADES ON THE UPPER FERRIS FORK
"Pristine Cascades"

"Pristine Cascades:" Fall #1

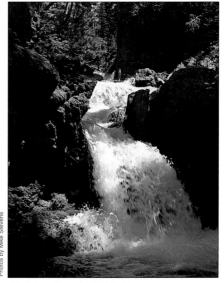

Photos by Mike Stevens

"Pristine Cascades:" Fall #3

LOCATION/FALL TYPE/HEIGHT:

FALL 1: 510787 4901867; Plunge; 22 feet

FALL 2: 511750 4902455; Cascade; 16 feet

FALL 3: 512133 4902563; Two-step Plunge; 19 feet

FALL 4: 512190 4902705; Plunge; 11 feet

STREAM: Ferris Fork of the Bechler River

MAP: Map of the Cascade Corner - C.H. Birdseye, 1922

ACCESS: Multiple-day off-trail hike.

Above Wahhi Falls, the Ferris Fork was, until now, an unknown entity. Shortly above upper Wahhi Falls, the stream has two branches. The smaller of the two (coming in from the south) flows from the Pitchstone Plateau and contains a medium-sized cascade. The larger of the two (coming in from the east) is the true Ferris Fork. It descends gradually through the forested region for some three miles before merging with its southerly tributary.

We now know that W.C. Gregg, Jack Haynes, and C.H. Birdseye did survey this far up the larger branch in 1921 and did indeed find waterfalls here. Birdseye's map of that trip shows four distinct "tick" marks on this stretch of creek within two miles of Wahhi Falls and within one mile of each other.

In August 1999 author Mike Stevens and park employee Lee Ramella surveyed the uppermost reaches of the Ferris Fork. They found Gregg and Birdseye's four other falls, along with several smaller cascades and falls. The four major features (#85–#88) are falls of 22, 16, 19, and 11 feet. They each carry their own unique feel of serenity and isolation. So seldom is this area visited that several ancient cans and remnants of an old campsite found by Stevens and Ramella likely belonged to Gregg, Haynes, and Birdseye themselves.

Our proposed name "Pristine Cascades" tries to capture the unspoiled quality of this remotest section of Bechler wilderness. Like the eight features of Quiver Cascade and the five steps of Tempe Cascade, we have chosen to identify this entire series of cascades under one designation in order to simplify an area already saturated with waterfalls.

Phillips Fork

The Phillips Fork is undoubtedly the most complex and confusing area in Yellowstone when it comes to waterfalls. The substantial creek has nine significant features on its length. In addition, its largest tributary, the "East Branch of the Phillips Fork," has three additional waterfalls for a total of 12 falls in the drainage. Completing this convoluted region is a thirteenth feature we call the "Weeping Wall." It is neither a waterfall, nor a cascade, but rather an entire hillside that oozes with springs. These string-like cascades slide swiftly into the Phillips Fork from the west.

Until this book was published, there was never a definitive explanation as to the locations and histories of the major features here, specifically Quiver Cascade and Hourglass Falls. Documentation of these two previously named falls has been riddled with historical inaccuracies, including miscaptioned photographs, incorrect or inconsistent heights, and misplacement on maps. The following entries are complicated and may not be easy to understand. It is our hope, however, that we can set the record straight as to the specific details of the Phillips Fork drainage. In an effort to aid the reader, we have included three detailed maps (see the third on page 117). that display all known features in the area. (Two of these maps were produced by author Paul Rubinstein using current USGS quadrangles, and the other is a portion of the historic 1922 Cascade Corner map by C.H. Birdseye.) We hope that inclusion of these maps will help clarify the intricacies of this part of Yellowstone.

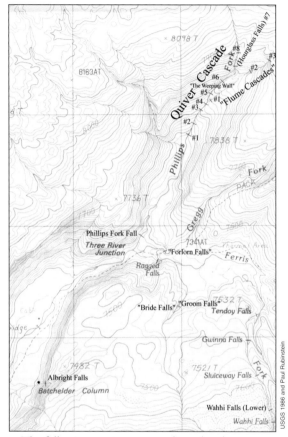

USGS 1986 and Paul Rubinstein

C.H. Birdseye, 1922

Portion of "Map of Cascade Corner"

89 PHILLIPS FORK FALL

Paul Rubinstein

LOCATION: 508583 4903828

FALL TYPE: Segmented Cascade

HEIGHT: 5 feet

STREAM: Phillips Fork of
the Bechler River

MAP: Map of the Cascade
Corner - C.H. Birdseye, 1922

ACCESS: Multiple-day
off-trail hike.

This waterfall, although only a meager five feet high, is included because it has an accepted historical name, given by W.C. Gregg in 1921. It is the first waterfall on the Phillips Fork above Three River Junction.[115]

A photo of this waterfall, Haynes photo 21055, was at one time available for sale to the general public. It could be ordered through the Haynes Bulletin beginning in February, 1922.

90-98 QUIVER CASCADE

Quiver Cascade #1

Paul Rubinstein

LOCATION/FALL TYPE/HEIGHT:

FALL 1: 509071 4904783; Plunge; 15 feet

FALL 2: 509116 4904921; Fan Cascade; 30 feet

FALL 3: 509147 4905003; Cascade; 30 feet

FALL 4: 509202 4905044; Cascade; 40 feet

FALL 5: 509254 4905185; Cascade; 25 feet

FALL 6: 509372 4905289; Cascade; 35 feet

FALL 7: (Hourglass Falls) - 509531 4905574; Horsetail Fan; 90 feet

FALL 8: 509559 4905663; Horsetail; 20 feet

STREAM: Phillips Fork of the Bechler River

MAP: Trischman Knob, Wyoming - 1986

ACCESS: Multiple-day off-trail hike.

Great confusion has surrounded not only this feature but also the whole of the Phillips Fork. The quandary is that on the fork there are eight cascades above Phillips Fork Fall (at the stream's mouth) and any of them could be Quiver Cascade.

The "cascade" was named in or about 1921 by explorers W.C. Gregg and Jack Haynes. They left only a notation on Birdseye's 1922 map (copied onto all subsequent maps) and a 1921 photo of the feature by Gregg that is listed as Haynes photo 21121. Although it seems to have disappeared from the records, this photo would identify the specific feature to which Gregg gave the name Quiver.[116]

We had much difficulty determining exactly which feature(s) is/are the proper Quiver Cascade. In 1978, USFWS researcher David Lentz explored the stream and named the seventh upstream cascade Hourglass Falls. Lentz apparently assumed Hourglass was upstream of Quiver Cascade. In 1984, John Barber published a photo labeled "Quiver Cascade" that was actually on a tributary stream to the Phillips Fork and not Quiver Cascade at all. Further confusion was added when a typing error in Lee Whittlesey's *Wonderland Nomenclature* placed Quiver Cascade above Hourglass Falls.

Paul Rubinstein

Quiver Cascade #2

This was the information we had when we began our research, and we were very confused. Finding no other historic references to clear things up, we began trying to determine which feature (or features) was the true Quiver Cascade.

The word "quiver" was our first clue. We long assumed the reason for the name was that the water had been seen to "quiver," but Mike Stevens believed that idea was incorrect. Instead, he theorized that "quiver" here referred to a container for arrows in archery. It happens that a round of arrows contains six arrows and that the six arrows are stored in a quiver; hence his theory that the name Quiver Cascade referred to the first six of the eight water features above Phillips Fork Fall. We knew Gregg's party had a pattern of sometimes naming a series of falls and cascades rather than individually. We also knew there were six falls and cascades below Hourglass Falls. In addition, several older USGS maps showed six tick marks for Quiver Cascade. Everything seemed perfect until we finally got a look at the original 1922 map. On it was the entry: "Quiver Cascade - 90 feet."

Upon seeing that one notation, Paul Rubinstein deduced what had happened. In 1922, Gregg and company found and named a 90-foot, steep, cascade-type fall Quiver Cascade. In 1978, researcher Lentz, using incorrectly marked USGS maps and thus believing he was above Quiver Cascade, named the same feature Hourglass Falls. The 90-foot reference was the key. Quiver/Hourglass is the only feature on the entire Phillips Fork even approaching that height. Rubinstein is convinced that when a copy of Haynes' original photo of Quiver Cascade does come to light, it will show the same feature Lentz called Hourglass Falls.

Faced with this historical confusion, and so many features to describe, we have decided to present all eight cascades of the upper Phillips Fork under one designation: Quiver Cascade. Although Gregg's party named only the largest cascade Quiver, they did map the other smaller drops with tick marks on their map. Descriptions of the eight features of the upper Phillips Fork follow.

About a mile above Phillips Fork Fall, the first fall of Quiver Cascade **(#90)** is a short plunge of about 15 feet. Several hundred yards beyond is

Quiver Cascade #4

Paul Rubinstein

the second cascade (#91). It is nearly twice the height of the first and nearly twice as wide. A short distance upstream from here is the third cascade (#92) of the Quiver system. It is a complex 25-foot cascade characterized by cliff walls on its northwest side and a 90-degree turn midway through its descent.

At Quiver Cascade #4 (#93), another 200 yards upstream, the stream hugs a cliff wall while the cascade splits and tumbles about 40 feet downward. The fifth Quiver Cascade (#94) sits amidst the most complex geography of the entire Phillips Fork. This 40-foot cascade is just above the point where an easterly branch of the stream feeds into it. Cascades at the mouth of this easterly branch flow directly into the Phillips Fork. The immediate area is a virtual waterfall crossroads with over a dozen falls within a one-mile radius in all directions. All five of these features are easily viewed, as opposed to the next feature upstream.

Quiver Cascade #6 (#95) is different; it sits in the bottom of a narrow trench, making it nearly impossible to photograph. Even more peculiar is a presence of a huge "Weeping Wall" (#98) on its west side. From the wall there are at least a dozen individual waterfalls streaming down the sidehill into the Phillips Fork. They range in height from 50–100 feet. All are ribbon-shaped but some fan out towards the bottom while others keep their rope-like appearances for their entire descent. The scene is rare, if not unique, in all of Yellowstone, particularly in an area that is already saturated with waterfalls.

This brings us to Quiver Cascade #7 (#96), the original inspiration for the name Quiver Cascade and more recently known as Hourglass Falls. This wispy falls is located at a vertical wall several hundred yards above Quiver Cascade #6. As mentioned earlier, it was individually named in 1978 by Lentz of the USFWS. Lentz stated he named it because "midway in its drop, the falling water is pinched off by rocks so that the flow narrows in the middle and spreads at the bottom, resembling a long hourglass."[117] Quiver #7/Hourglass Falls is by far the most impressive feature found on all of the Phillips Fork tributary system. With over 90 feet of nearly vertical plunge, it dwarfs the other waterfalls described in the drainage.

Fifty yards above the brink of Hourglass Falls is the eighth and final feature of Quiver Cascade (#97). It is a 20-foot nearly vertical falls and is the farthest upstream feature the authors found in any of their surveys of the Phillips Fork drainage. It is a cascade-type fall, followed by a long, lazy section of rapids. Like the lower Wahhi Falls, hikers can easily miss this waterfall. The cliffs that surround it obscure it from view.

Quiver Cascade #7 (Hourglass Falls)

Moving upstream beyond this eighth and final fall, the Phillips Fork continues to contain numerous small cascades from 10–12 feet. Some are direct drops while others twist and slide through small gorges and canyons. Of all the named streams in Yellowstone, the Phillips Fork houses the highest concentration of cascades and falls.

"East Branch of the Phillips Fork"

The Phillips Fork's largest tributary is an unnamed stream that runs almost parallel to it before entering it two miles above its mouth between the fourth and fifth features of Quiver Cascade. We refer to this important stream as the "East Branch of the Phillips Fork." To further complicate matters, this branch contains three additional, separate waterfalls, all of which were mapped by C.H. Birdseye in 1922. In an effort to simplify the overwhelming complexities of this area, we present these three features of the "East Branch of Phillips Fork" under one name: "Flume Cascades." This procedure is similar to what we have done with Quiver Cascade and Tempe Cascade.

99–101 UNNAMED SERIES OF FALLS ON THE "EAST BRANCH OF THE PHILLIPS FORK" "Flume Cascades"

LOCATION LOWER (#99):
509250 4905138 (lower)
LOCATION MIDDLE (#100):
509402 4905261 (middle)
LOCATION UPPER (#101):
509830 4905507 (upper)

FALL TYPE: Three Cascades

HEIGHT: 25, 15, & 80 feet

STREAM: "East Branch Phillips Fork"

MAP: Map of the Cascade Corner - C.H. Birdseye, 1922

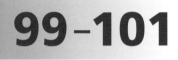

ACCESS: Multiple-day off-trail hike.

"Flume Cascades" (lower)

Mike Stevens

The first of these three drops **(#99)** is the most historically important. The 25-foot cascade rushes steeply down a rocky ravine at the very spot where the "East Branch" meets the Phillips Fork. A photograph of this waterfall appeared in John F. Barber's 1984 *Ribbons of Water* under the heading of "Quiver Cascade." This feature is not Quiver Cascade; in fact, it is not even on the Phillips Fork. The photographic error by Barber is understandable however.

In late season the water levels of both streams run so low at times that without the proper maps it is difficult to discern which stream is the true Phillips Fork. Because the photo was published with the caption "Quiver Cascade," we were confused when we first surveyed this area. Now after four separate visits to the drainage, we feel confident in our assessment.

The next section of the flume **(#100)** is within 50 yards of the first. It is a small falls of no more than 15 feet. It does however provide a direct link to the grandest sight the "East Branch" has to offer just one-quarter mile farther upstream.

The third waterfall **(#101)** of the "East Branch" is the reason for the name "Flume Cascades." It is far and away the most impressive on the stream. Physically similar to Ouzel Falls, the churning water slides down a steep rock face for the majority of its descent before finally dropping free at the end. This bottom plunge is perhaps 15 feet on its own, while the upper section is more than 40 feet in length. Ranger David Rothenburger thought the scene was reminiscent of a water-park ride where an artificial log careens down a fast track until it is slowed by a bottom pool, hence our proposed name.

"Flume Cascades" (middle)   *"Flume Cascades" (upper)*

Gregg Fork and "Aviator Creek"

102 UNNAMED FALLS ON GREGG FORK
"Forlorn Falls"

Paul Rubinstein

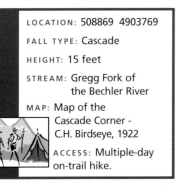

LOCATION: 508869 4903769

FALL TYPE: Cascade

HEIGHT: 15 feet

STREAM: Gregg Fork of the Bechler River

MAP: Map of the Cascade Corner - C.H. Birdseye, 1922

ACCESS: Multiple-day on-trail hike.

"Forlorn Falls" is the first waterfall of the Gregg Fork. Several hundred yards above the creek's mouth at Three River Junction, it is almost always overlooked. It is a well-defined falls with a uniform and relatively straight descent of about 15 feet.

Unfortunately, this beautiful little waterfall is another example of a fine feature missed by perhaps hundreds of hikers per season. There are several reasons for this. Although the trail passes within yards of it, "Forlorn Falls" is tucked neatly out of view into a small ravine that also muffles its roar. Secondly, the prominence of Ragged Falls only 100 yards to the south draws most people's attention. Combine this with the fact that this falls has appeared on only one park map (shown as a "tick" on the C.H. Birdseye 1922 Map of Cascade Corner) and we see why it has been historically ignored.

We believe it deserves more notice and a name. It should be a prime attraction in the area. Hikers take note: "Forlorn Falls" is a rightful participant in the Cascade Corner.

103 UNNAMED CASCADES IN GREGG CANYON

There is an extensive stretch of cascades (#103) in the first large canyon of the Gregg Fork above its mouth at Three River Junction. It is a long series, on the order of hundreds of feet, seen by few due to an absence of decent vantage points. The canyon walls are vertical on the river here, making travel next to the stream impossible. However a portion of these impressive cascades can be seen from above, by walking several feet off the Bechler River trail.

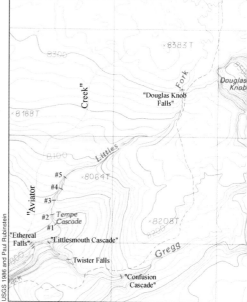

USGS 1986 and Paul Rubinstein

104 UNNAMED FALLS AT THE MOUTH OF "AVIATOR CREEK" "Ethereal Falls"

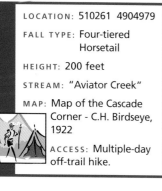

LOCATION: 510261 4904979

FALL TYPE: Four-tiered Horsetail

HEIGHT: 200 feet

STREAM: "Aviator Creek"

MAP: Map of the Cascade Corner - C.H. Birdseye, 1922

ACCESS: Multiple-day off-trail hike.

"Ethereal Falls" is located on an unnamed, permanent stream that enters Gregg Fork from the north, at a point about one-fifth mile below the mouth of the Little's Fork. This impressive feature is a four-tiered horsetail falls with intermixed cascades. It drops directly into the Gregg Fork and totals at least 200 feet in

Top two tiers of "Ethereal Falls"   Mike Stevens

height. The feature appears from a distance to be organized into tall, multiple, vertical falls, each twisted to face a different direction.

In 1922, W.C. Gregg and his party saw this falls, as indicated by the "double-tick" on their map of that year. It appears, however, they did not survey the stream but rather saw "Ethereal Falls" from a distance, as their map does not show any water-course above the falls. In 1990, Paul Rubinstein, Mike Stevens, and a party of six others surveyed the entire stream. They fell onto it at its headwaters west of Douglas Knob and followed it downstream where they saw "Ethereal Falls." Ethereal means "light and airy." It also means "celestial or heavenly." Either reference is applicable.

We propose the name "Aviator Creek" for the stream. On its headwaters, at a point 1.6 miles west of Douglas Knob and 1.9 miles south of Trischman Knob, a U.S. Air Force B-47 airplane crashed in 1963 killing three U.S. airmen. The wreckage of the plane remained on the site until removed by the NPS in 1993.[118]

105 TWISTER FALLS

LOCATION: 510628 4904846

FALL TYPE: Cascade

HEIGHT: 55 feet

STREAM: Gregg Fork of the Bechler River

MAP: Shoshone Geyser Basin, Wyoming - 1986 (Reversed with "Confusion Cascade")

ACCESS: Multiple-day on-trail hike.

Paul Rubinstein

There has long been confusion between this falls on the Gregg Fork and another one a short distance upstream that we have called "Confusion Cascade." Many recent maps show the name "Twister" on the wrong feature. The true Twister Falls, as mapped in 1921 and named by explorer W.C. Gregg, is three-quarters of a mile downstream from "Confusion Cascade" and closer to the mouth of Little's Fork.

This original Twister Falls makes a characteristic twist as the water drops and has a height of

55 feet.[119] A spur trail from the Bechler River Trail gives a good view of this falls, but the better view is from the opposite side, directly facing the falls. About 10 yards above Twister Falls is an upper, vertical fall with a height of only 10 feet.

Which Falls Was First?

Three River Junction is the point where the Ferris, Gregg, and Phillips Forks merge at virtually the same place to form the Bechler River. Within two miles of this junction are no less than 33 waterfalls, undoubtedly the heaviest concentration in the park. In 1876, F.V. Hayden constructed the first Yellowstone map showing a feature there. On it, the notation "falls" appeared near the headwaters of what his men labeled "Bechlers R." It wasn't much, but it was the first indication that this region was a treasure trove of waterfalls. It remained the only mapped waterfall in the vicinity of Three River Junction for the next 45 years, yet today, we are uncertain which falls it was.

What makes this particularly important is that no waterfall in the vicinity of Three River Junction was known to have been discovered before W.C. Gregg surveyed the area with C.H. Birdseye and Jack Haynes in 1920–21. The map's implication is that at least one waterfall was known 45 years earlier. This mysterious notation ("falls") remained on nearly all park maps until the Gregg expedition, at which time nearly a dozen new falls appeared with their accompanying new names including Tendoy Falls, Gwinna Falls, and Twister Falls.

How could explorers in the 1870s have mapped only one waterfall when there are so many to be found there? The answer may be contained in a description of the first documented visit to the Bechler drainage by Dr. Frank Bradley and chief topographer Gustavus Bechler in 1872. While camped at Madison Lake, the source of the Firehole River, Bradley described a detour that he and Bechler took as the main survey party moved east toward Shoshone Lake:

> Our hunter, Frank Mounts, had reported a valley about two miles south of us, through which a stream flowed westward. Accordingly, while the train moved about three miles due east, to a new camp on Shoshone Lake, Mr. Bechler and I crossed the southern divide to the head of the newly reported river. We found it to be a large stream, formed, within a short distance, from the abundant flow of numerous large springs bursting from low down in the sides of a high plateau of very porous volcanic sandstones, which we afterward found to extend for several miles to the southward.[120]

Apparently Bradley and Bechler fell onto the Little's Fork from the north before turning east to meet their main party. They did not survey downstream far enough to find the numerous waterfalls and cascades that they were so close to. But at least one waterfall was seen.

106 UNNAMED FALLS ON THE UPPER GREGG FORK "Confusion Cascade"

LOCATION: 511092 4904687

FALL TYPE: Fan Cascade

HEIGHT: 25 feet (130 feet with cascades)

STREAM: Gregg Fork of the Bechler River

MAP: Shoshone Geyser Basin, Wyo. - 1986 (Reversed with Twister Falls)

ACCESS: Multiple-day on-trail hike.

Paul Rubinstein

"Confusion Cascade" is a fan-type, 25-foot drop followed by a long, curving cascade of 80–100 feet. The north side of the creek is steep and open with unstable footing. The Bechler Trail once passed by this falls, but has since been rerouted. To see the falls, follow the old unmaintained trail from campsite 9D2 upstream about three-eighths of a mile.

With this name we hope to clear up an important historical mapping error in Yellowstone. Since 1959, the USGS 15-minute quadrangles and many other park maps have shown two falls on the Gregg Fork: "Twister Falls" and "Falls." The inaccuracy is that these names have been reversed. We cite the error here and wish not only to correct it but also to suggest the name "Confusion Cascade" for the upper falls in keeping with this inaccurate mapping history.

107-108

UNNAMED FALLS AT THE MOUTH OF THE LITTLE'S FORK "Littlesmouth Cascade"

LOCATION: 510450 4905002

FALL TYPE: Cascade

HEIGHT: 45 feet

STREAM: Little's Fork of the Bechler River

MAP: Unmapped

ACCESS: Multiple-day off-trail hike.

Paul Rubinstein

An impressive cascade (#107) is found at the mouth of the Little's Fork. It is neither mapped nor previously photographed in any publication. Its only known documentation is in the USFWS *Annual Project Report* for 1979. The report says: "The Little's Fork flows over frequent cascades and receives several spring tributaries culminating with an unnamed 15.2m falls near the mouth."

Paul Rubinstein and Mike Stevens each came up with the suggested name, "Littlesmouth Cascade," independently. After viewing it, they each thought its location on the stream was the most distinguishing characteristic. Hikers should be aware that when facing Twister Falls, they are only yards away from several wonderful vantage points of this surprisingly significant cascade.

At the bottom of "Littlesmouth Cascade", the Little's Fork and the Gregg Fork merge. Less than five feet upstream and spanning the entire width of the Gregg Fork is a six-foot waterfall (#108) that did not meet our height criterion for inclusion as its own entry. However we take the opportunity to mention it here. We affectionately refer to it as "Fusion Falls" because it is at the spot where the two creeks "fuse" together as one.

109–113 TEMPE CASCADE

Tempe Cascade #1   Paul Rubinstein

LOCATION/FALL TYPE/HEIGHT:

FALL 1: 510550 4905130; Cascade; 20 feet

FALL 2: 510462 4905235; Cascade/Plunge;
          20 feet

FALL 3: 510488 4905351; Cascade/Fan; 25 feet

FALL 4: 510535 4905470; Cascade; 15 feet

FALL 5: 510580 4905502; Cascade; 30 feet

STREAM: Little's Fork of the Bechler River

MAP: Shoshone Geyser Basin,
        Wyoming - 1986

ACCESS: Multiple-day off-trail hike.

Tempe Cascade was originally named in 1922 by explorer W.C. Gregg, who suggested "Cavern" as the name. The USBGN changed the name-form to Tempe, a Shoshone Indian word for "cavern," to create a more noticeable difference between this name and Cave Falls to the south.

The 1986 maps show four "falls" marks here while the 1956 and 1961 maps show three. But there are actually five features on Little's Fork, above "Littlesmouth Cascade," which comprise "Tempe Cascade." Moving upstream, the five, each within 100 yards of the next, are as follows: a 20-foot cascade (**#109**), a 20-foot cascade/plunge (**#110**), a 25-foot cascade/fan (**#111**), a 15-foot cascade (**#112**), and a 30-foot cascade (**#113**). The second feature, which has a true cave immediately adjacent to it, is most likely the feature Gregg and Haynes named the entire cascade for and which is depicted in the park's black photo albums, a collection of 30 scrapbooks containing many photos.

Ranger Scotty Chapman described the cave in 1964: "Though not very deep, it is large enough in which to erect a tent. The rangers did so years ago and used it as an emergency camp several times while on winter patrols in this area."[121]

Tempe Cascade #2   Paul Rubinstein

114 UNNAMED FALLS SOUTHWEST OF DOUGLAS KNOB "Douglas Knob Falls"

LOCATION: 511661 4906435

FALL TYPE: Segmented Cascade

HEIGHT: 25 feet

STREAM: Little's Fork of the Bechler River

MAP: USFWS Map of Bechler River Headwaters - 1979

ACCESS: Multiple-day off-trail hike.

Paul Rubinstein

As the name suggests, "Douglas Knob Falls" can be found less than a half-mile southwest of its namesake Douglas Knob on the Little's Fork. It drops sharply for at least 18 feet before cascading for at least seven more. Its only previous documentation is in the USFWS *Annual Project Report* for 1979. The report's hand-drawn map shows the notation, "6m falls."

"Douglas Knob Falls" sits in a small, narrow canyon. This is probably why it has gone essentially unnoticed until now, even though it is close to a heavily used hiking trail. Its waters twist and tangle for roughly 25 feet around rocky bluffs and through stacked, downed timber. In this stretch of the Little's Fork, the creek makes an S-shaped pattern. The top of the falls is segmented into multiple sections, a condition we suspect is prevalent for most of the season.

Finding this falls is easy as it is less than a 10-minute walk from the Bechler River Trail at Douglas Knob. The forest here is thin and footing is not a problem.

Boundary Creek and Tributaries

The most visited stretch of Boundary Creek is in its lower reaches in Bechler Meadows. However, to truly appreciate Boundary Creek as one of the most scenic streams in Yellowstone, one must explore the portion from Dunanda Falls upstream. There the water churns and tumbles for miles through a seemingly endless stretch of small cascades and foaming rapids. At numerous points along the Boundary Creek Trail the hiker encounters the stream's whitewater as it rushes over the uneven bedrock. This diverse creek also receives runoff from numerous thermal springs that extend from Dunanda Falls for miles upstream.

Boundary Creek takes its name from its geographical proximity to the Wyoming-Idaho border, as noted by the Hague Survey in 1904. However, 30 years earlier, independent surveyor A.V. Richards had given it the appropriate name of Cascade Creek (a name that survives today on one of Boundary Creek's upper tributaries), most likely due to the numerous small falls on its upper reaches. Although only four of its more prominent drops are detailed in this book, there are many smaller falls and picturesque rapids that contribute to the magnificence of this stream. We highly recommend this beautiful and often overlooked part of Yellowstone.

Dunanda Falls

Mike Stevens

115–116

UNNAMED FALLS ON LOWER BOUNDARY CREEK
"Confederate Falls"

"Confederate Falls"

Mike Stevens

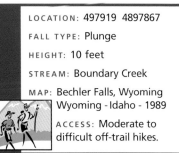

LOCATION: 497919 4897867

FALL TYPE: Plunge

HEIGHT: 10 feet

STREAM: Boundary Creek

MAP: Bechler Falls, Wyoming
Wyoming - Idaho - 1989

ACCESS: Moderate to difficult off-trail hikes.

A mile below Dunanda Falls, this 10-foot-high, 50-foot-wide waterfall (#115) is a real surprise. Its waters flow over an abrupt wall giving the illusion of a much taller falls than its height would indicate. It is mapped, and for that reason we include it here even though it is somewhat shorter than our height criterion of 15 feet. Its location is also surprising given that it sits within Bechler Meadows, an area of relatively flat topography. The surrounding forest is sparse and the immediate terrain is normally bathed in sunlight, making the approach to this falls quite easy. One need only bushwhack several hundred yards to the west of the Boundary Creek Trail just before the footpath begins climbing towards the Madison Plateau.

Years ago, ranger Dunbar Susong referred to this waterfall as "Alice's Pool Falls" for his wife who loved to bathe in the stream at its base. The name "Confederate" was suggested by Mike Stevens in 1995. He explains:

> There is a sidestream coming into Boundary Creek from the west about 20 yards below the base of the falls. It contains a small, unnamed fall of similar height. I viewed this merging of streams as somewhat like the geography at Union Falls in that two waterfalls on separate streams drop in close proximity to each other. Thus I took advantage of this geographical anomaly to use the obvious Union-Confederate play on words.

We fondly refer to the fall on the second (smaller) stream as "Confederate's Compatriot" (#116)

117 DUNANDA FALLS

LOCATION: 498099 4899218

FALL TYPE: Plunge

HEIGHT: 150 feet

STREAM: Boundary Creek

MAP: Bechler Falls,
Wyo.-Idaho - 1989

ACCESS: Moderate to
difficult on-trail hike.

The discovery of this exquisite, 150-foot, plunge-type falls (**#117**) has always been credited to explorer W.C. Gregg in 1920. "One splendid falls with a straight drop of one hundred and thirty feet," wrote Gregg that year, "is yet without a name."[122] The following year Gregg returned to the area and noted that "few human beings have looked on this fall, which for centuries has shown its beauties only to its Creator and his dumb creatures."[123] He and/or Jack Haynes originally proposed the name "Ranger Fall" for the feature, but the USBGN changed the name to "Dunanda" from the Shoshone Indian word meaning "straight down."[124]

We have learned that, contrary to the existing record, Dunanda Falls was seen and recorded more than 40 years before Gregg's party. The entry "cascade" appears on two maps from the 1870s based on the surveys of Alonzo V. Richards. (One is Richards own 1874 sketch map and the other a General Land Office map of 1876 using information provided by him.) Richards was assigned the monumental task of determining the exact coordinates of the west boundary of the Territory of Wyoming and his travels took him through this immediate area. He surveyed and named Boundary Creek, calling it Cascade Creek. He did not put forth a name for either Dunanda or Silver Scarf Falls (which he may not have seen).

In 1904, Dunanda Falls began to appear on most official park maps as "falls," even though it would not be named by the USBGN until 17 years later.

Paul Rubinstein

118 UNNAMED CASCADE ON UPPER BOUNDARY CREEK "Horseshoe Cascade"

LOCATION: 497399 4902392

FALL TYPE: Serial Cascade

HEIGHT: 30 feet

STREAM: Boundary Creek

MAP: Buffalo Lake, Idaho - Wyoming - 1986

ACCESS: Multiple-day on-trail hike.

Farther upstream on Boundary Creek is another picturesque locale that we call "Horseshoe Cascade." It is located about twelve miles above the Bechler Ranger Station.

Throughout its descent, Boundary Creek makes an uncharacteristic horseshoe turn around a prominent vantage point. Our suggested name is a description of the bend in the river's direction during the cascade's decline. This area is best viewed from the promontory outcropping high above the "horseshoe." The total elevation loss of the stream here is about 30 feet.

"Horseshoe Cascade" may be unique in Yellowstone in that, as the river doubles back on itself, it also cascades. As a result, it is extremely difficult to photograph (even with a wide-angle lens) and must be seen in person to be appreciated.

119–120

UNNAMED FALLS ON UPPER BOUNDARY CREEK
"Deep Pool Falls"

LOCATION: 496945 4906144

FALL TYPE: Plunge

HEIGHT: 15 feet

STREAM: Boundary Creek

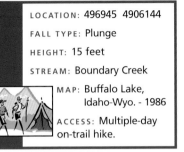

MAP: Buffalo Lake, Idaho-Wyo. - 1986

ACCESS: Multiple-day on-trail hike.

Mike Stevens

On Boundary Creek's most upper reaches is a gorgeous 15-foot falls (**#119**) that should not be missed. It is alongside the main trail about three miles southeast of Buffalo Lake. Its first documentation appears to have been in 1978 when a party of fishery biologists passed through the area while searching for barriers to fish migration. They found it dry.[125]

While "Deep Pool Falls" has no doubt been seen by a fair number of hikers through this remote part of the park, we can find no names ever suggested for it. For this book, it was visited in 1995 and again in 1997. Mike Stevens recalls:

> From high above, perhaps 50 feet, we were looking nearly straight down at a beautiful, calm, slightly greenish, but exceedingly clear, deep pool. The green tint was like the refreshing green of Lake Louise in the Canadian Rockies. The water was clear and inviting, 20 to 30 feet deep. It seemed serene and out of character with the rest of the local semi-arid environment. The five of us were impressed. On the rim of its canyon I said something like 'that should be the easiest falls to ever name, Deep Pool Falls.' All four others agreed.

A small canyon begins where "Deep Pool Falls" plunges 15 feet. Above the falls is an even larger (and probably deeper) pool. The scene is striking for its beauty and volume of water in an area that is primarily dry.

Just downstream from "Deep Pool Falls," the creek reaches the end of an even deeper canyon. In it exists a much larger unnamed cascade (**#120**) of at least 100 feet in length.

121 SILVER SCARF FALLS

LOCATION: 498336 4899088

FALL TYPE: Cascade

HEIGHT: 250 feet

STREAM: "Silver Scarf Creek"

MAP: Bechler Falls, Wyoming - Idaho - 1989

ACCESS: Moderate to difficult on-trail hike

Paul Rubinstein

Located only one-quarter mile east of Dunanda Falls, Silver Scarf Falls is on an unnamed tributary of Boundary Creek (for which park geologist Rick Hutchinson proposed the name "Silver Scarf Creek" in his report "Monitoring of Thermal Activity in Southwestern Yellowstone National Park and Vicinity, 1980–1993"). A 250-foot sloping cascade, it first appeared on a 1907 park map, although it is not known who recorded it at that time. It was seen in 1920 by explorer W.C. Gregg and named the following year by Dr. Henry Van Dyke, an ex-minister to Holland who originally called it "Silver Scarf Cascade." A quick scramble to the top of this falls affords the hiker superb views of the Tetons to the south with the vast Bechler Meadows in the foreground.

The unnamed stream on which Silver Scarf Falls is located originates many miles north in a large, open valley that we call the "Valley of Death." This area contains massive numbers of unmapped, boiling thermal springs with numerous runoff channels and extremely thin crusts. One misstep on its fragile surface could be disastrous. Hence, the "Valley of Death" moniker.

122–123

UNNAMED FALLS ON LOWER "SHANGRI-LA CREEK" "Verdant Falls"

"Verdant Falls"

Paul Rubinstein

LOCATION: 499536 4899073

FALL TYPE: Two-tiered Cascade

HEIGHT: 15 feet

STREAM: "Shangri-la Creek"

MAP: Unmapped

ACCESS: Multiple-day off-trail hike.

One mile due east of Silver Scarf Falls is a very significant and picturesque stream that we call "Shangri-La Creek." It reminds us of the hidden paradise of the same name in James Hilton's novel, *Lost Horizon.*

The stream contains no less than four waterfalls. The first of these is a pretty, double drop that we dubbed "Verdant Falls" **(#122)** for the lush greenery that immediately surrounds it. Its two steps total 15 feet, but even by itself the lower step is quite picturesque. To see the entire falls, one must wade out into the center of the refreshing creek.

Only several hundred feet west of "Verdant Falls" is another waterfall **(#123)** of about 20 feet in height. A cascade-type falls, it is not on "Shangri-La Creek" proper, but rather on a 100-yard-long side (spring) tributary that literally gushes from the hillside. "Springside Falls" seems an obvious name.

124 UNNAMED FALLS ON "SHANGRI-LA CREEK" "Birdseye Falls"

LOCATION: 499640 4899382

FALL TYPE: Cascade

HEIGHT: 100 feet

STREAM: "Shangri-La Creek"

MAP: Bechler Falls, Wyoming-Idaho - 1989

ACCESS: Multiple-day off-trail hike.

"Birdseye Falls" is one of the most impressive waterfalls in all of the Yellowstone backcountry. It is surprising that a falls this large was not discovered or mentioned in early park accounts. The stream was never even surveyed by the USFWS. Its only documentation seems to be the notation "falls" on the 1989 Bechler Falls 7½-minute quadrangle and the following description of it in a 1987 memo from North District Naturalist Tim Manns to Superintendent Bob Barbee as they considered which feature to name "Albright Falls":

> Falls on a branch of Boundary Creek approximately one mile east of Dunanda and Silver Scarf Falls, about 1 mile off trail. Dunbar [Susong] has not been to this falls but believes it is over 100 feet high. The area overlooks the Bechler Valley to some degree, an argument in favor of naming it for Albright since his actions as superintendent helped preserve that part of Yellowstone.

Author Paul Rubinstein considers it one of the five best waterfalls he has seen in the entire Cascade Corner region. He proposed the name "Birdseye Falls" for Claude Hale Birdseye. Birdseye, a topographer for the USGS, accompanied W.C. Gregg and Jack Haynes into the Bechler region in the early 1920s. Their historic trips revealed many of the region's waterfalls to the world for the first time and helped to ultimately save the area from Idaho developers who wanted the place turned into a reservoir. Birdseye drew the first detailed map of the region in 1922.

A second reason for the name is that views from the brink of this falls and the open hillside to its southwest give one a "birdseye" view of the entire Bechler Meadows and of the Grand Tetons to the south.

125–126

TWO UNNAMED FALLS ON UPPER "SHANGRI-LA CREEK" "Woodland Falls" and "Graceful Falls"

"Woodland Falls"

"Graceful Falls"

#125 "WOODLAND FALLS"

LOCATION: 499591 4899682

FALL TYPE: Cascade

HEIGHT: 18 feet

STREAM: "Shangri-La Creek"

MAP: Unmapped

ACCESS: Multiple-day off-trail hike.

#126 "GRACEFUL FALLS"

LOCATION: 499803 4899982

FALL TYPE: Fan/Cascade

HEIGHT: 25 feet

STREAM: "Shangri-La Creek"

MAP: Unmapped

ACCESS: Multiple-day off-trail hike

On "Shangri-La Creek," "Birdseye Falls" should be reward enough for anyone, but more lies in wait upstream. The first attraction, about one-quarter mile above "Birdseye" is a steep if not vertical falls of 18 feet (#125). It is tucked into a steep canyon and in deep forest, so one has to be alert for it. These dark woods were the inspiration for its name, "Woodland Falls."

Moving farther upstream, the hiker will be able to see across the stream to an unnamed tributary of nearly as much flow coming in from the east. Almost exactly at the two streams' convergence, this tributary steps down 25 feet to the level of "Shangri-La Creek," creating the second significant falls (#126 in the drainage. We call this descent "Graceful Falls." This fan-shaped feature grows wider as it steps down from 15 to 25 feet.

On the uppermost reaches of "Shangri-La Creek" the stream contains multiple branches. Springs litter the base of the cliffs that line the southwestern side of the Madison Plateau. Traversing this area, one will encounter a plethora of small spring-fed cascades. We hoped to find a 300-foot falls here shown clearly on the topographic maps (although that portion of the stream is seasonal). Instead, the immediate area is a pocket of rich, green growth, all the more refreshing for the abundance of cold, pure water seemingly flowing everywhere.

127 UNNAMED FALLS NORTHWEST OF OUZEL FALLS "Purgatory Falls"

LOCATION: 501605 4901579

FALL TYPE: Multi-step Plunge

HEIGHT: 60–70 feet

STREAM: "Acheron Creek"

 MAP: Trischman Knob, Wyoming - 1986

ACCESS: Extremely strenuous off-trail hike.

Mike Stevens

Of the many images in this book, "Purgatory Falls" has the distinction of being the only "dry" falls we have included. Why a dry falls? Simply put: it is on the map and when it flows it must be positively gorgeous!

The USGS mapped this feature in 1986. It shows on the 7½-minute Trischman Knob quadrangle as "cascade," on the first creek west of Ouzel Creek. Park employees Mike Stevens and Lee Ramella surveyed this stream in mid-July 1998 in an effort to determine what the USGS saw. What they found was a dry rocky gorge, except for detached stagnant pools at the bottom. They speculate from the severity of erosion that this may be a place where water once came from a large spring that has transferred its flow elsewhere. During spring runoff there must be nearly 100 feet of plunges here. The first vertical falls is 25 feet. Just upstream is a chambered, undercut, pure vertical fall of 50 to 65 feet depending on how deep and full its plunge pool is. Even when the streambed is dry, this area is spectacular in its own right.

Ramella suggested the name for the feeling that the area conveys. It is so stark, rugged and harsh that Purgatory seemed appropriate. Ramella vowed to return to the site even though it is a long and difficult hike. If he can ever get there when water is flowing, it might indeed seem that he has served his time in purgatory and truly arrived in heaven.

128 UNNAMED FALLS WEST OF OUZEL FALLS "Acheron Falls"

LOCATION: 500082 4897384

FALL TYPE: Horsetail/Fan

HEIGHT: 27 feet

STREAM: "Acheron Creek"

MAP: Unmapped

ACCESS: Multiple-day off-trail hike.

Zachary Park

About one mile west of Lake Wyodaho, the unnamed stream that contains our "Purgatory Falls" drops through a V-shaped notch in the plateau wall and falls 27 feet. It then cascades another 25 feet and abruptly disappears underground.

Park employees Zachary Park, David Powell, and Chris Reis visited this falls on August 29, 1999, and showed us photos taken from a distance. They revisited on October 2 to take a series of closer pictures, and then proposed the name "Acheron Falls." They described the locale as having huge, jumbled, conglomerated boulders; it was a spot at once stark and foreboding.

In Greek mythology, Acheron (pronounced ACH-er-ron) was one of the rivers that surrounded the underworld and gave access to Hades. The name, which means "river of woe," is often used metaphorically for Hades itself.

It was "upon the dismal shores of Acheron" that the demon Charon, with his eyes of fire, loaded boats full of the naked and weeping souls of the unfortunates damned to Hades in order to ferry them across to the Gates of Hell.

Because Acheron was a mythological river that sank underground into Hell, we propose that this sinking stream be called "Acheron Creek" and its falls "Acheron Falls." These are appropriate names, for on the upper reaches of the stream lies our "Purgatory Falls;" some 120 yards below "Acheron Falls," the stream sinks underground. (The two names, Acheron and Purgatory, were arrived at independently by separate parties and the fact that they are related is pure coincidence.)

129 UNNAMED FALLS ON ROBINSON CREEK "Robinson Canyon Falls"

LOCATION: 493365 4896682

FALL TYPE: Cascade

HEIGHT: 30 feet

STREAM: Robinson Creek

MAP: Bechler Falls, Wyoming-Idaho - 1989

ACCESS: Moderate to difficult on-trail hike.

Paul Rubinstein

This is Yellowstone's only waterfall in the state of Idaho. Its cascading nature is similar to that of Wraith Falls or Virginia Cascade. An even better description would be that it is a larger version of Little Gibbon Falls.

Our proposed name is geographical, but from the canyon rather than the creek. Robinson Canyon is a significant park feature, stretching for miles on Robinson Creek and growing wider and deeper as the stream flows southwest out of Yellowstone. The canyon in the vicinity of the falls is gentle and weathered, in stark contrast to the massive, sheer-walled section downstream.

The maintained West Boundary Trail runs alongside the falls eight miles from the Bechler Ranger Station. This waterfall has obviously been visited by many, but reported by few. Photography is also not a problem because the area receives plenty of sunlight and there is a good, reliable flow of water in the stream.

The Backcountry

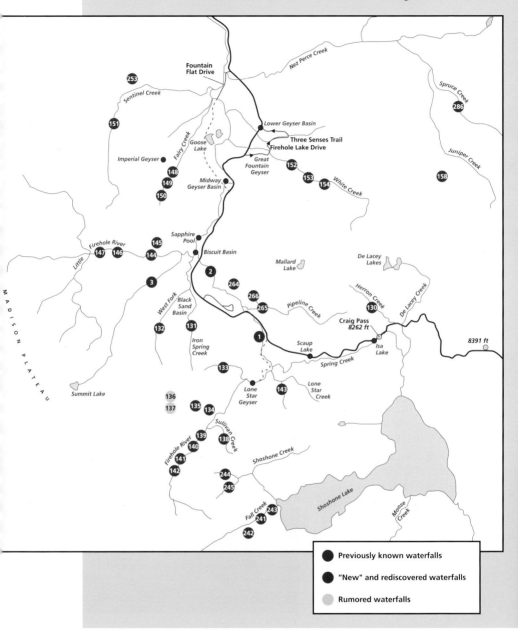

Fountain Flat Drive

Nez Perce Creek

Spruce Creek

253

Sentinel Creek

286

151

Lower Geyser Basin

Three Senses Trail
Firehole Lake Drive

Juniper Creek

Fairy Creek

Goose Lake

Great Fountain Geyser

Imperial Geyser

148

152

158

149

Midway Geyser Basin

153

150

154

White Creek

Sapphire Pool

De Lacey Lakes

145

147 146

Firehole River

Biscuit Basin

Mallard Lake

Little

144

Herron Creek

130

De Lacey Creek

MADISON PLATEAU

2

264

3

266

Pipeline Creek

West Fork

265

Craig Pass
8262 ft

8391 ft

Black Sand Basin

132 131

1

Scaup Lake

Isa Lake

Iron Spring Creek

133

Spring Creek

Summit Lake

136

Lone Star Geyser

143

Lone Star Creek

137

135 134

Firehole River

139

Sullivan Creek

140

138

141

Shoshone Creek

142

244

245

Shoshone Lake

Moose Creek

Fall Creek

243

241

242

- ● Previously known waterfalls
- ● "New" and rediscovered waterfalls
- ● Rumored waterfalls

Craig Pass

130 UNNAMED FALLS ON HERRON CREEK
"Sundial Falls"

LOCATION: 521904 4922256

FALL TYPE: Cascade

HEIGHT: 15 feet

STREAM: Herron Creek

MAP: Unmapped

ACCESS: Moderate to difficult off-trail hike.

Mike Stevens

Just north of Craig Pass lies a charming little fall that we refer to as "Sundial Falls." It is located on Herron Creek about a mile upstream from where it crosses the Grand Loop Road. The stream is hardly noticed as one crosses it on the highway between De Lacy Creek and Isa Lake.

A nearly vertical cascade, the falls has a towering, sheer outcropping of rhyolite on its immediate right bank at the brink. The abrupt cliff throws a sharp shadow over the falls for much of the day. This slow, creeping silhouette gradually encompasses the falls in such a way that it resembles a sundial marking time. The area surrounding the falls is characterized by small but extremely rugged canyons and gorges.

The authors learned of this falls through park employees Marek Hrebicek and Steve Wiechmann, who surveyed the area in July 1998. They describe Herron Creek as "a wet and difficult creek to follow in the darkness of late evening." Wiechmann notes: "We came to a point where large rhyolite boulders, uncommon to the rest of the relatively flat creek, jut up 35–40 feet on each side of the stream. We were able to skirt down the east side between the creek and the rocks, entering what seemed like some sort of animal den. As we did so, we found ourselves at the bottom of a fall about 15 feet high."

Old Faithful

131 FERN CASCADES

LOCATION: **512475 4921339**

FALL TYPE: **Three-serial Cascade**

HEIGHT: **10, 20, & 70 feet**

STREAM: **Iron Spring Creek**

MAP: **Old Faithful, Wyoming - 1986**

ACCESS: **Easy to moderate on-trail hike.**

Paul Rubinstein

You can spot a series of cascades on Iron Spring Creek only a few short miles south-west of Old Faithful Geyser. Its name, Fern Cascades, is characteristic of the luxuriant ferns that grow in this moist area. The feature is a three-step cascade with drops of 10, 20, and 70 feet. In 1977, the USFWS surveyed this portion of the stream and reported that Fern Cascades was "over 100 vertical feet in 100 horizontal yards."

The name "Fern Falls" was applied locally until 1956 when chief naturalist David Condon proposed Fern Cascades. Portions of this lengthy stretch of whitewater can be seen from the Fern Cascades Loop Trail. Unfortunately good views are only available of the 10- and 20-foot sections. Some tricky navigation down a steep and slippery slope is required to view the lower 70-foot section pictured here. It is by far the most scenic segment of this pleasant cascade.

132 UNNAMED CASCADE SOUTHWEST OF OLD FAITHFUL "Sidedoor Cascade"

LOCATION: 511388 4921261

FALL TYPE: Segmented Horsetail/Cascade

HEIGHT: 80 feet

STREAM: Unnamed Tributary of the West Fork of Iron Spring Creek

MAP: USFWS Map of Iron Spring Creek - 1978

ACCESS: Moderate to difficult off-trail hike.

Paul Rubinstein

A fine, steep cascade can be seen just over a mile upstream from the government corrals. The cascade is actually on an unnamed side stream that springs out of the Madison Plateau and flows only a couple hundred yards before falling into the West Fork.

How could Yellowstone explorers have missed this one for 122 years? Surely, as close as it is to Old Faithful, many people must have viewed it at some time. However, the only recorded evidence is in one of the park's USFWS reports. Fishery biologists saw it in 1977 and marked it on their hand-drawn map.[126]

In 1994, after carefully studying maps of the area (and unaware of the USFWS report), Paul Rubinstein formed the opinion that a waterfall of some size was located on the upper reaches of the West Fork of Iron Spring Creek. He sent Mike Stevens and park employee Jeremy Muraski up the West Fork looking for waterfalls. Although they found none on the main stream, they were rewarded with the discovery of this cascade on a side stream. Two large boulders framed the brink of the towering cascade. The formation reminded them of a door. The stream's flow comes out at the base of the "door," much as a "pet door" is built into the bottom of a larger door. Because the high rock outcroppings shade sun from the south, the feature is best photographed during the summer solstice.

Upper Firehole River and Tributaries

133 UNNAMED CASCADE WEST OF LONE STAR GEYSER "Lone Star Cascade"

LOCATION: 513883 4918823

FALL TYPE: Cascade

HEIGHT: 130 feet

STREAM: Unnamed Tributary of the Firehole River

MAP: USFWS Map of Creek 1624 - 1978

ACCESS: Moderate to difficult off-trail hike.

Paul Rubinstein

"Lone Star Cascade," near Lone Star Geyser, is remarkable not so much for its appearance, which is formidable at almost 130 feet, but also for its location at less than one mile from one of the most heavily traveled trails in the park. The cascade is a plunge-type falls for its first 30 feet as it drops from the eastern edge of the Madison Plateau (looking much like Rustic Falls) and then begins a long, twisting, C-pattern cascade for another 100 feet.

It was first noted in 1872 by the second Hayden Survey. Dr. Bradley of the survey party described the cascade: "A small stream which comes on from the west near our camp, has a fine cascade, 130 feet high, about a quarter mile from the river. Its supply apparently comes from the flow of the numerous small ponds among the hills before mentioned."[127] Its only additional documentation seems to be a brief mention by a USFWS survey during their overall study of the upper Firehole drainage in the summer of 1977.[128]

"Lone Star Cascade" is located on the first watercourse you encounter when walking west from campsite OA1 (about 200 yards). By turning right (north) and following this small creek less than a mile, even the novice hiker cannot fail to find this magnificent surprise. The approach is heavily forested with old-growth lodgepole pine. In addition, many swamps line either side of the stream. The falls is not visible until just moments before you reach it. However, the sound of falling water can be plainly heard several hundred yards before you see it. The woods open up nicely at the falls' base. The best views are from its bottom and along the north slopes. We surveyed above the falls a short distance, but found no other falls.

Our suggested name is geographical. Its close proximity to Lone Star Geyser, one of the most popular backcountry features in all of Yellowstone, makes this designation an obvious choice.

134–137

UNNAMED FALLS WEST OF CAMPSITE OA3 "Leaping Falls" and "Dashing Falls"

#134 "LEAPING FALLS"

LOCATION: 513032 4916747

FALL TYPE: Plunge

HEIGHT: 30 feet

STREAM: Unnamed Tributary of the Firehole River

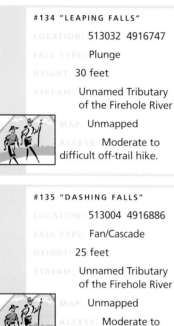

MAP: Unmapped

ACCESS: Moderate to difficult off-trail hike.

#135 "DASHING FALLS"

LOCATION: 513004 4916886

FALL TYPE: Fan/Cascade

HEIGHT: 25 feet

STREAM: Unnamed Tributary of the Firehole River

MAP: Unmapped

ACCESS: Moderate to difficult off-trail hike.

"Leaping Falls"

Mike Stevens

Leaping Falls (#134) and Dashing Falls (#135) are two of the most perplexing waterfalls we found in our extensive fieldwork, not because of their appearance or location, but because we found them at all. They are on an unnamed tributary of the Firehole River about two miles south/southwest of the Lone Star Pool footbridge. Although we were pleased to find them, they are not what we set out to find.

The general areas in question were the distant cliffs west of campsite OA3, themselves southwest of Lone Star Geyser. The original destinations of our search were two waterfalls discovered by the USFWS in 1977. They were shown on another of the now-familiar hand-drawn maps from their upper Firehole River survey and were tantalizingly marked as a 40-foot (#136) and a 100-foot (#137) plunge falls dropping next to each other from cliffs at the rim of the Madison Plateau. We imagined something so special that it would be unique to all of Yellowstone: two completely independent, large waterfalls on parallel streams that could be photographed together, falling side by side. We gave them the working name of "Double Falls" and visualized them as one of the great hidden treasures of the park. Unfortunately, not only did we not find them, we did not even find the streams these alleged falls were supposed to be located on. What we found instead were two other waterfalls on a different surveyed stream, one the USFWS hand-drawn map showed as having no falls at all.

The falls we found are on what the USFWS calls Creek 1626. The first we call "Leaping Falls." It is a pleasing, south-facing, 30-foot plunge from between large

rhyolite boulders. We suspect it turns into
a split-fall in late summer. At its brink,
"Leaping Falls" leaps off the rocks and free-
falls into a meadowy bottom. The two best
views of this lovely waterfall are from its base
and from the rim of the 40-foot cliffs that
line its western side.

Just one-quarter mile upstream we
found what we call "Dashing Falls." It is an
80-degree, sloping, fan-type falls typical of
many in this area of the park. Facing east,
this 25-foot falls starts off narrow, less than
five feet wide, and flares out to both sides
symmetrically on its way down.

We continued our survey up Creek
1626 for at least a mile until we reached the
top of the Madison Plateau, but we found
no other waterfalls. The country, however,
was positively gorgeous: forested canyons,
alpine views, and plenty of snow. Other
unnamed streams to the north and south
did not yield any clues as to the whereabouts of our mysterious "Double Falls."

Thus, we were left with two baffling
questions that day. How did we miss the
"Double Falls" and its two parallel streams?

"Dashing Falls"   Paul Rubinstein

And how did the USFWS miss the two beautiful waterfalls that we are reporting here
on Creek 1626? In answering the first question, Paul Rubinstein remains convinced
that it was not a survey error; he believes their maps to be correct. Either the "Double

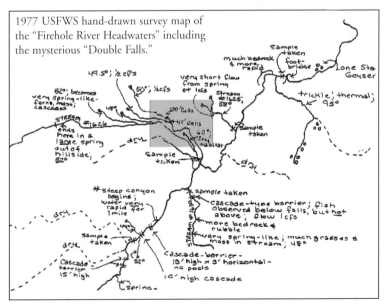

1977 USFWS hand-drawn survey map of
the "Firehole River Headwaters" including
the mysterious "Double Falls."

Falls" remain hidden somewhere in this area, or perhaps they were located on spring-fed streams that have since dried up. The Firehole River has no less than a dozen tributaries flowing off the Madison Plateau in this area, and Rubinstein believes the "Double Falls" remain concealed on two of them. If anyone feels inspired enough to make the trek to this baffling area and resolves the mystery of the "Double Falls," please let us know.

Study any attempt to reach this area thoroughly beforehand. Maps and a compass are a must.

"Leaping Falls" Lost to History!

In November 1998, Lee Whittlesey made an amazing discovery while at the archives of the Union Pacific Railroad in Omaha, Nebraska. He and Union Pacific archivist Don Snoddy came across a set of 21 previously unknown 1924 photographs numbered 2869 through 2889 and labeled "The New Falls near Old Faithful." Both Whittlesey and Snoddy were stumped as to what falls it was. Days later, after careful inspection, Mike Stevens realized that this was actually our "Leaping Falls." We were surprised this most obscure falls had a history at all, let alone photographs. This appears to be the only documentation anywhere of the existence of this obscure park feature.

The photographer of the falls is uncredited but two people in one of the photos are identified as Charles Van Tassell and Mildred "Fuzzy" Alberts. We do not know who Mildred was, but the name Charles Van Tassell is well-known in Yellowstone history. Van Tassell was a noteworthy park stagecoach driver. He began his career in 1906 and continued to interpret through the 1920s. He published several editions of a guidebook under the name *Truthful Lies of Yellowstone Park* that sold in gift shops around Yellowstone. It contained snippets of his stagecoach repertoire. Van Tassell's knowledge was so well-known in park circles at the time that officials from Union Pacific sought out his services during their visit to the park.

UPRR Archives

138 UNNAMED FALLS ON SULLIVAN CREEK "Grant's Pass Cascade"

LOCATION: 513189 4915402

FALL TYPE: Cascade

HEIGHT: 25 feet

STREAM: Sullivan Creek

MAP: USFWS Map of Firehole River Headwaters - 1978

ACCESS: Moderate to difficult off-trail hike.

Paul Rubinstein

This sloping cascade on Sullivan Creek in the upper Firehole River drainage lies in one of a series of densely forested drainages, about a mile northwest of Grant's Pass. Because it has no major distinguishing characteristic, we are proposing the geographical name of "Grant's Pass Cascade."

In a survey of Sullivan Creek, the USFWS Annual Project Report for 1977 stated, "a cascade-type fall of unknown height is located on the stream, south of the Firehole in the vicinity of Grant's Pass." We have found no other documentation of this charming little treasure.

Sullivan Creek is a rather obscure place name in Yellowstone and does not appear on current park maps. It was named in 1882 by S.P. Panton, Carl Hals, Charles Loud, and other Northern Pacific Railroad surveyors and so shown on their map of that year.[129] The name was given for one of two Sullivans (and perhaps both of them) in the employ of the railroad. It is the second creek from the south end of the meadow north of Grant's Pass and it is the largest.

139-142

UNNAMED CASCADES ON THE UPPER FIREHOLE RIVER
"Quadruple Cascades"

LOCATION/FALL TYPE/HEIGHT:

FALL 1: 512077 4914883; Cascade; 15 feet

FALL 2: 512013 4914781; Split Cascade; 15 feet

FALL 3: 511800 4914636; Cascade; 20 feet

FALL 4: 511766 4914483; Plunge; 15 feet

STREAM: Firehole River

MAP: USFWS Map of Firehole River
Headwaters - 1978

ACCESS: Moderate to difficult off-trail hike.

Near the headwaters of the Firehole River, in a steep, narrow canyon only one and one-half miles due west of Grant's Pass are the "Quadruple Cascades" (#139-#142). They were mentioned at length by the USFWS in 1977 as four distinct cascades with drops of 15 feet, 15 feet, 20 feet, and 15 feet, respectively, over the course of less than a half mile.[130] They described the water in the cascades as "torrential" even in late August. Of the canyon the report says: "there are many springs in the area; the water is very rapid; 90% bedrock causes many cascades—10% rubble and sand." The most down-stream cascade was originally reported by the 1872 Hayden Survey and marked as "falls" on their map of that year.[131]

Paul Rubinstein

"Quadruple Cascades" Fall #1

In 1998, Paul Rubinstein and Lee Whittlesey visited the cascades and made much the same observations as the USFWS. The one notable exception was the presence of a long step-down rapid between the second and third cascade that the 1977 survey failed to mention. This rapid was at least one-quarter mile long but did not classify as either a waterfall or a true cascade. In addition, Rubinstein and Whittlesey noted the presence of a large cave just above the third cascade on the river's eastern side.

"Quadruple Cascades" Fall #3

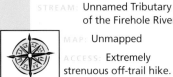

143 UNNAMED CASCADE SOUTH OF SPRING CREEK "Hundred Step Cascade"

LOCATION: 517162 4917933

FALL TYPE: Multi-step Cascade

HEIGHT: 100 feet

STREAM: Unnamed Tributary of the Firehole River

MAP: Unmapped

ACCESS: Extremely strenuous off-trail hike.

Paul Rubinstein

Although relatively close to developed areas, "Hundred Step Cascade" can be tricky to find. It is hidden in dense forest, about a mile north of the old Howard Eaton (Spring Creek) Trail and less than two air miles east-northeast of Lone Star Geyser. This cascade is definitely heard before seen. Facing north in a notched, V-shaped canyon, large boulders line its sides on the lower end with forested slopes on its upper half. Its waters "step down" the face at least 100 times, hence its proposed name. Photographing its entire drop is difficult, if not impossible, due to dense forest. One can only hope to partially capture its grandeur.

Visitors to this waterfall will encounter thick foliage, low visibility, and challenging navigation even with a compass. Furthermore, the presence of a second creek in the immediate area makes this locale even more confusing. The terrain is also quite varied. Many small side canyons and ravines cut this region.

The 1977 USFWS survey made no mention of this cascade in either its writings or maps. However it does appear on one of their charts labeled "Barriers to Fish," shown as a 100-foot barrier on Creek 1618. Confused as to which of the two creeks in this area was Creek 1618, we surveyed both. The second creek, known as Lone Star Creek (the name was used by fishermen at least as early as 1920, no doubt derived from nearby Lone Star Geyser) does not contain any significant waterfalls. At the base of "Hundred Step Cascade," Creek 1618 flows into Lone Star Creek and then through a small valley for about three-quarters of a mile, before emptying into the Firehole River.[132]

Little Firehole River

144–145 MYSTIC FALLS

LOCATION: 510120 4925441

FALL TYPE: Multi-tiered
Cascade/Plunge

HEIGHT: 70 feet

STREAM: Little Firehole River

MAP: Old Faithful,
Wyoming - 1986

ACCESS: Easy to
moderate on-trail hike.

Mike Stevens

Located on the Little Firehole River, Mystic Falls (#144) was originally called "Little Firehole Falls" by the 1872 Hayden Survey. Its present name, given in 1885 by the Hague Survey, is probably merely fanciful and imaginative. It has long been a favorite short hike of Old Faithful area visitors and employees, and 1930s visitors often swam at its base. With several actual drops and a widening at its base, it is a striking feature.

Thermal features are located in the rocky banks of Mystic Falls, as well as downstream. Steam can often be seen rising from them as rivulets of hot water feed into the river. As a bonus, a second, seasonal waterfall (#145) drops from cliffs to the north of Mystic Falls on an unnamed tributary of the Little Firehole River. More visible since the 1988 fires, it appears each spring above and west of Biscuit Basin. By the end of June this second waterfall has usually dried up.

The short trip to Mystic Falls is one of the most popular hikes in Yellowstone. An easy, well-maintained trail leaves the boardwalk at the far end of Biscuit Basin and winds through lodgepole pines for a short mile before reaching the falls.

146   UNNAMED FALLS ON THE LITTLE FIREHOLE RIVER "Precipitous Falls"

Paul Rubinstein

LOCATION: 506793 4925590

FALL TYPE: Plunge

HEIGHT: 25 feet

STREAM: Little Firehole River

MAP: USFWS Map of Little Firehole River - 1978

ACCESS: Moderate to difficult off-trail hike.

In August 1978, the USFWS surveyed the Little Firehole River. Some two miles above Mystic Falls they encountered a significant waterfall, estimated at between 20 and 25 feet high. A vertical plunge, it was a good deal wider than it was tall. Its waters featured a split in the river and interesting interplay with the trees and boulders.

In 1992, Paul Rubinstein and Mike Stevens viewed this falls while hiking in the area. Unaware of the previous USFWS survey, they found the falls by accident. As the Little Firehole River trail descended from the Madison Plateau to a point where it met the river, they heard a distant but plainly audible roar. After bushwhacking their way towards the sound for about a quarter mile, they broke out onto a precipice and were treated to a splendid view of the falls. With the name "Precipitous" we hope to convey the ruggedness of the rocky cliffs above this spot on the river.

Even though this waterfall is only a short distance from the heavily used footpath, it is a bit tricky to reach. You can only see it from well above the river. Use extreme caution on these cliffs when attempting to view "Precipitous Falls."

147 UNNAMED FALLS ON THE LITTLE FIREHOLE RIVER "Lovely Falls"

LOCATION: 506167 4925492

FALL TYPE: Plunge

HEIGHT: 8–10 feet

STREAM: Little Firehole River

MAP: USFWS Map of Little Firehole River - 1978

ACCESS: Moderate to difficult on-trail hike.

This absolutely gorgeous but small waterfall can be found on the Little Firehole River at campsite OD3, some two and one-half miles above Mystic Falls. The short vertical plunge terminates in a beautiful, round pool of sparkling water. The area surrounding the falls is particularly appealing. Its bowl shape creates a feeling of isolation and serenity. Because the falls is located directly adjacent to a designated campsite, it is not visible from the main trail, further adding to its privacy.

As a twice-documented falls, we felt an obligation to include this small gem, even though it fell below our height criterion. It appears on one of the obscure hand-drawn maps of the USFWS surveys of the mid-1970s. More importantly, it is mentioned in one of the park's significant hiking guides. Mark C. Marschall's book *Yellowstone Trails* contains the following passage: "The trail continues to climb through lodgepole pine forest for 2 more miles. It then descends to the Little Firehole River just downstream from a lovely waterfall." We follow Marschall's lead in proposing the name "Lovely Falls" based on his original impressions of it.

Lower Geyser Basin

148 FAIRY FALLS

Paul Rubinstein

LOCATION: **510363 4930002**

FALL TYPE: **Plunge**

HEIGHT: **197 feet**

STREAM: **Fairy Creek**

MAP: **Lower Geyser Basin, Wyoming - 1986**

ACCESS: **Easy to moderate on-trail hike.**

Located south of Twin Buttes, Fairy Falls plunges almost 200 feet from the Madison Plateau. Captain John Barlow named it in 1871, "from the graceful beauty with which the little stream dropped down a clear descent of 250 [sic] feet."[133] Fairy Falls was rediscovered in 1900–1901 and an unsuccessful attempt was made to rename it "Lost Falls."[134]

Physically, Fairy Falls is unmatched in Yellowstone. Its high free fall on such a narrow stream gives the waterfall an extremely thin appearance. The delicate waters don't seem to vary throughout the entire summer season. Whether viewed in June or October, Fairy Falls remains consistent in level of flow.

About halfway down the face of the falls, there appears to be a great deal of water pouring out of the center of the cliff wall itself. This seepage in effect forms a fall behind the fall. We suspect that this geologic anomaly may be the early stages of a natural bridge formation. Eventually this secondary seepage could erode away enough of the rhyolite cliff to form a tunnel and effectively cut off Fairy Falls. The result will be that all the waters of Fairy Creek will flow through this tunnel and pour from the middle of the cliff wall rather than over the top as it does now.

The two-mile hike to Fairy Falls is one of the park's most popular. An inviting plunge-pool at its bottom seems to beckon to bathers, although the water is usually chillingly cold.

Hine took this photo of Fairy Falls on the day of its discovery in 1871.

The Forgotten Thomas J. Hine

Photographer Thomas J. Hine accompanied Captain John W. Barlow on Barlow's 1871 Yellowstone expedition. Barlow was assigned by General William Tecumseh Sherman to make a reconnaissance of the Yellowstone country at the same time as Dr. F.V. Hayden's survey. Just as William Henry Jackson was Hayden's photographer, Hine was Barlow's. Unfortunately the bulk of Hine's photos were destroyed in the Chicago fire of October, 1871. Mr. Hine saved 16 prints he had made a few days previously, but even those somehow disappeared. Approximately 200 photos were destroyed, including not only lake and mountain scenes but also many images of the largest Yellowstone geysers taken while they were in eruption. Had those photos survived, they would have vied with Jackson's for prominence in the establishment of Yellowstone. The fact that Jackson's pictures were the only ones published in 1871, is, according to Jackson, "something for which I have to thank Mrs. O'Leary's cow."[135]

Remarkably, seven of Hine's Yellowstone photos have been recently found by frontier photo historian Dr. James Brust at the New-York Historical Society. They include the earliest known photograph of Old Faithful, as well as the stereoview photo shown above, "Fall of the Fairies," Fire Hole Basin.

149 UPPER FAIRY FALLS

LOCATION: **510361 4929944**

FALL TYPE: **Fan/Cascade**

HEIGHT: **20 feet**

STREAM: **Fairy Creek**

MAP: **USFWS Map of Sentinel and Fairy Creeks - 1976**

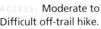

ACCESS: **Moderate to Difficult off-trail hike.**

A pleasant plunge of Fairy Creek is hidden just above its more famous sister, Fairy Falls. It is tucked out of sight in a forested, little pocket canyon that you can reach by ascending an animal trail that begins a couple hundred yards east of Fairy Falls.

In 1871, this falls was also visited by Captain John Barlow following his discovery and naming of Fairy Falls below it. Barlow wrote: "A very pretty cascade was discovered a few yards above the brink of the [Fairy] fall."[136]

Upper Fairy Falls is seldom visited. It is difficult to photograph because it does not face the sun and is surrounded by burnt forest. The scale of the modest drop and small flow of water, along with the unavoidable nearness of the viewer, make for a pleasant experience. The name Upper Fairy Falls has apparently been in local usage for years.

Mike Stevens

150

UNNAMED FALLS ON FAIRY CREEK
"Fairyslipper Falls"

LOCATION: 509249 4929674

FALL TYPE: Plunge

HEIGHT: 15 feet

STREAM: Fairy Creek

MAP: USFWS Map of Sentinel and Fairy Creeks - 1976

ACCESS: Moderate to difficult off-trail hike.

Mike Stevens

Near the headwaters of Fairy Creek is a delicate, vertical falls. The third of three waterfalls on the stream, it is roughly half a mile above Upper Fairy Falls. The geology at its brink is characterized by a long, straight, ancient volcanic flow that is perpendicular to the stream flow. This natural dike is responsible for the waterfall. The forest here was severely burned in 1988, thus the falls is not blocked from long views. The creekside downstream is full of seeps.

We propose the name "Fairyslipper Falls" for three reasons. First, the falls is located on Fairy Creek. Second, it has a fragile nature. And third, the fairyslipper (a.k.a. the Calypso Orchid—*Calypso bulbosa*) is a flower found throughout the park that has never had its name attached to any park feature. This falls' only documented history is its inclusion on a hand-drawn map in the USFWS *Annual Project Report* for 1975. This is one of several entries in this book in which the years of the USFWS maps and reports do not match. This discrepancy occurs because the reports were published a year after the collection of stream data.

151   UNNAMED FALLS ON SENTINEL CREEK "Sentinel Falls"

LOCATION: 507095 4933907

FALL TYPE: Multi-tiered Cascade

HEIGHT: 150 feet

STREAM: Sentinel Creek

MAP: USFWS Map of Sentinel and Fairy Creeks - 1976

ACCESS: Moderate to difficult off-trail hike.

Paul Rubinstein

One of the more intriguing waterfalls in Yellowstone is "Sentinel Falls." It is on Sentinel Creek where the stream spills off the rim of the Madison Plateau, about two miles upstream from the end of the Sentinel Meadows/ Queen's Laundry Trail. Lee Whittlesey came to know of this falls in the late 1970s while reading the USFWS *Annual Project Report* for 1975. He surveyed the stream soon after. Since that time, this complex, 150-foot, spiraling falls has been revisited on three separate occasions by the authors.

"Sentinel Falls" is hard to describe and even harder to photograph. The falls divides several times on its way down. It tumbles in stages and cascades, twisting within itself as it careens down the narrow canyon. Sadly, the waterfall is impossible to see in its entirety. Although the forest is not thick, tall pines block the falls from every angle. When one gets close enough to avoid the trees, views of the upper two-thirds are cut off by a formidable cliff. The result is that this fantastic feature can only be observed in sections.

The approach is not difficult if you navigate up Sentinel Creek. Well-worn buffalo trails actually lead almost to the falls itself. The only downsides to this walk are that the forest is burnt and the meadows remain swampy for much of the season.

152-154   WHITE CREEK FALLS

Bob Berry Collection

LOCATION: 516549 4930667

FALL TYPE: Plunge

HEIGHT: 6 feet

STREAM: White Creek

MAP: Map of the Lower Geyser Basin - Gustavus Bechler, 1872

ACCESS: Easy to moderate off-trail hike.

Although this small vertical falls (#152) on White Creek above Black Spring is only six feet high, it is included here because it bears the historical proper name of White Creek Falls. The name was used by photographer T.W. Ingersoll in 1888 (from a trip probably made in 1887) on his stereo photograph 1208, shown above. He captioned the photograph "White Creek Falls, Boiling Water," a reference to the fact that White Creek contains hot water.

Sixteen years earlier in 1872, Gustavus Bechler mapped this falls at 10 feet and another small falls (#153) at 14 feet just upstream on his Map of the Lower Geyser Basin. It is not known how he arrived at these measurements, but neither estimate is currently correct.

You can access a worn trail across the road from Great Fountain Geyser and follow it up White Creek about half a mile to both of these small falls. In recent years this trail has become obscured and some bushwhacking is now required. Hikers should also know there is yet a third waterfall (#154) in this area. Just another quarter-mile upstream from White Creek Falls, a 20-foot cascade of thermally heated water falls into the stream from an unnamed tributary to the south. Anyone hiking up White Creek should use extreme caution in this area due to the numerous, dangerous hot springs surrounding the trail and creek.

The Backcountry

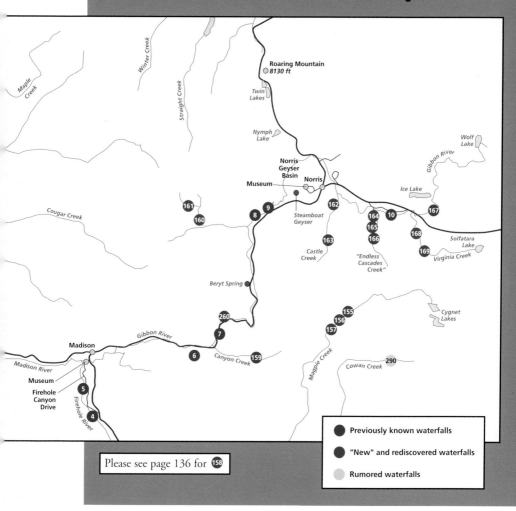

Roaring Mountain
⊙ *8130 ft*

Winter Creek

Straight Creek

Maple Creek

Twin
Lakes

Nymph
Lake

Gibbon River

Wolf
Lake

Norris
Geyser
Basin

Museum

Norris

Ice Lake

161
8 **9**
160
162

164
10
167

165

166
168

Cougar Creek

Steamboat
Geyser

163

169

Castle
Creek

"Endless
Cascades
Creek"

Solfatara
Lake

Virginia Creek

Beryt Spring

260
7

Gibbon River

Madison

155

156
157

*Cygnet
Lakes*

Madison River

Museum

Firehole
Canyon
Drive

6
Canyon Creek
159

Magpie Creek

Cowan Creek
290

5

4

Firehole River

○ Previously known waterfalls

● "New" and rediscovered waterfalls

○ Rumored waterfalls

Please see page 136 for **158**

Magpie Creek

Magpie Creek is one of the major tributaries draining the park's central interior. It flows west out of Cygnet Lakes and empties some 11 miles later into Nez Perce Creek, just after passing under a small footbridge on the Mary Mountain Trail. For most of its length, it is a placid, meandering stream passing through a mixture of medium-density forest and small meadows. The one notable exception is in the creek's middle section. Here the water tumbles with much force off the rim of Central Plateau in a series of three waterfalls. In 1996, the three of us, along with six other park employees (Stephanie Anderson, Keith Humphrey, Andy Krumm, Nels Peterson, Michelle M. Serio, and Kristie Wiederholt), trekked to the upper Magpie from the Paintpot Hill area to photograph these falls.

155 UNNAMED FALLS ON MAGPIE CREEK
"Mosquito Falls"

LOCATION: 525080 4945187

FALL TYPE: Two-tiered Cascade

HEIGHT: 15 feet

STREAM: Magpie Creek

MAP: USFWS Map of Magpie Creek - 1978

ACCESS: Moderate to difficult off-trail hike.

At the smallest and upper-most fall on Magpie Creek, the water rushes down two small steps, totaling 15 feet in height. We had some trouble coming up with a distinctive name for this pleasing spot. One of our hiking party, Andy Krumm, blurted out "Mosquito Falls," almost as a joke because of a terrible concentration of the little pests right in the vicinity of this waterfall. Although he barely remembers saying it, Krumm had the best suggestion and we present it here for consideration.

Paul Rubinstein

156 UNNAMED FALLS ON MAGPIE CREEK "Angled Falls"

LOCATION: 525023 4945150

FALL TYPE: Two-tiered Cascade

HEIGHT: 25–30 feet

STREAM: Magpie Creek

MAP: USFWS Map of Magpie Creek - 1978

ACCESS: Moderate to difficult off-trail hike.

Paul Rubinstein

"Angled Falls" is the second of three previously little-known falls on Magpie Creek. It has two distinct sections. At its brink, it is pinched between a pair of large rhyolite boulders where Magpie Creek "angles" from a southerly to a westerly course. A white spray fans out steeply down a smooth rock face for a distance of 17 feet. The creek then "angles" back to a southerly direction where it immediately falls another eight to 10 feet in a narrow, vertical descent. The USFWS *Annual Project Report* for 1977 described "Angled Falls" as a "cascade with a 15-foot rise in 5 feet." That brief notation was our only clue to the existence of this rewarding locale.

Like "Mosquito Falls," this falls sits in an oasis of sorts. Lush, green pines surround the vicinity in an otherwise burnt area of the park. This part of the Central Plateau suffered heavy fire impact during the 1988 Yellowstone fires.

Just yards downstream the woods open up with a spectacular overlook to the south. This is actually the brink of the third and largest falls of Magpie Creek, "Elysian Falls." From this incredible overlook one can see as far south as the area near De Lacy Lakes and Craig Pass.

157 UNNAMED FALLS ON MAGPIE CREEK "Elysian Falls"

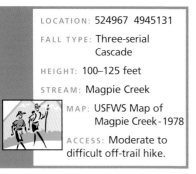

LOCATION: 524967 4945131

FALL TYPE: Three-serial Cascade

HEIGHT: 100–125 feet

STREAM: Magpie Creek

MAP: USFWS Map of Magpie Creek-1978

ACCESS: Moderate to difficult off-trail hike.

Upper half of "Elysian Falls"   Paul Rubinstein

The single most impressive thing about this falls is the height it exhibits for its location. "Elysian Falls" is about 125 feet high, yet it is in an area of relative overall flatness. A reference to a "torrential" 100–125 foot cascade in the USFWS *Annual Project Report* for 1977 put Paul Rubinstein on the trail of this feature.

"Elysian Falls" tumbles in a chaotic fashion. Huge, black boulders cover the bed of the stream, and the south canyon wall is largely composed of this black rock. The effect is one of tumultuous beauty and great size.

As we were leaving the spot, Lee Whittlesey said, "I really hate to leave such a beautiful place!" That sentiment became the impetus for the name "Elysian," chosen later. "Elysian" comes from "Elysium," in classical Greek mythology any place or state of perfect happiness. Because of this happiness, "Elysium" was also the abode of the blessed after death.

Rossiter Raymond, a visitor to the park in 1871, experienced a similar reaction to a waterfall as he was leaving it. "To bid farewell to such a scene is like descending from the heights of heaven," he wrote. "Precious indeed is the memory of so fair a vision."[137]

Juniper Creek

158 UNNAMED FALLS IN THE JUNIPER CREEK DRAINAGE "Hanging Falls"

LOCATION: 524446 4930801

FALL TYPE: Two-step Plunge

HEIGHT: 20 feet

STREAM: Unnamed Tributary of Juniper Creek

MAP: Unmapped

ACCESS: Extremely strenuous off-trail hike.

Paul Rubinstein

"Hanging Falls" is located on an unnamed tributary in the Juniper Creek drainage in the difficult, trailless country south of Nez Perce Creek. Its small canyon is approximately two miles south-southwest of the confluence of Juniper and Spruce Creeks. The country surrounding "Hanging Falls" is some of the most seriously burnt we have encountered in all of Yellowstone. Ten years after the fires of 1988, this area was still severely scorched and scarred.

Photography is tricky here as the double waterfall faces north. Its unnamed stream and the stream into which it flows are both hot streams. Numerous thermal seeps characterize this remote, desert-like region. Our name "Hanging Falls" comes from the type of small canyon it is nestled in, a spot where the larger stream has cut a groove deeper than its smaller tributary coming in from the south. We know of no history to this falls. It was seen by the authors along with park employees Tom Murphy and Phil Lerman during a survey of Spruce and Juniper Creeks in August 1998.

Canyon Creek

159 JORDAN FALLS

LOCATION: 520325 4943517

FALL TYPE: Cascade

HEIGHT: 40 feet

STREAM: Canyon Creek

MAP: USFWS Map of Canyon Creek - 1975

ACCESS: Moderate to difficult off-trail hike.

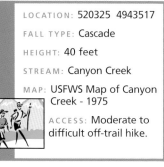

Paul Rubinstein

Jordan Falls, an attractive, sliding cascade, is nestled in a narrow pocket on Canyon Creek about two miles above its mouth. Its west-facing location in deep shade makes it difficult to photograph, but it exhibits a beautiful if delicate display for a falls on a small stream.

The name was suggested in 1975 by John Varley, then of the USFWS, in memory of David Starr Jordan (1851–1931). Jordan was a fish expert and the first fish investigator in Yellowstone Park, as well as a naturalist, teacher, university president, and peace advocate. During his day he was the greatest living authority on fish. Jordan made a reconnaissance of Yellowstone streams and lakes in 1889 to ascertain which waters were barren of fish. As a result of his visit, a program began that year to stock the park's lakes and streams with game fish. As the first scientist to ascend Canyon Creek, after his visit Jordan wrote "The Story of a Strange Land," a tribute to Yellowstone as a whole but especially to its waterfalls, which he was interested in as barriers to fish migration.[138]

A 1915 publication, "The Fishes of Yellowstone National Park," contains a brief reference to this feature (though not by name.)[139] In 1975, the USFWS survey and rehabilitation project on Canyon Creek was one of the more extensive of any in the entire program. A hand-drawn map from that study shows Jordan Falls (by name) and is the only map reference the authors have found of this significant waterfall.

Gibbon Meadows

160-161

UNNAMED CASCADE WEST OF GIBBON MEADOWS
"Slide Cascade"

LOCATION: 517344 4950716

FALL TYPE: Cascade

HEIGHT: 20 feet

STREAM: Unnamed Tributary of the Gibbon River

MAP: USFWS Map of Gibbon River & Tributaries - 1975

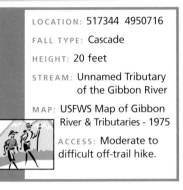

ACCESS: Moderate to difficult off-trail hike.

Paul Rubinstein

A medium-sized unnamed stream flows into Gibbon Meadows from the west. Two miles from the mouth of this stream a nearly vertical 20-foot cascade (#160) seems somewhat diminutive until one descends into its small canyon. Only after being examined from the base does its true size become apparent. This cascade was first documented by the USFWS in 1974.

Paul Rubinstein, Mike Stevens, park employee Lee Ramella, and visitors Gil and Brian Lesko visited this canyon in 1998. Their observations led to the working name of "Slide Cascade" for the white, turbulent waters that seem to slide for the falls' entire length.

Just upstream from "Slide Cascade" another 20-foot cascade (#161) can be seen. A narrow feature, it is actually on a smaller, secondary stream that comes in from the west. This entire area sits on the rim of an immense thermally active zone extending all the way to Norris Geyser Basin. Although they are widely scattered, numerous small hot seeps exist in the vicinity of these two falls.

Castle Creek

162 UNNAMED FALLS ON CASTLE CREEK
"Picnic Falls"

LOCATION: 525243 4951109

FALL TYPE: Two-step Cascade

HEIGHT: 25 feet

STREAM: Castle Creek

MAP: USFWS Map of Castle Creek - 1980

ACCESS: Easy to moderate off-trail hike.

Paul Rubinstein

We originally learned of this falls from an almost incidental remark in a USFWS aquatic report for Castle Creek. This obscure stream flows northeast from Gibbon Hill into the Gibbon River about a mile southeast of Norris Junction. By 1972, NPS maintenance workers used the name Castle Creek, probably for the castle-like rock formations on the stream.[140]

On their first survey of the stream in 1997, Lee Whittlesey and Mike Stevens missed this fall, instead finding the previously unknown "Sweetwater Falls" a mile upstream. In 1999, during a second survey, Paul Rubinstein alertly spotted and then correctly identified this falls as the same one the USFWS saw in their previous survey. Surprisingly, a full-sized picnic table had been placed overlooking the 25-foot cascade (most likely put there by an NPS maintenance person).

A majority of Yellowstone's backcountry waterfalls are extremely difficult for the weekend hiker to visit. This is not the case with "Picnic Falls." It may in fact be one of the easiest. A short 15-minute walk up the second service road east of Norris Junction will bring one very close to this falls. The key to finding it is to leave the service road and stay on Castle Creek once the service road begins its steep climb to the east. At this point the hiker should follow the remnants of an older service road on the west bank of Castle Creek for about 100 yards. "Picnic Falls" will quickly come into view. Although technically a cascade, we have designated this feature as a falls because this was the label given by the USFWS upon their first observations of it.

163 UNNAMED FALLS ON CASTLE CREEK
"Sweetwater Falls"

LOCATION: 526229 4950035

FALL TYPE: Plunge

HEIGHT: 16 feet

STREAM: Castle Creek

MAP: Unmapped

ACCESS: This is a Bear Management Area, no travel allowed.

This comely little falls plunges over a sheer wall on Castle Creek about two miles above its junction with the Gibbon River. It has no documented history.

The creek was at one time the water-supply stream for the Norris area and, because of sulphurous thermal features in most of the vicinity, it is some of the only potable water in the area. For that reason, we proposed the name "Sweetwater Falls" in 1997.

A service road paralleling Castle Creek ends about one mile short of "Sweetwater Falls." The original USFWS map of Castle Creek shows three more small cascades below "Sweetwater Falls." There is no indication, however, that they surveyed this far up the stream.

Mike Stevens

164
UNNAMED CASCADE ON "ENDLESS CASCADES CREEK"
"Devil's Elbow Cascade"

LOCATION: 527563 4950793

FALL TYPE: Cascade

HEIGHT: 16 feet

STREAM: "Endless Cascades Creek"

MAP: USFWS Map of Gibbon River & Tributaries - 1975

ACCESS: Easy to moderate off-trail hike.

Paul Rubinstein

This attractive cascade is located just above the mouth of the large stream we call "Endless Cascades Creek" and is visible from the Gibbon River. We call it "Devil's Elbow Cascade" because of its proximity to the hairpin curve on the old stagecoach road known as "Devil's Elbow."

During stagecoach days in Yellowstone, a sharp, 180-degree bend in the road became known as the "Devil's Elbow." In his 1900 road report, engineer Hiram Chittenden called the hill and curve here "a positive menace to the lives of travelers." Said Chittenden, "Several accidents have occurred here and one life has been lost. Stage drivers [from the east] are often compelled to make passengers alight and walk down the hill."[141] On the hill south of "Devil's Elbow" another 25-foot unnamed cascade falls on a secondary stream.

165 UNNAMED CASCADE ON "ENDLESS CASCADES CREEK" "Slippery Rock Cascade"

Paul Rubinstein

LOCATION: 527782 4950324

FALL TYPE: Cascade

HEIGHT: 40 feet

STREAM: "Endless Cascades Creek"

MAP: USFWS Map of Gibbon River & Tributaries - 1975

ACCESS: Moderate to difficult off-trail hike.

This sliding cascade, which resembles Wraith Falls, is on "Endless Cascades Creek" about one-half mile above "Devil's Elbow Cascade." A three-segment drop, its middle and largest segment is the most "rock hugging" of the three. The footing was bad at the base of this cascade when surveyed by the authors in 1997, hence the name.

166 UNNAMED CASCADE ON "ENDLESS CASCADES CREEK" "Endless Cascades"

LOCATION: 527823 4950058

FALL TYPE: Cascade

HEIGHT: 150 feet

STREAM: "Endless Cascades Creek"

MAP: USFWS Map of Gibbon River & Tributaries - 1975

ACCESS: Moderate to difficult off-trail hike.

These lengthy cascades have a run of at least 250 yards during a descent of about 150 feet, concluding just yards above "Slippery Rock Cascade." Much of the length of this stream is composed of cascading whitewater.

Near the base of "Endless Cascades," the authors had a discussion as to whether this long, narrow cascade was worthy of inclusion in our book. It was too closely surrounded by forest to be photogenic, it was not a vertical fall, and it was not clear how extensive it would prove to be. In its defense, Mike Stevens, who had been farther upstream, remarked: "It isn't just a cascade; it's an endless cascade." That seemed to be convincing, so much so that we eventually applied the name to the entire stream.

Paul Rubinstein

167 LITTLE GIBBON FALLS

Paul Rubinstein

LOCATION: **530502 4951469**

FALL TYPE: **Cascade**

HEIGHT: **25 feet**

STREAM: **Gibbon River**

MAP: **Crystal Falls, Wyo. - 1986**

ACCESS: **Easy to moderate on-trail hike.**

A delicate little cascade, Little Gibbon Falls is shown on several park maps as "falls." It is located on the Gibbon River a half-mile southeast of Ice Lake. Originally called "Upper Falls of the Gibbon" and given its present name in 1939 by fish researcher John Seamans, Little Gibbon Falls resembles Gibbon Falls on a smaller scale.[142]

Today, you can reach Little Gibbon Falls via a short maintained trail that begins from a somewhat obscured departure point just off the west end of Virginia Meadows on the north side of the Canyon-Norris Road.

A Memorable Search for Little Gibbon Falls

In the spring of 1990, authors Paul Rubinstein and Mike Stevens were still in the early stages of their Yellowstone explorations. Yet even then, Stevens already had a long-term theme to his wilderness travel. He wanted to see every waterfall in the Yellowstone backcountry. Having spent many seasons in the Sierra Nevadas of California, it is not surprising that the quest for unsullied falling waters is his first love.

By spring of that year, Stevens believed he was nearing his goal. One June afternoon the two were perusing a leaflet publication they had obtained from one of the park's visitor centers entitled "Ribbons of Water." It was a collection of photographs purporting to present a majority of Yellowstone's mapped falls. As the two flipped from page to page checking off the falls Stevens had seen, they came to a falls that neither of them knew of. It was called Little Gibbon Falls.

Little Gibbon Falls? Where was Little Gibbon Falls? Aside from one small photograph, the book offered no other description or explanation as to its location, instead only captioning the image with some of the author's feelings as he sat on its banks. In the coming days Stevens and Rubinstein checked all available park maps and talked with several Old Faithful rangers, but to no avail. Little Gibbon Falls seemed unknown to everyone they spoke to.

Determined, the two decided to try to find it anyway. Judging by the name "Little Gibbon" and the amount of water in the stream, they guessed it must be on the Gibbon River somewhere. The following Saturday they steadfastly searched sections of the Gibbon River where some topographic relief seemed possible. They concentrated in particular around the Norris Geyser Basin.

By 3 p.m. they had spent the majority of the day slogging through swamps, skirting fragile thermal areas, and climbing over deadfall; still there wasn't a hint of a falls. What if it wasn't on the Gibbon River at all? By now Rubinstein realized that without more information they could spend a week on this river and its tributaries and never find the falls. Already late in the afternoon, they called off the quest and decided instead to head up to the northern part of the park for some sightseeing.

By the time they reached Mammoth, the weather had become nasty. The temperature dropped considerably and lightning filled the sky. Pulling into the

continued on next page

parking area of the Horace Albright Visitor Center, they figured at least they could seek respite from the rain and perhaps do some browsing. However, once inside, it seemed that every tourist in Yellowstone had the same idea. It was pandemonium! Many people were crammed around the books, while many others clamored at the information desk for attention. Two haggard-looking rangers tried their best to accommodate this sea of cranky visitors.

Not wanting to stay any longer than necessary, Rubinstein and Stevens thought they might as well see if any of these rangers knew the whereabouts of Little Gibbon Falls. As they pressed their way closer to the desk, the intensity of the questions in front of them became louder and more frantic. Where are the campsites? How do I get to Old Faithful? What time does the park close? On and on it went, yet these two rangers kept their cool through it all and politely and calmly answered all the interrogators' questions with patience and dignity.

When the two finally jostled their way to the front, a woman cut between them from seemingly nowhere and barked at the ranger: "I saw a sign that said 'Closed, Bear Management Area.' Does that mean the bears are going crazy?" Rubinstein's jaw nearly hit the floor. "How do they stand it?" he wondered aloud.

A bewildered ranger, just now digesting the bizarre bear inquiry, asked Stevens, "Can I help you?" Stevens spoke softly and calmly. "I know this might be an odd question. We are employees and (holding up his copy of "Ribbons of Water") we are searching for a waterfall named Little Gibbon Falls, but are having no luck using this book. Have you ever heard of it?"

The ranger paused for an instant, then his eyes lit up as if he had been waiting for this moment all his life. For a split-second Rubinstein thought the man was going to leap across the counter. The next few seconds were a blur. The ranger spoke so quickly, with so much information streaming forth, it was as if a mountain of gold nuggets had come collapsing down and the two men couldn't gather them all up in time. He told them of waterfalls they had never heard of. There were stream names and fall names: Sentinel, Golden Fleece, Shallow, Thorofare; a hundred feet here, two hundred feet there. The ranger came flying around the counter. In a flash he had pushed his way through the herd of visitors and led the men to a white reference book on the far wall. He whipped through the pages so fast they never even saw the title. Within what seemed like milliseconds he stopped on a page and pointed to an entry listed as "Little Gibbon Falls"!

Finally, his frenzied pace slowed and a relative stability returned to the situation. It was then he turned and said, "I wrote this book. My name is Lee Whittlesey."

And the waterfalls project was born.

Virginia Creek

168 UNNAMED FALLS ON VIRGINIA CREEK "Duet Falls"

LOCATION: 529583 4949145

FALL TYPE: Two-tiered Plunge Fan

HEIGHT: 12 and 16 feet

STREAM: Virginia Creek

MAP: USFWS Map of Gibbon River & Tributaries - 1975

ACCESS: Moderate to difficult off-trail hike.

Paul Rubinstein

"Duet Falls" is located some two miles above the mouth of Virginia Creek where it flows into the Gibbon River at Virginia Meadows. This double falls is actually two completely separate waterfalls. The upper section falls about 12 feet between a series of huge rhyolite boulders that obscure it from most vantage points. Several yards downstream the lower falls plunges 16 feet into the opening at the bottom of the oddly shaped rocks. Getting a perfect view of both falls is most challenging because of the shape of the stones. Some of the free-falling water is always obscured no matter what the angle.

We were tipped off to the possibility of a falls on this stream by biologist Bob Gresswell, who surveyed this area many years ago with the USFWS. The suggestion for a name came from a member of our party, archivist-volunteer Joanne Sides. Due to its two steps she suggested "Double-Decker Falls" or "Duet Falls."

The terrain in the immediate vicinity of "Duet Falls" is comprised of rolling hills and medium-density lodgepole forest. Reaching the falls by navigating up Virginia Creek is not difficult, but 7½-minute quadrangles and a compass should be carried by anyone exploring this area of the park.

169 UNNAMED FALLS ON VIRGINIA CREEK "Cloistered Falls"

Joanne Sides

LOCATION: 530213 4948773

FALL TYPE: Plunge

HEIGHT: 15 feet

STREAM: Virginia Creek

MAP: USFWS Map of Gibbon River & Tributaries - 1975

ACCESS: Moderate to difficult off-trail hike.

This elegant plunge is roughly two and one-half miles above the mouth of Virginia Creek and only a half-mile above "Duet Falls."

Inspired by a rock chamber that formed a roofed passageway of rare excellence, the name "Cloistered" means "hidden away in spiritual beauty." A group consisting of Paul Rubinstein, Mike Stevens, Melissa Frost, and Joanne Sides visited this spot in 1997 and were ecstatic about it.

Our name suggestions were all aimed at capturing the sense of the rock-formed room. Sides tried "Sanctuary," and Frost offered Hermitage." Stevens threw out "Sanctum" and "Chambered," but the name that received the biggest response was his "Cloistered Falls." Cloistered also means a covered passage.

An endearing feature near the base of this falls and within the rock chamber is a lovely, grassy peninsula that protrudes into the plunge pool. It serves as a beautiful vantage point and adds immeasurably to the feeling generated here—that this is somehow sacred ground.

Lower half of "Elysian Falls"; Photo by Paul Rubinstein

The Backcountry

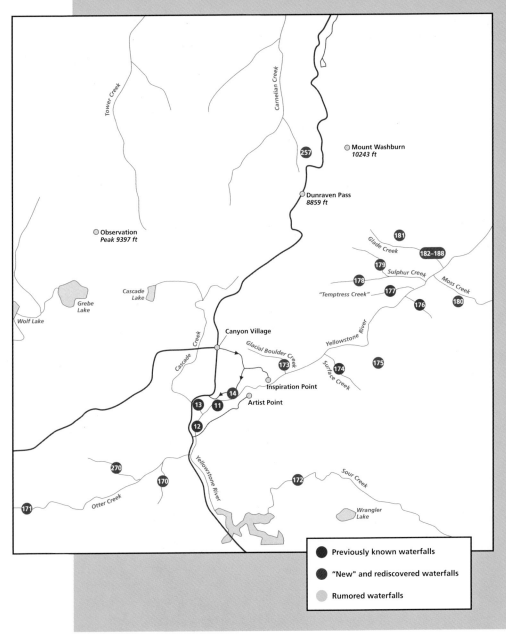

Otter Creek

170 "BEAR FEEDING FALLS"

A half-mile west of the mouth of Otter Creek is a dainty seasonal falls, height 25 feet. Situated on an unnamed stream that flows northeast into Otter Creek, the unnamed stream passes the site of the famous NPS "Bear Feeding Shows," which were held at the old Otter Creek Amphitheater during the summer seasons of 1931 through 1941.[143] Park visitors to these shows must have routinely looked at this falls while watching bears feed, yet no one seems to have mentioned it in any park literature.

The NPS established "Bear Feeding Shows" during a time when it was thought that feeding bears was an acceptable way to entertain tourists in Yellowstone. When garbage was dumped onto a large concrete platform at Otter Creek, numerous grizzly bears would amble out of the nearby forest and begin to eat it to the delight of assembled park visitors.

The fact that three different people (David Rothenburger, Paul Rubinstein, and Lee Whittlesey) came up with the name "Bear Feeding Falls" independently, suggests that it is a natural one. The falls splits near the top and then cascades in a fragmented manner to its muddy bottom.

"Bear Feeding Falls" dries up in mid to late summer but is included here because of its unique location in a dually historic setting: park bear feeding shows and the spot where William Tesinsky was killed by a grizzly bear in 1986. It is also the closest waterfall to the spot where, in 1877, Nez Perce Indians fought with a party of Helena tourists.

171 UNNAMED FALLS ON OTTER CREEK
"Double Grotto Falls"

LOCATION: 535465 4948019

FALL TYPE: Two-tiered
Plunge/Cascade

HEIGHT: 45 feet

STREAM: Otter Creek

MAP: USFWS Map of
Otter Creek - 1983

ACCESS: Moderate to
difficult off-trail hike.

Paul Rubinstein

"Double Grotto Falls" is a superb double plunge that changes direction by 90 degrees during its tumultuous descent. Located on Otter Creek three to four miles above its mouth, it was visited in June 1996 by authors Paul Rubinstein and Lee Whittlesey along with park employees Sarah Dykes, Michelle Serio, Steve Smith, and Barbara Totschek. The falls is located in a deep canyon at a spot fairly difficult to access.

Whittlesey arrived at the falls first and exclaimed to the others that it was a "double grotto," hence the name suggested here. A large and fairly deep cave overlooks the falls from a high point some 10 feet above it.

This is the only waterfall that we found to be mismapped by the USFWS. On their 1982 hand-drawn map of Otter Creek, "Double Grotto Falls" is shown in the lower of two canyons on the stream. It is in fact nestled deep in the upper canyon of Otter Creek. During our 1996 survey, we nearly abandoned our efforts due to the error of this map. Any trips are best made in June or July. By late summer, "Double Grotto Falls" loses much of its water and along with it, its powerful, thundering, character.

Hayden Valley

172 UNNAMED FALLS ON SOUR CREEK
"The Falls of Hayden Valley"

Mike Stevens

LOCATION: **542464 4948614**

FALL TYPE: **Segmented Cascade**

HEIGHT: **15 feet**

STREAM: **Sour Creek**

MAP: **Canyon Village, Wyo. - 1986**

ACCESS: **Easy to moderate on-trail hike.**

We are proposing this name for Hayden Valley's only mapped waterfall. The cascade-type falls is on Sour Creek just above where the Howard Eaton (Canyon-Fishing Bridge) Trail crosses that stream. Similar in shape to Knowles Falls, this feature has appeared on two maps. The 1986 Canyon Village 7½-minute quadrangle shows this falls as a "rapids," while a 1982 USFWS hand-drawn map marks it as "waterfall."

The setting is an unlikely candidate for a waterfall in that most of Hayden Valley is fairly flat. Moreover, there is little rock in the valley, but there are large rocks here. In spring, this waterfall is quite powerful.

Grand Canyon of the Yellowstone

173 UNNAMED FALLS ON GLACIAL BOULDER CREEK "Castle Ruins Falls"

LOCATION: 542129 4952567

FALL TYPE: Plunge

HEIGHT: 30 feet

STREAM: Glacial Boulder Creek

MAP: Unmapped

ACCESS: Dangerous off-trail hike, not recommended.

Chris Benden

"Castle Ruins Falls" on Glacial Boulder Creek plummets 30 feet just northeast of Inspiration Point. It is formed when the stream drops over a colorful, hydrothermally-altered rhyolitic ledge into the Grand Canyon of the Yellowstone River. After its brief plunge, it then cascades for hundreds more feet. We propose the name from the waterfall's proximity to the "thousand castellated pinnacles" nearby that writer Olin Wheeler named Castle Ruins in or about 1897.[144] Wheeler stated that the yellow colors "run riot" here, because of the chiseling of the forces of erosion.

174-175 SILVER CORD CASCADE

Mike Stevens

LOCATION: 543546 4952592

FALL TYPE: Horsetail

HEIGHT: 1,200 feet

STREAM: Surface Creek

MAP: Canyon Village, Wyoming - 1986

ACCESS: Easy to moderate on-trail hike.

Perhaps Yellowstone's tallest waterfall, Silver Cord Cascade (#174) plummets some 1,200 feet. It is located on Surface Creek at the point it enters the Grand Canyon of the Yellowstone from the south. Hikers can view it from the Glacial Boulder Trail near Inspiration Point, one mile east of Glacial Boulder. In addition, the Ribbon Lake Trail leads to the brink of this falls, but there you must exercise much caution.

Silver Cord Cascade was probably at least partly responsible for early stories of waterfalls 1,000 feet or more high on the Yellowstone River. Western explorers beginning with Lewis and Clark knew such tales. In 1870, N.P. Langford wrote: "We had been told by trappers and mountaineers that there were cataracts in this vicinity a thousand feet high; but, if so, they must be lower down the cañon, in that portion of it which . . . we failed to see."[145]

Cornelius Hedges noted that "the wild, floating stories about falls 1,000 feet in height are no doubt exaggerations as applied to the main stream. That there are small streams . . . that fall the distance of 1,000 feet or more, perpendicular, is true and such were seen by some of our party."[146]

Silver Cord Cascade was first named "Silverthread Fall" by Ben Stickney and Sam Hauser of the 1870 Washburn party. While superintendent Norris called it "Sliding Cascade" in 1883, members of the USGS gave the present name in 1885. In 1897, a newspaper article referred to Silver Cord Cascade as "maybe the highest waterfall in the world" at 1,800 feet.[147] That figure was too high, and it is now known that Angel Falls in Venezuela is far taller at over 3,200 feet. A similar but seasonal 1,000-foot cascade (#175) is present just downstream from Silver Cord Cascade.

176-177 TWIN FALLS

LOCATION NORTH(#176):
546699 4954866

LOCATION SOUTH (#177):
546755 4955225

FALL TYPE: Segmented Horsetail/
Series of Cascades

HEIGHT: 200 and 200 feet combined

STREAM: Unnamed Tributaries
of the Yellowstone River

MAP: "Map of the Yellowstone
National Park" - P.W. Norris,
1880, 1881

ACCESS: Moderate to
difficult on-trail hike.

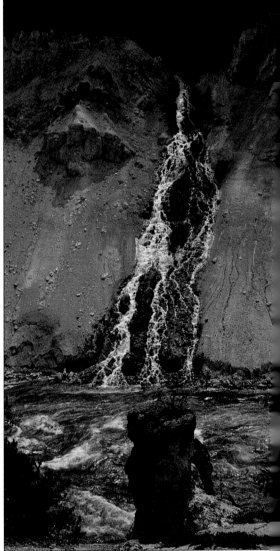

Twin Falls (south)

Mike Stevens

Near Seven Mile Hole a long, steep cascade (#176) horsetails into the Yellowstone River. Its drop of at least 200 feet can best be seen from the area near Safety Valve Geyser. The unnamed stream enters the Yellowstone River from the south.

Just upstream from this point on the north side of the Yellowstone River is a second unnamed stream, which we call "Temptress Creek." Unlike its predecessor, this stream does not contain any 200-foot cascades. Instead it descends unevenly in a series of 15- to 30-foot cascades over a period of about half a mile (#177). These seemingly routine streams and their unnamed cascades are actually part of a legendary duo of waterfalls known as Twin Falls.

In 1880, park superintendent P.W. Norris named them while riding his horse through the canyon. Norris wrote, "Some of these streams [which run into the Grand Canyon] descend by beautiful cascades or in dark narrow cañons, and others, as the Twin Falls, by cañons to the remnants of old [rock] slides, and thence by a clear, beautiful leap of some two hundred feet, reach the river nearly opposite..."[148]

Norris evidently had found two separate waterfalls nearly opposite each other on the Yellowstone River. So taken was he with the spot, he immediately built the first

A portion of Twin Falls (north)

Mike Stevens

trail to the area. (Originally called the "Twin Falls Trail," it is today known as the Seven Mile Hole Trail.) Norris's discovery was reported in park guidebooks in 1882 and 1883.[149] Mysteriously, within several years of discovery, Twin Falls faded into obscurity. The two falls were then essentially forgotten for 105 years until Lee Whittlesey mentioned them in his 1988 book, *Yellowstone Place Names*. Unfortunately, Whittlesey had the location incorrect and did not realize that Norris had been referring to multiple waterfalls, so it was not until 1999 that the original Twin Falls were re-identified (see "The Twin Falls Controversy"). Had Norris more accurately described his Twin Falls at their initial discovery, then perhaps they would have remained in park literature to this day.

The Twin Falls Controversy

There is no question that sometime in 1879 or 1880 P.W. Norris named and mapped a waterfall in the Grand Canyon of the Yellowstone that he called Twin Falls. It appeared on his 1880 and 1881 maps as well as on several other park maps for some six years before disappearing like a number of other named features of the time. In searching for Norris's Twin Falls, we extensively surveyed every seasonal and perennial stream in the Grand Canyon for some six miles below Lower Falls. Yet for more than 10 years we were not able to settle the key question to our satisfaction. Where exactly was Norris's Twin Falls?

Author Lee Whittlesey originally faced this problem while writing *Yellowstone Place Names* in the mid-1980s. During his research, he came upon the only known quote describing Twin Falls. Norris penned that brief description in his annual report for 1880.

In 1980, with only that single citation and Norris's 1880 map, Whittlesey made an attempt to determine the location of Twin Falls. Although the hundred-year-old map showed Twin Falls near the mouth of Sulphur Creek, he found no waterfall there. After carefully weighing all the possibilities, he theorized that it was a mapping error and that Twin Falls must have been located on the next large stream down the canyon: Glade Creek. So in 1988, Twin Falls appeared in Yellowstone literature for the first time in more than a century, in Whittlesey's book *Yellowstone Place Names.*

The Twin Falls issue seemed resolved until 1995 when Paul Rubinstein and Mike Stevens hiked into the Glade Creek drainage to photograph it for this book. As they surveyed downstream on Glade Creek, they found no 200-foot waterfall. Puzzled, the two continued east along the canyon rim and within minutes found an unmapped stream that contained one of the most beautiful waterfalls they had ever seen in Yellowstone.

Not only was the falls at least 200 feet in height, it appeared to them that at least 400 feet of cascades continued below the falls. Also, its waters fell free for at least 100 feet before striking rocks and splitting into a dual or "twin" plunge to the canyon bottom. Surely, they thought, this was Twin Falls. The height was correct, the falls took on a twin appearance (at least on its lower half) for much of the season, and it was in the Glade Creek drainage (if not on Glade Creek itself). Thus ended the mystery of Twin Falls. Or so we believed.

Over the next four years, as our research continued on the park's other falls, we never gave a second thought to the Twin Falls controversy. We were happy believing we had solved a 100-year-old mystery.

For Rubinstein, however, something did not seem right. In his heart he still wasn't sure. He was bothered by several disturbing questions:

• Why was the Twin Falls notation always shown near the mouth of Sulphur Creek? This was true on all maps that showed it. If it were a mapping error, it was never corrected.

• Why did an 1883 guidebook published by Herman Haupt Jr. describe the location of Twin Falls as follows: "4½ miles down-stream [from Lower Falls] is the Twin Falls, a veil of water 200 feet high, which may be reached by a scramble down from the top of the canon"?[150] Where did Haupt get this distance? Again, that figure would put Twin Falls near Sulphur Creek, not Glade Creek.

- Why did all maps that showed Twin Falls also show an additional 200-foot fall downstream on the canyon's south side? Where was this waterfall and why had we never seen or read any more about it?

In addition, Rubinstein noted several problems with the falls near Glade Creek: it was not in the correct map location according to Norris, and for much of the season it did not take on a "twin shape" appearance. Moreover, Norris never mentioned Glade Creek, even though he himself had named it.

Rubinstein also continued to be bothered by the notation "200 foot falls," which routinely appeared downstream of Twin Falls on the canyon's south side during the 1880s. The only south-side fall we knew of approaching that height was one we had surveyed in the area around Seven Mile Hole. It was a steep, cascade-type fall that split into multiple branches during its descent. Because it had no historic name known to us, we had tentatively called it "Meadowsweet Cascade."

Perhaps this was actually Twin Falls? Rubinstein felt that this theory wasn't right either, but he did notice several interesting coincidences:

- Norris described Twin Falls as being 200 feet high. "Meadowsweet Cascade" was 200 feet high.

- Herman Haupt's 1883 guide stated that Twin Falls was four and one-half miles downstream from Lower Falls. "Meadowsweet Cascade" was four and one-half miles downstream from Lower Falls.

- Norris did build a trail to the area around Seven Mile Hole in 1880. "Meadowsweet Cascade" is (and was) visible from this trail.

- "Meadowsweet Cascade" does split at its top, thus giving a twin and sometimes triple appearance as it cascades down the open slopes of the canyon.

Still struggling with the inconsistencies, Rubinstein decided that these were indeed just coincidences, because they did not explain why maps only showed Twin Falls on the canyon's north side. Norris's description of Twin Falls ("and others, as the Twin Falls, by cañons to the remnants of old [rock] slides, and thence by a clear, beautiful leap of some two hundred feet, reach the river")[151] did not accurately depict "Meadowsweet Cascade," which does not leap. Further, in the mid-1880s, some park maps completely omitted Twin Falls, while the "200 foot falls" notation on the south side of the canyon remained. After pondering the evidence for many months, Rubinstein decided to leave well enough alone and give in to the fact that the 200-foot plunge near Glade Creek was the better choice for Twin Falls.

Then, in July 1999 Rubinstein apparently solved this 119-year-old mystery. He happened to be rereading Norris's annual report for 1880 and came across the now-familiar quote describing Twin Falls. Although he had seen the quote many times before, something caught his eye as being different. It was different! In its original form the quote read: "Some of these streams descend by beautiful cascades or in dark narrow cañons, and others, as the Twin Falls, by cañons to the remnants of old slides, and thence by a clear, beautiful leap of some two hundred feet, reach the river nearly opposite; while there is a similar fall from the eastern terrace less than a mile below."[152]

continued on next page

continued from previous page

There were two additional words, "nearly opposite," as well as an entire sentence that had been omitted from the Twin Falls entry in *Yellowstone Place Names* in 1988. But what did those two words mean? "Nearly opposite" of what? Rubinstein immediately questioned Lee Whittlesey as to why these two words had been left out of *Place Names*. Whittlesey said that they had made no sense to him. Thinking they would only confuse the reader, he left them out of the final draft. Rubinstein and Whittlesey pondered this new twist for several hours but could reach no definitive answer. What did Norris mean by "nearly opposite?"

Leaving that problem for a later time, Rubinstein focused on the additional sentence. Unlike the "nearly opposite" riddle, it proved to be an immediate and major clue. Analyzing Norris's statement "while there is a similar fall from the eastern terrace less than a mile below," Rubinstein concluded that Twin Falls and the 200-foot falls downstream were not the same falls. Even more importantly he now felt that Twin Falls could not possibly be in the Glade Creek drainage. The distances and directions were all wrong. It once again put Twin Falls somewhere near the mouth of Sulphur Creek.

Within hours more clues were found in the Norris report. Rubinstein next discovered that Norris had included a trail mileage chart in the rear of the report as a reference. Most interesting were the distances along what Norris called the "Twin Falls Trail." Judging by the locations this trail passed by, it was the same as today's Seven Mile Hole Trail. The critical item was the reference that the distance between Twin Falls and Safety Valve Geyser was one mile (with Twin Falls being downstream from Safety Valve). Here was a new Twin Falls reference coming to light, and yet things were still confusing. Although Twin Falls was always mapped on the north side of the Yellowstone River, there was no waterfall on the canyon's north side a mile downstream from Safety Valve Geyser. But there was a 200-foot waterfall on the south side: the one we had been calling "Meadowsweet Cascade." Rubinstein believed the answer was getting closer, but knew he still didn't have it precisely.

Finally, in the late afternoon, he found the last piece of the puzzle. While studying (for what seemed like the hundredth time) the 1880 Norris map (the earliest map to show Twin Falls), he noticed something he hadn't before. With the aid of a large magnifying glass he discovered that Norris had included extremely small "tick" marks on this map to indicate his waterfalls. This was unusual, as Norris had apparently never used them on any other maps. What Rubinstein saw was that at precisely the spot where all the evidence said Twin Falls should be located, there were "tick" marks on both sides of the Yellowstone River. Not only that, but they were located exactly opposite each other. It hit him in a flash that this was what Norris had meant when he said "nearly opposite." This also meant that the idea that Twin Falls was a single, plunging fall was and always had been erroneous. In fact, Twin Falls were two separate waterfalls on opposite sides of the canyon, each falling into the Yellowstone River, and apparently so-mapped by Norris.

But where was the second 200-foot waterfall on the canyon's north rim? Norris's map indicated that the stream containing this second fall is actually an unnamed short-lived stream that emerges from the canyon side along the Seven Mile Hole Trail. Fortunately, we were familiar with this small creek and had surveyed it thoroughly. It steps downward in a series of small falls and cascades before sliding into the Yellowstone River. It does not have any feature approaching 200 feet. However, the sum total of all of its features does approach this figure (Whittlesey confirmed this on foot in September 1999). We believe that Norris unfortunately gave a brief and confusing description of these features and that it has contributed to the confusion of the history of the area.

We now believe the correct scenario goes like this. In 1880, P.W. Norris discovered and named two waterfalls in the Grand Canyon of the Yellowstone. One was approximately 200 feet in height, and the other a series of small drops totaling nearly 200 feet. Their unnamed streams entered the Yellowstone River nearly opposite each other. So taken with these features was Norris that he built a trail to them later that year, calling it the "Twin Falls Trail." Shortly thereafter, we think the few visitors who ventured to Twin Falls were confused and puzzled by what they saw. The evidenced is in the fact that, by 1881, Norris abruptly dropped the name "Twin Falls Trail" and instead simply called it the "Bridal Trail." His maps then applied the name Twin Falls only to the remaining fall on the southern side—the same one we photographed years later and called "Meadowsweet Cascade." We theorize that this is why Twin Falls disappeared from park maps so early in its history. As subsequent observers went into the area, they found that there was nothing on the northern side to be seen approaching 200 feet. When Norris's confusing description of the falls is taken into account, it is no wonder that the entire name was deleted from subsequent literature.

Portion of Yellowstone map featuring Twin Falls

But what of Norris's other 200-foot fall on "the eastern [southern] terrace less than a mile below"? This riddle too was soon solved. Less than a mile below Twin Falls on the canyon's southern side flows Moss Creek, a stream we had long suspected contained a large falls. Rubinstein later confirmed this when he sighted, through his telescope from the Washburn Hot Springs overlook on the Grand Loop Road, a plunge of unknown proportions on Moss Creek.

In our Twin Falls entry we have now given you what we believe is the correct answer as to what feature(s) Norris actually named Twin Falls. We have otherwise searched in vain for any other 200-foot fall in the Sulphur Creek area. There is definitely no fall approaching a 200-foot leap on the north side of the canyon, as mapped by Norris. Again, we suspect it was his poor description that led to all this confusion for more than a century.

Unfortunately, the answer will never be absolute unless new information comes to light—another old map or Norris's lost diary. We know he kept a diary, but it has never been located. Finding it would, in all likelihood, settle the question of Twin Falls once and for all.

178 UNNAMED CASCADES ON THE SOUTH BRANCH OF SULPHUR CREEK "Brimstone Cascades"

LOCATION: 545405 4956088

FALL TYPE: Two Serial Cascades

HEIGHT: 30 and 70 feet

STREAM: Sulphur Creek (South Fork)

MAP: Unmapped

ACCESS: Moderate to difficult off-trail hike.

Mike Stevens

The lower, 70-foot portion of "Brimstone Cascades"

The "Brimstone Cascades" are a double cascade located on the south branch of Sulphur Creek about one-half mile above its junction with the north fork. They are hidden deep in a side canyon of the Grand Canyon of the Yellowstone. The upper of the two cascades is a drop of 30 feet in perhaps 100 feet of flow. After 30 yards of relatively tranquil water, the lower portion then drops more steeply for another 70 feet.

What makes these cascades special is the brightness of the surrounding yellow bedrock and the small thermal features contained within. In places the rock is embedded with geode-like stones. The steep, high canyon above the creek includes numerous vertical pinnacles. The stream is joined by a variety of springs, some cool, others warm and sulphurous, hence the name "Brimstone." Photography of both cascades together is difficult due to the narrowness of the canyon and the configuration of the twisting and dipping cascades.

179 UNNAMED FALLS ON SULPHUR CREEK "Xanadu Falls"

Mike Stevens

Joe Mangiantini

"Xanadu Falls" in spring   *"Xanadu Falls" in autumn*

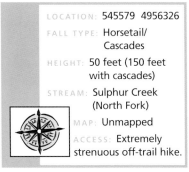

LOCATION: 545579 4956326

FALL TYPE: Horsetail/
Cascades

HEIGHT: 50 feet (150 feet
with cascades)

STREAM: Sulphur Creek
(North Fork)

MAP: Unmapped

ACCESS: Extremely
strenuous off-trail hike.

This waterfall is set in a fairytale-like locale. We did not know for certain that it existed, but we long suspected it.

Travel in Yellowstone's Grand Canyon is potentially dangerous at any time and this trip was no exception. We reached the falls by traveling upstream on Sulphur Creek, a difficult route.

This is a 50-foot falls with more than 100 feet of steep cascades below it that tumble over brightly colored yellow and brown rocks. The stream appears to be lined with sulphur vents as well as colorful springs actually in the creek. Also apparent is a small, side catch-basin where the waters collect from both a hot and a cold source. Lee Whittlesey saw a cave on the cliff-face to the left of the falls and at first suggested calling the falls, "Sulphur Cave Falls."

In time, however, we settled on "Xanadu Falls" for the spectacular setting of this small canyon within a canyon. Xanadu is the enchanted land in a poem called "Kubla Khan" by Samuel Taylor Coleridge (1772–1834) which begins as follows:

> *In Xanadu did Kubla Khan*
> *A stately pleasure dome decree;*
> *Where Alph the sacred river ran*
> *Through caverns measureless to man*
> *Down to a sunless sea.*

Like the land described in the poem, the country below "Xanadu Falls" seems enchanted. Small hot-spring streams break out to flow into Sulphur Creek in jet-black rivulets that contrast with the green of a spruce forest covered with luxuriant ferns, verdant mosses, and huge boulders.

This place, with its caves, walls and towers, sacred rivers, and sunny spots of greenery, all located within "a deep, romantic chasm," evoked for us visions of Xanadu. As the poem says, it is "a savage place, holy and enchanted," and indeed, while there, we thought we saw a "damsel with a dulcimer." Coleridge could have been writing specifically about this spot. Those who choose to visit here should make it a point to read "Kubla Kahn."

But we must re-emphasize the potential danger here. We attempted to leave the spot by scaling a wall to the immediate west of "Xanadu Falls." The ascent was steep and difficult. As we attained the summit, we were suddenly confronted with the fact that the wall was only three feet wide and we were facing a 300-foot vertical drop into an adjacent canyon, the south branch of Sulphur Creek. Sick with fear, we managed to crawl several hundred feet up this narrow "catwalk" onto the forested Grand Canyon rim and safety. We sat in the forest for some time, trembling, even though we had, as Coleridge said, "drunk the milk of paradise."

180 MOSS CREEK CASCADES

We have seen portions of these cascades from the brink of "Citadel of Asgard Falls." They are located on Moss Creek where it plunges over the south rim of the Grand Canyon of the Yellowstone some 10 miles downstream from Lower Falls. They are not as vertical as Silver Cord Cascade, but they do plummet over 1,000 feet as the stream makes a series of cascades and horsetails before joining the Yellowstone River.

The only documentation of any feature on Moss Creek is the notation "200-foot falls," which appears on several of P.W. Norris's 1880s maps. An individual falls approaching this height is visible on Moss Creek from the Grand Loop Road at the Washburn Hot Springs overlook. Using strong optics, a sharp-eyed person can see a distant waterfall plummeting into the Grand Canyon from the opposite side.

In July 1999, Mike Stevens partially surveyed Moss Creek. His conclusion is that at least one and possibly several other significant falls and cascades are hidden in the forest just upstream from where the creek plunges into the canyon. Unfortunately, he could not access any good vantage points of these cascades or of the main 200-foot fall.

Glade Creek

High on the southeastern slopes of Mount Washburn are the rivulets of an innocent looking stream called Glade Creek. It was named in or about 1881 by park superintendent P.W. Norris, probably for the large open meadow on its southerly and larger branch.[153] The drainage has a rather complex geography. Mapped as only a north and south fork, it actually contains at least a dozen tributaries (the majority being seasonal).

The largest and most important creek in the system is actually Glade Creek's south fork. Flowing to the southeast, it gently descends through the alpine slopes of the Washburn Range before entering the aforementioned meadow. Here the stream turns due east and enters the forest for the remainder of its journey to the Yellowstone River.

A short distance into these woods, the stream reaches the rim of the Grand Canyon of the Yellowstone. A turbulent but little-explored stream, it is rife with waterfalls. Five falls grace its length, four of them occurring on the stretch of stream located within the Grand Canyon of the Yellowstone. Unlike the narrow canyon upstream at Upper and Lower Falls, here the Grand Canyon is nearly two miles across. This widening of the canyon creates a topography unique to the park. Over the

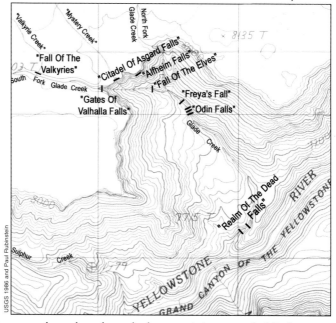

next mile, Glade Creek journeys through perhaps the last remaining stronghold of massive, undiscovered, Yellowstone waterfalls.

We believed this heretofore-unexplored region deserved a theme worthy of its outstanding beauty and chaotic nature. We chose the title "Valhalla" to represent the canyon country of this most important drainage, and we selected only names from Norse mythology to identify the individual features contained within. Valhalla, "Hall of the Slain" in Norse mythology, was the hall presided over by the Norse god Odin. At the entrance to Valhalla, a wolf guarded the western door and an eagle hovered over it. It was to here that women called Valkyries, Odin's messengers and spirits of war, brought the heroes who died on the battlefield.

Yellowstone has a long tradition of taking place names from mythology. This hallowed tradition befits the park's status as a world heritage site and underscores its role in sublime spectacle and mythical splendor. The idea of using Norse mythological names perfectly captures the spirit of this exceptional area. Norse mythology is about nature, and Yellowstone represents nature on the grandest of scales. The magical themes depicted in Norse mythology suggested to us places in this enchanted area of Glade Creek, a world-class area that deserves no less than to be celebrated in history, poem, and song. We noted the contrast between the pastoral meanderings of the upper parts of Glade Creek and the ferocity of the stream's lower reaches. Norris, the namer of the stream and a man who knew this difficult but fascinating area, would not have been surprised at this contrast.

Though we did not discover this fact until after we had selected the name, we are not the first to propose the name "Valhalla" for this magnificent canyon. Legendary western writer Owen Wister shared his similar vision of Valhalla while visiting the park in 1891. In describing the upper end of the Grand Canyon of the Yellowstone he wrote: "The place is at once romantic, exquisite, and wholly sublime. The South is not in it, nor anything of Homer, but you can easily believe Monsarrat is round the next corner or expect to see the Gods stretch a rainbow somewhere and march across to Valhalla."[154]

As we pondered over what designations the individual waterfalls deserved, we asked ourselves: what feelings did these sites evoke in us and what aspects of Norse mythology most closely captured those emotions? We tried to select the names of Norse mytho-logical lands and gods that most closely epitomized those feelings while still reflecting the natural geography of the waterfalls and their immediate surroundings.

The diversity of features here is positively staggering: the mighty three-step "Odin Falls," named for the powerful king of all Norse gods; the wispy "Fall of the Elves," honoring a race of beings that seems to dissolve into the dark woods; the towering "Citadel of Asgard Falls," the grandest spectacle Valhalla has to offer; the perplexing "Alfheim Falls," a falls whose stream has no beginning and no end and seems to appear out of nowhere, then vanish without a trace. Unquestionably, this is Yellowstone's greatest concentration of magnificent, little-known waterfalls.

The most superb feature, "Citadel of Asgard Falls," is visible from the canyon rim, but the rest require a hazardous descent into the canyon. The region's sheer number of waterfalls and dangerous and slow travel conditions, required us to make many trips to grasp the area's complexity and to photograph its features. This part of the Grand Canyon of the Yellowstone was a siren-temptress to us, but a place that simultaneously cried out for much caution. It is easy to forget prudence during captivation. This is a world where one can be easily injured.

Still, Valhalla was a land where warriors were rewarded with eternal life, and the "brave warrior" who makes the pilgrimage here will be blessed with panoramic vistas of perhaps the most stunning, unheralded region in all of the Yellowstone backcountry. "Valhalla" is without a doubt our favorite place in the park for waterfalls. It contains some of the finest scenery Yellowstone has to offer.

181 UNNAMED FALLS ON "VALKYRIE CREEK"
"Fall of the Valkyries"

LOCATION: 546686 4957254

FALL TYPE: Two-tiered Plunge

HEIGHT: 15 feet

STREAM: "Valkyrie Creek"

MAP: Unmapped

ACCESS: Moderate to difficult off-trail hike.

Paul Rubinstein

This small, pretty two-drop falls is located on an unnamed creek that enters the south fork of Glade Creek about one-half mile above "Gates of Valhalla Falls." One crosses this unnamed stream when hiking along the north side of south Glade Creek. The name "Fall of the Valkyries" is suggested from its proximity to "Valhalla," Yellowstone's waterfall-laden side-canyon just a half-mile to the east. We also suggest the name "Valkyrie Creek" for its small stream. (This stream is missing from maps, but appears to flow for most if not all of the season.)

In Norse mythology, Valkyries were warrior-maidens mounted on winged steeds and armed with helmets, shields, and spears, who conducted the souls of brave warriors to the ultimate reward of Valhalla. As they rode upon their winged horses—sometimes wolves—their armor caused the strange flickering light that today we call Aurora Borealis.[155] "Val" means "slain," and the Valkyries were the "choosers of the slain," desirable virgins who selected the bravest of warriors for Valhalla.

Like the Valkyries themselves, this falls and stream are located on the way to Valhalla. Any hiker who reaches this delicate falls will be rewarded with vistas of epic proportions a short distance beyond.

182 UNNAMED FALLS ON GLADE CREEK
"Gates of Valhalla Falls"

LOCATION: 547060 4957178

FALL TYPE: Three-tiered Plunge

HEIGHT: 100 feet

STREAM: Glade Creek (South Fork)

MAP: Unmapped

ACCESS: Dangerous off-trail hike, not recommended.

Paul Rubinstein

This three-step falls is world-class in its setting and beauty. A tiered falls with vertical steps, it is at least 100 feet high with at least 100 feet of cascades below it. It is located on the south fork of Glade Creek, which enters the Grand Canyon of the Yellowstone below Mount Washburn.

This is another of those waterfalls that for years we had suspected existed. The falls cannot be seen in its entirety or photographed well from its brink, but travel to the brink is the only logical way to reach it. We obtained photographs by a difficult descent into the canyon. The photo shown here was secured during the high-water period of spring while the falls is torrential, but we also photographed it in autumn when its volume is much smaller. As we continued our research in the Grand Canyon of the Yellowstone, visiting Twin Falls, "Xanadu Falls," and others, it became apparent to us that the panoramic vistas here are some of the most pristine and spectacular of anywhere on Earth. The three authors arrived at the name "Gates of Valhalla," and, after extended discussion, decided to suggest it for this falls, which overlooks such spectacular country.

The view from its brink is superb, as one looks southeast over some 60 square miles into the most rarely visited section of the Grand Canyon. In the foreground, a natural bowl is actually formed by Glade Creek proper. The spot seems to be a natural portal that looks into an area also containing "Fall of the Elves," "Freya's Fall," and "Citadel of Asgard Falls," among others. The panoramic vista makes one think he or she is standing at some mighty entrance, perhaps looking into Valhalla, the mythological and paradisiacal hall of slain heroes in Asgard, the mountain-home of gods and goddesses of Norse mythology.

183 UNNAMED FALLS ON "MYSTERY CREEK" "Citadel of Asgard Falls"

Upper half of "Citadel of Asgard Falls"

Paul Rubinstein

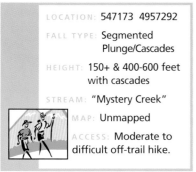

LOCATION: 547173 4957292

FALL TYPE: Segmented
Plunge/Cascades

HEIGHT: 150+ & 400-600 feet
with cascades

STREAM: "Mystery Creek"

MAP: Unmapped

ACCESS: Moderate to
difficult off-trail hike.

This breathtaking and world-class waterfall is located on an unnamed stream between the north and south forks of Glade Creek. The stream plunges at least 150 feet onto a bench in the Grand Canyon of the Yellowstone and then cascades for hundreds of feet more. During and after its plunge, it is wispy and elegant. Rising hundreds of feet, imposing rock walls reminiscent of citadels and battlements surround this waterfall and form an alcove that have kept it and its dramatic ramparts from public view until now.

We first saw this falls in 1995 while searching for Twin Falls. For four years we believed this magnificent spectacle to be Twin Falls. Because it is located in an alcove within an alcove, it is not easily visible from the air, nor is it visible from any obvious or developed vantage points. It wasn't until information

came to light in July 1999 that the true Twin Falls was identified and the undocumented nature of this wonderful cataract became apparent.

Its stream, an unmapped, middle branch of Glade Creek, is fed by cold springs that keep it running most years. Joe Mangiantini of one of our parties proposed the name "Mystery Creek" for the stream because it puzzled us for so long as to what stream it was.

Our height figure reflects only the first absolutely vertical plunge and does not include hundreds of feet of cascades. Because of these, this is a very tall waterfall; in fact, we initially thought it might be taller than 300 feet.

It is virtually impossible to see the bottom of "Citadel of Asgard Falls" from anywhere along the north rim. Only a dangerous trip into the canyon to visit the base of the falls allowed us to finally see its entire drop.

"Citadel of Asgard Falls"   Paul Rubinstein

Our proposed name is meant to capture the magnificence of this astounding falls. Asgard, in Norse mythology, was one of the nine worlds and the homeland of the Aesir, the race of warrior gods. Considered the highest level of the Norse universe and a place of gold and silver palaces, it was located at the end of the rainbow and could be reached only by crossing a rainbow bridge (appropriate for waterfalls). In addition, it was a citadel surrounded by a high wall of closely fitted stone blocks, much as this falls is. Also found on this level were the worlds of Alfheim (see "Alfheim Falls") and Valhalla (see "Glade Creek" and "Gates of Valhalla Falls"). The view of the Grand Canyon from the brink of "Citadel of Asgard Falls" is as spectacular a view as any in the park. It epitomizes Yellowstone wilderness. From here, on the canyon's opposite side you can view a portion of the "Moss Creek Cascades," a 1,000-foot-tall series of cascades that rival Silver Cord Cascade in total height.

"Valhalla" viewed from the brink of "Citadel of Asgard Falls"

Paul Rubinstein

184

UNNAMED FALLS IN A WALL OF THE GRAND CANYON OF THE YELLOWSTONE
"Alfheim Falls"

LOCATION: 547289 4957299

FALL TYPE: Plunge

HEIGHT: 30 feet

STREAM: underground spring

MAP: Unmapped

ACCESS: Dangerous off-trail hike, not recommended.

Paul Rubinstein

Yellowstone is truly special with regard to waterfalls; it seems to have everything imaginable. Can one even conceive of a waterfall with no stream leading to it nor a stream leading away from it? "Alfheim Falls" is such a waterfall, a "magic" falls that seems suspended in space. It is unbelievable, surreal, almost otherworldly, and certainly fantastic beyond belief. As such, after learning of it from us, Paul Schullery elected to describe it in his important book, *Searching for Yellowstone.*

The fairness and novelty of this mystical little falls rests in its setting: it is located in the Grand Canyon of the Yellowstone River. Its unnamed stream comes out of the center of the canyon wall from a cave, drops 30 feet over a ledge, and then disappears underground in a boulder field. The spot is accessible only by a dangerous scramble into the canyon below "Citadel of Asgard Falls."

Alfheim, in Norse mythology, was one of the nine worlds of the Gods and Goddesses. It was located on the highest level of the Norse universe. Alfheim (or "Elf Home") was the place where the goddess Freya ruled over the fairies and the homeland of the Elves of Light (see "Fall of the Elves" and "Freya's Fall"). It was a secret, unfathomable, occult land in that its location was always mysterious.

"Alfheim Falls" is also such a place. It is extremely tricky to locate. It is not seen or heard until one stumbles upon it among the dense spruces and firs. Like the mystic land it is named for, "Alfheim Falls" hides cryptically in the north wall of the canyon a few hundred yards northeast of the middle fork of Glade Creek ("Mystery Creek") after that stream drops over "Citadel of Asgard Falls."

185 UNNAMED FALLS ON LOWER GLADE CREEK "Fall of the Elves"

LOCATION: 547361 4957183

FALL TYPE: Plunge

HEIGHT: 17 feet

STREAM: Glade Creek
(South Fork)

MAP: Unmapped

ACCESS: Dangerous off-
trail hike, not
recommended.

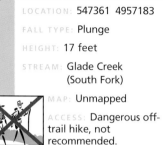

Mike Stevens

Well into the canyon is a vertical plunge of the south branch of Glade Creek. Its waters plummet straight down, just 30 yards above the stream's confluence with "Mystery Creek" (see "Citadel of Asgard Falls") and some 600 yards below "Gates of Valhalla Falls."

We refer to this well-hidden gem as the "Fall of the Elves." In Norse mythology, there was a mysterious race of beings known as elves. The race was split into two separate groups, the Elves of Light and the Elves of Darkness. They lived in the lands of Alfheim (Elf home) and Svartalfheim. The Elves of Light had fair, golden hair and sweet musical voices, and they wore delicate, gossamer garments. Carrying golden harps and invisible to humans, they loved to dance in the woods, on hillsides, and in meadows. The elf-dancers had to disappear before cockcrow or they would remain stationary but invisible, and anyone who touched them unawares would inherit sickness and pain. The Elves of Darkness, by contrast, lived in caves and clefts and avoided light, appearing only at night because sunlight could turn them into stone. They were ugly, long-nosed dwarves of a dirty brown color. Females could produce ravishing music, irresistible to susceptible youth, that produced fatal results.

This particular waterfall straddles the border between the open, well-lit, rock-lined cliffs of the upper canyon and the dark, complex forest of the lower canyon. The fall's proximity to these two microenvironments (light and dark) was our genesis for the proposed Norse name.

Our first encounter with this undocumented waterfall was in 1995 when we viewed it in the distance from the canyon rim. We did not travel to it at that time. In 1997, ranger David Rothenburger, along with Mike Stevens, descended the canyon and photographed it from close range. You can spot this falls from above, along the north rim of the Grand Canyon of the Yellowstone, at a vantage point approximately one-half mile northeast of "Citadel of Asgard Falls."

186 UNNAMED FALLS ON LOWER GLADE CREEK "Freya's Fall"

LOCATION: 547637 4957026

FALL TYPE: Plunge

HEIGHT: 38 feet

STREAM: Glade Creek

MAP: Unmapped

ACCESS: Dangerous off-trail hike, not recommended.

Mike Stevens

On June 19, 1997, ranger David Rothenburger took a solo trip to the base of "Citadel of Asgard Falls." From there he began surveying the south branch of Glade Creek. Soon his exploration took him farther downstream then any previous surveys for this book. It was in this densely forested area of the lower reaches of Glade Creek proper that he discovered a 38-foot plunging fall.

It is not clear exactly how many falls he saw that day, but he certainly was the first known person to view this well-hidden terraced fall that we call "Freya's Fall." Its brink is 200 yards downstream from the junction of the north and south branches of Glade Creek. Although it is certainly debatable, Rothenburger believes he was the first Euro-American ever to see this falls: "Until the moment of my discovery of it, I believe the only other living things that ever saw this beautiful waterfall were squirrels, birds, and other animals due to its extremely remote location."

Our proposed Norse name is for the goddess Freya, the goddess of love and fertility, and the most beautiful and auspicious of the goddesses. She loved music, spring, and flowers, and was particularly fond of elves, whom she ruled over in the land of Alfheim (see "Fall of the Elves" and "Alfheim Falls"). She was also the receiver of half the souls of the slain warriors who fell in battle, with the other half going to the Norse god Odin (See "Odin Falls") at Valhalla. Friday was named for her, originally called "Freya's Day."[156]

187 UNNAMED FALLS ON LOWER GLADE CREEK "Odin Falls"

LOCATION: 547694 4956941

FALL TYPE: Two-step Plunge/ Cascade

HEIGHT: 70, 30, and 30 feet

STREAM: Glade Creek

MAP: Unmapped

ACCESS: Dangerous off-trail hike, not recommended.

Upper plunge of "Odin Falls"

Mike Stevens

Just below "Freya's Fall" is a double plunge with an additional cascade that we call "Odin Falls" in tribute to the leader of the Norse gods and goddesses. This spectacular three-step falls is located in one of the most difficult-to-travel areas in Yellowstone. Hiking along lower Glade Creek is slow, laborious, and difficult, at times with few or no places to walk. Our progress was slowed by sheer rock faces with crumbling rhyolite, precipitous slopes of unstable ground, severe cut banks, jumbled boulders, multitudinous and wicked deadfall, alder thickets, and a thick understory of thorny gooseberry and raspberry bushes. All that was made worse by day-long, intermittent showers that made the footing viciously slippery. It is one of those places where hikers talk about doing "hours per mile" rather than "miles per hour." The stream itself is deep, wide, and seemingly angry; it rushes madly among house-sized boulders.

As our party of nine park employees (including Julie Guarino, Mark Lehman, Louise Mercier, Ashea Mills, Lee Ramella, Adina Smith, and Keri Thorpe) stood at "Freya's Fall" in June 1999, we looked downstream over our shoulders to see the stream abruptly disappearing over a precipitous brink.

"I remember shouting something like 'It's ours,'" says Whittlesey. "I knew that the chances of any Euro-American, or even an Indian, having seen it were few. This place, hidden in a canyon within the Grand Canyon, was simply too difficult to reach."

Later, we decided on the name "Odin Falls" for this extraordinary spectacle. Norse mythology exemplifies nature and daring, and reaching "Odin Falls" combined both of those things in an unforgettable way.

Odin, the father of all Norse gods, was the god of war and death but also of poetry, prophesy, wisdom, the wind, and magic. His throne was located in Asgard, the mountain citadel where many of the gods and goddesses lived, but he also resided with the Valkyries (see "Fall of the Valkyries") in Valhalla, the great hall where the bravest of warriors were taken after death in battle. Odin could make the dead warriors speak in order to question the wisest among them. Generally depicted with two wolves by his side, Odin also had two ravens named Thought and Memory whom he sent out to the world of men every day to gather knowledge for him.

Sometimes called Alfadir (All Father), Odin was often depicted as an old man with a long, white beard who wore a cloak with a hood "as blue as the sky," and who had only one eye, because he had traded the other one for a drink from the Well of Wisdom in order to gain immense knowledge. Other paintings showed him as a war lord with a gold helmet, his spear in one hand and breastplate in the other. Odin possessed a spear that never missed its mark, a bow that unleashed ten arrows with every pull, a wonderful steed with eight legs, and a magic ring that created nine of itself every night.

Both plunges of "Odin Falls"

Mike Stevens

In all ways, he was mankind's benefactor, and from his Anglo-Saxon name we get Woden's Day or Wednesday. We propose the name Odin for this waterfall from its power, its poetry, its magic, the wind around it that seems ever present, and its difficulty of access.

188 UNNAMED SERIES OF FALLS ON LOWER GLADE CREEK "Realm of the Dead Falls"

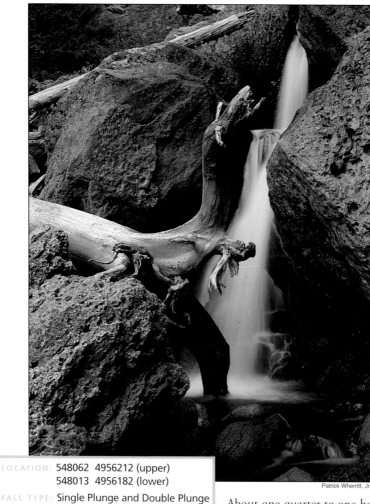

Patrick Wherritt, Jr.

LOCATION: 548062 4956212 (upper)
548013 4956182 (lower)

FALL TYPE: Single Plunge and Double Plunge

HEIGHT: 35–40 and 20 feet

STREAM: Glade Creek

MAP: Unmapped

ACCESS: Dangerous off-trail hike, not recommended.

About one-quarter to one-half mile above the mouth of Glade Creek are two waterfalls that together we call "Realm of the Dead Falls" from the mysterious place in Norse mythology for the dead who did not die bravely on the battlefield.

During the low-water time of autumn, hikers to Seven Mile Hole can walk the beach of Yellowstone River from Sulphur Creek to Glade Creek and then up Glade Creek to "Realm of the Dead Falls." But when the waterfalls look their best (times of higher water in spring and summer), travel to "Realm of the Dead Falls" is very difficult.

Reaching the mouth of Glade Creek can be accomplished in two ways. One is by ascending the hill east of Sulphur Creek's mouth, traveling around the head of a deep and colorful silt canyon, across a timbered bench, and then east to Glade Creek through a treacherous area of unstable rhyolite pinnacles that lie above, and east of, the timbered bench. We do not recommend this route to anyone.

The other route is more sensible but still difficult, involving descending into the canyon via North Glade Creek, then following Glade Creek to its mouth. That route, too, is difficult and prohibitively long for day-hikes. And, once you arrive at "Realm of the Dead Falls" and the mouth of Glade Creek, you are still faced with the problem of reaching the Seven Mile Hole Trail for exit purposes, a near impossibility during the high-water months of spring and summer. You will likely run out of daylight, even during the long days of summer. And you will subject yourself to extreme danger if you attempt the pinnacles route or a route near the river that requires scaling a soft-sided and steep butte. Plummeting hundreds of feet or drowning in the Yellowstone River could be the results of attempting to reach "Realm of the Dead Falls." After that, the name of the place would have more real meaning than you probably want.

We saw "Realm of the Dead Falls" during high-water times only once, and then only from a distance. The lower falls, choked with large boulders and fully 35–40 feet high, is probably spectacular during high water. The upper falls consists of two drops that together are 20 feet high.

The Realm of the Dead was one of the nine worlds of Norse mythology. While battlefield warriors went to Valhalla, all other dead persons went to the Realm of the Dead, also known as Helheim, where Hel the goddess of the underworld ruled supreme, and from which we probably get our word "Hell." Half alive and half dead, Hel's face and body were those of a living woman, but her thighs and legs were those of a corpse, mottled and moldering. Her dish was Hunger, her knife was Starvation, her attendants were Delay and Slowness, and the decorative hanging in her domicile was Falling Peril. The Realm of the Dead was a cold, dark, misty, and ice-bearing abode of the nonliving, located at the lowest level of the Norse universe. No one could ever leave this place because of the impassable river Gjoll that encircled it. The entrance to the Realm of the Dead was guarded by Garm, a monstrous hound resembling a wolf, and Hraesvelg, a giant eagle who made the wind continually blow by flapping his wings.

Our proposed name "Realm of the Dead Falls" has meaning for several reasons. Like the Norse Realm of the Dead, these two waterfalls are located near the lowest part of the Grand Canyon of the Yellowstone. Like the river Gjoll, the Yellowstone River makes it difficult for persons to enter or leave this place. In line with Hraesvelg, the wind seems ever to blow in this low canyon region. And of course the references to cold, dark, hunger, delay, slowness, and falling are well-known to hikers in Yellowstone and especially in the canyon.

Norse mythology is romantic in that it combines nature with daring heroes. Certainly hiking to any of the waterfalls on Glade Creek requires some daring. It also rewards the adventurer with some of the most spectacular features and nature experiences in all the world. But please use caution here.

"Valhalla" section of Glade Creek; "Valhalla Fall"
is visible at the top and "Fall of the Elves" is
visible at the bottom. Photo by Paul Rubinstein

The Backcountry

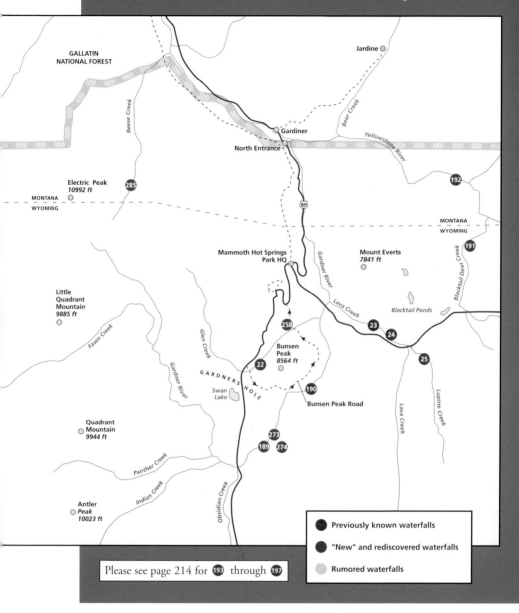

GALLATIN
NATIONAL FOREST

Jardine

Reese Creek

Bear Creek

Gardiner

Yellowstone River

North Entrance

Electric Peak
10992 ft   285

MONTANA
WYOMING

89   192

MONTANA
WYOMING

191

Mammoth Hot Springs
Park HQ

Mount Everts
7841 ft

Little
Quadrant
Mountain
9885 ft

Fawn Creek

Glen Creek

Gardner River

Lava Creek

Blacktail Deer Creek

Blacktail Ponds

258

Bunsen
Peak
8564 ft

23

24

GARDNERS HOLE   22   25

190

Swan
Lake

Bunsen Peak Road

Lava Creek

Lupine Creek

Quadrant
Mountain
9944 ft

273
189   274

Panther Creek

Indian Creek

Obsidian Creek

Antler
Peak
10023 ft

Previously known waterfalls

"New" and rediscovered waterfalls

Rumored waterfalls

Please see page 214 for 193 through 197

189 UNNAMED FALLS ON THE GARDNER RIVER "Tukuarika Falls"

LOCATION: 522773 4971195

FALL TYPE: Cascade

HEIGHT: 25 feet

STREAM: Gardner River

MAP: Unmapped

ACCESS: Easy to moderate off-trail hike.

Mike Stevens

In the winter of 1996–97, the authors received a letter from writer/photographer Lee Silliman of Deer Lodge, Montana. It contained a picture of a waterfall on the Gardner River that he suggested we investigate. He described it as being about half a mile downstream from the Sheepeater Cliff parking lot. He also offered that there might be more cascades even farther down the river. In a second letter, Silliman suggested giving the feature the name "Sheepeater Falls" for the only tribe of Native Americans to reside in Yellowstone year-round and who were undoubtedly present at one time in the immediate area of this waterfall. He went on to propose the new name be established not in English, but rather as the Sheepeater Shoshones themselves probably spoke it: "Tukuarika" (pronounced TOOK-wu-REE-ku).[157]

"Tukuarika Falls" looks much like the Cascades of the Firehole, but it is steeper and longer. Park employee Joanne Sides was most pleased with its surroundings. She stated: "The setting, with the stately lodgepole pines and snow-capped mountains caused us to linger to truly appreciate yet another awe-inspiring vantage point."

190 OSPREY FALLS

LOCATION: 525232 4974860

FALL TYPE: Plunge

HEIGHT: 150 feet

STREAM: Gardner River

MAP: Mammoth, Wyo.-Mont. - 1986

ACCESS: Moderate to difficult on-trail hike.

Members of the Hague party named this 150-foot waterfall in 1885 for the osprey or fishhawk (*Pandion haliaetus*) that frequents Yellowstone Park. Although it is on a major park stream, hikers only occasionally visit it. You can reach it via the Osprey Falls Trail, which is accessed by the Bunsen Peak loop drive (which is no longer open to motor vehicles but available for bicycles and foot travel). Hikers should be aware that this is a steep trail with many switchbacks as it descends over 700 feet into the heart of Sheepeater Canyon.

Traveler George Wingate saw Osprey Falls on his 1885 trip and noted: "It was a magnificent and most picturesque sight . . . The white fall, the tumbling water, and the dark shadows of the cañon, make a striking picture."[158]

Mike Stevens

191 HIDDEN FALLS

LOCATION: 532841 4981384

FALL TYPE: Cascade

HEIGHT: 20 feet

STREAM: Blacktail Deer Creek

MAP: Blacktail Deer Creek, Wyoming - 1986

ACCESS: Moderate to difficult on-trail hike.

Paul Rubinstein

Nameless for many years and appearing on maps only as "falls," this 20-foot falls was first documented by Captain John Barlow on July 24, 1871. Over 100 years later the falls reappeared under the name "Hidden Falls" in the 1984 publication *Ribbons of Water.* It is easy to miss this falls even though it is only a short distance from the Blacktail-Yellowstone River Trail. That fact was responsible for the name that was suggested for the falls in approximately 1980 by John Barber and Lee Whittlesey.[159] In his 1996 book *Waterfalls of Yellowstone,* Charles Maynard referred to it as "Blacktail Deer Falls," but "Hidden Falls" has priority because it is older.

192   KNOWLES FALLS

LOCATION: 532001 4984166

FALL TYPE: Cascade

HEIGHT: 15 feet

STREAM: Yellowstone River

MAP: Ash Mountain, Montana - 1987

ACCESS: Moderate to difficult on-trail hike.

Knowles Falls is also informally known as the "third falls of the Yellowstone River." Had this waterfall not been on the Yellowstone River, it probably would never have received a name at all, for it is only 15 feet high and not really vertical. During the high water of spring, the "falls" almost disappears completely, becoming only turbulent rapids. It is accessed by the Black Canyon Trail, which runs nearby about three miles below Crevice Lake. The trail provides a short spur to a fine vantage point of the falls. The best time for photographs is during the lowest water possible. April and October are usually the best months in which to see the actual plunge of Knowles Falls.

Called "Cañon Fall" by Lt. G.C. Doane in 1876, Knowles Falls was given its present name sometime around 1930 by NPS personnel or other local persons. Their name was for John S. Knowles, a miner who lived illegally in a cabin at the mouth of Crevice Creek near this falls for more than 20 years. Knowles was engaged in placer mining along Crevice Creek from about 1880 to 1900.[160]

Paul Rubinstein

193 UNNAMED FALLS ON GARNET CREEK
"Apron Falls"

LOCATION: 541571 4979293

FALL TYPE: Plunge/Fan

HEIGHT: 39 feet

STREAM: Garnet Creek

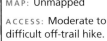

MAP: Unmapped

ACCESS: Moderate to difficult off-trail hike.

This delicately beautiful, plunge-type falls is located on Garnet Creek within half a mile of its confluence with the Yellowstone River at Black Canyon. The name was suggested in 1996 by ranger David Rothenburger because "the drop looked like a full apron that one would wear when out doing an outdoor barbecue."

The spot is idyllic in its verdancy and overall setting. "Apron Falls" drops over a sheer wall of basalt that begins a small canyon, that then extends on to the Yellowstone River.

Although the old Howard Eaton Trail passes just south of this hidden treasure, there is no record of this waterfall's existence in any previous trail guides or publications.

Mike Stevens

194 UNNAMED FALLS ON GARNET CREEK
"Luxuriant Falls"

LOCATION: 541507 4979447

FALL TYPE: Cascade

HEIGHT: 20 feet

STREAM: Garnet Creek

MAP: Unmapped

ACCESS: Moderate to difficult off-trail hike.

Mike Stevens

Located less than 50 yards from the mouth of Garnet Creek in the Black Canyon of the Yellowstone is "Luxuriant Falls." This 20-foot, cascade-type falls does include a 15-foot, steep drop in its center section. Our suggested name relates to the spectacular verdancy of the surrounding vegetation. In fact, its deep forest setting and dense understory make it difficult to reach. Views of this falls are sometimes unrewarding due to heavy deadfall.

Hikers are advised not to try to access "Luxuriant Falls" directly from "Apron Falls." Walking is difficult, especially along the creekside. It is better to make the approach from downstream.

195 UNNAMED FALLS ON COYOTE CREEK
"Tempestuous Falls"

LOCATION: 545512 4982689

FALL TYPE: Serial Cascade/ Plunge

HEIGHT: 75 feet

STREAM: Coyote Creek

MAP: USFWS Map of Hellroaring Creek - 1981

ACCESS: Moderate to difficult off-trail hike.

Upper half of "Tempestuous Falls"

Paul Rubinstein

This raging, rollicking series of falls and cascades is located on Coyote Creek in a deep canyon a few hundred feet above its mouth. Its stormy, indeed violent and tumultuous nature, particularly in its upper half, is responsible for the name we suggested in 1997.

Surveyed and mapped by the USFWS in 1980, "Tempestuous Falls" has a height of 50-75 feet. Its lower 30 feet is vertical and its upper 45 feet is a 70- to 80-degree cascade. It can be seen from the Hellroaring Creek Trail on the opposite side of that stream, and an unmaintained spur trail leads almost to its base if one hikes to campsite 2H8.

196 UNNAMED FALLS NEAR TOWER JUNCTION "Anniversary Falls"

LOCATION: 546524 4977476

FALL TYPE: Horsetail

HEIGHT: 227 feet

STREAM: Unnamed Tributary of the Yellowstone

MAP: Unmapped

ACCESS: Moderate to difficult off-trail hike.

David Rothenburger

This waterfall was noticed in 1997 by ranger David Rothenburger who found it while hiking the Garnet Hill loop trail about two miles north of Roosevelt Lodge. He measured its upper and lower drops at 30 and 197 feet, respectively.

The unnamed stream drops almost directly into the Yellowstone River on the east side of the river. Because the falls' stream is set into its cliff, the falls seems to hide from view, so one must look hard for it.

We worried initially that this stream might be a temporary one, but it seems to keep its water well into autumn. Because Rothenburger found it in 1997, the 125th anniversary year of the park, he proposed the name "125th Anniversary Falls." We propose to shorten that to "Anniversary Falls."

197 SLOUGH CREEK RAPIDS

A short distance above Slough Creek Campground a stretch of whitewater cascades through a small gorge. It is known informally as "Slough Creek Rapids."

Another of our "rediscovered" features, it was originally documented more than 100 years ago. Surprisingly, this roaring section of the large creek has never been officially named. Pioneer researcher and stream surveyor Barton Evermann first noted these rapids in 1893. In his "A Reconnaissance of the Streams and Lakes of Western Montana and Northwestern Wyoming" appears the following entry: "Several waterfalls are located in narrow canyon of Slough Creek." The "Slough Creek Rapids" are mapped, appearing on the 1986 Lamar Canyon 7½-minute quadrangle as "rapids."

The Backcountry

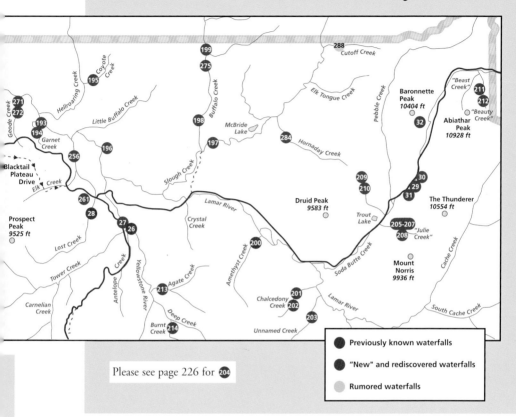

Previously known waterfalls

"New" and rediscovered waterfalls

Rumored waterfalls

Please see page 226 for 204

Buffalo Creek has proven difficult to assess in the writing of this book. The stream flows from some of the highest peaks in Montana and enters the park from the north before emptying into Slough Creek just below the Slough Creek Campground. Surveyed by the USFWS in the early 1980s, their descriptions of the stream were vague, stating only that "a series of falls and cascades are present on Buffalo Creek." Needing a more detailed account, we asked ranger David Rothenburger to survey this stream in September 1996. He reported more than 12 waterfalls, yet many of them sounded borderline when it came to our 15-foot criterion. In an effort to clarify the situation, author Mike Stevens and archivist-volunteer Joanne Sides made a third survey in August 1997. This made matters even more complicated when their data did not match Rothenburger's. It was only after the three authors sat down and analyzed all field notes, topo maps, and photographs that we grudgingly accepted the fact that there were only two features that, for this book, would truly pass as waterfalls on Buffalo Creek. We stress, however, that the stream does contain many fine cascades and small falls that ranger Rothenburger took the time and trouble to document. And although spots like "Six Falls," "Flag Pole Falls," and "Lower Buffalo Cascades" did not meet our height parameters, we are deeply grateful for all of his efforts and research there.

Buffalo Creek

198 UNNAMED FALLS ON BUFFALO CREEK "Enduring Falls"

Mike Stevens

LOCATION: **554550 4979076**

FALL TYPE: **Plunge**

HEIGHT: **15–18 feet**

STREAM: **Buffalo Creek**

MAP: **Unmapped**

ACCESS: **Moderate to difficult off-trail hike.**

In the large, lower canyon of Buffalo Creek about two miles north of the Slough Creek campground, this interesting plunge has a distinct characteristic. During the summer of 1997, several large logs formed an awning in front of the falls. During ranger David Rothenburger's hike up Buffalo Creek, he was so taken with these logs that he proposed the name "Log Bridge Falls." Lee Whittlesey pointed out, however, that features such as logjams can change in the blink of an eye. This particular log bridge could last for 20 years, but it also could be washed away in 20 days. For this reason we chose instead "Enduring Falls."

With this selection not only have we suggested a designation that will stand the test of geologic time, but also a name that matches in spirit the other significant fall on Buffalo Creek farther upstream. Both names allude to the granite (uncommon in the park) in their surroundings and particularly to the slow geologic processes that seem to be at work in this area of Yellowstone.

199 UNNAMED FALLS ON BUFFALO CREEK "Granite Falls"

Mike Stevens

LOCATION: 554935 4985809

FALL TYPE: Plunge/Fan

HEIGHT: 20 feet

STREAM: Buffalo Creek

MAP: Unmapped

ACCESS: Moderate to difficult off-trail hike.

Simply put, "Granite Falls" is one of the most scenic little waterfalls in Yellowstone. Given the rarity of granite in the park, few if any are like it. Because it flows over the smooth granite, the water has a clearer, almost invisible appearance. When viewed in good light with a blue-sky background, "Granite Falls" is a truly gorgeous sight.

The water in this falls tumbles steeply for a distance of some 20 feet in an open, alpine setting accented with massive boulders. Park employee Joanne Sides suggested the name for the startling granite formations in the area. We personally feel that it is the prettiest of the park's Montana falls.

Lamar Valley

200 FAIRIES' FALL

LOCATION: 558872 4970107

FALL TYPE: Plunge

HEIGHT: 32 feet

STREAM: Amethyst Creek

MAP: Unmapped

ACCESS: Moderate to difficult off-trail hike.

Michelle M. Serio

Not to be confused with Fairy Falls west of Midway Basin, this beautiful plural-possessive name was given to a plunge of Amethyst Creek about 1880, probably by stereo photographer Henry Bird Calfee, whose published stereoview 119 used the name. Park writer Herman Haupt immediately placed the falls, located in a small canyon a quarter-mile above the creek's mouth, in his guidebook of 1883. At that time the main road to Cooke City passed just below the falls on the south bank of the Lamar River. An attempt was made around 1903 to rename it "Amethyst Falls."[161]

The name is characteristic of the graceful and delicate appearance of the small waterfall, just the type of idyllic spot that could be inhabited by fairies. The tree-clad alcove that hides this falls is otherwise surrounded by the open country of Lamar Valley. It can actually be seen in the distance from the Mammoth-Cooke City Road by standing a few dozen yards west of the entrance to the Yellowstone Institute.

Hallam Webber Collection

No.119 Specimen Creek, Fairies Fall

Stereoview of Fairies' Fall by Henry Bird Calfee

201-202

UNNAMED FALLS ON CHALCEDONY CREEK
"Little Eden Falls"

LOCATION LOWER (#201):
562021 4965496

LOCATION UPPER (#202):
561978 4965461

FALL TYPE: Plunge/Double Plunge

HEIGHT: 20 and 16 feet

STREAM: Chalcedony Creek

MAP: USFWS Map of Chalcedony Creek - 1985

ACCESS: Moderate to difficult off-trail hike.

These are actually two separate waterfalls of Chalcedony (pronounced cal-SED-o-nee) Creek just south of the central Lamar Valley.

The lower fall (#201) is a 20-foot vertical plunge. It has a similar feel to "Lovely Falls" on the Little Firehole River in that it is delightful on a small, up-close-and-personal scale.

Between 50 and 100 yards upstream from it is a second fall (#202) with a 16-foot double drop.

Originally the name "Breccia Falls" was suggested for these falls because of the pronounced nature of the cliff face on which the lower of the two is situated. Upon consulting with park geologist Rick Hutchinson, we learned that it was not a breccia formation but rather conglomerate. We agreed on a name related to the surrounding terrain. Both of these waterfalls seem to be nestled in lush oases of deep forest, yet surrounded by a more common, open grassland. It is the paradisiacal nature of the setting that inspired the name "Little Eden Falls."

The two falls were mapped in 1984 by the USFWS, but no other documentation of these beautiful works of nature has been found.

Our survey of Chalcedony Creek yielded another unexpected discovery. Downstream from the lower falls were the remnants of an elaborate, long-abandoned corral. It was constructed with five horizontal, parallel rails that made a fence five to six feet high. It appeared to have been built from young lodgepoles even though we were in more of a climax forest. The fence was so long, we could not see its end. Nails up to a foot long had been hammered into standing trees and into erected

Lower "Little Eden Falls"   Mike Stevens

posts. Many of these rails had fallen in a random fashion, but about 40 percent of them could still be seen. This fence was probably used in early park days to corral a portion of the Yellowstone bison herd here in the lower Lamar area.

203 UNNAMED FALLS ON UNNAMED CREEK "Wild Rose Falls"

LOCATION: 563675 4964831

FALL TYPE: Three-tiered Plunge

HEIGHT: 70 feet

STREAM: Unnamed Creek

MAP: Unmapped

ACCESS: Moderate to difficult off-trail hike.

Mike Stevens

Paralleling much of the Specimen Ridge Trail as it climbs towards the summit of Amethyst Mountain from the Lamar River is a stream known as Unnamed Creek—its actual name, as shown on the 1989 Opal Creek 7½-minute map. "Wild Rose Falls" lies several miles up this oddly named watercourse at a point just beyond where the trail leaves the stream. This nearly vertical, three-tiered falls is difficult to appreciate in photographs because its upper two sections slant away from the camera and do not appear as tall as they actually are. We estimated the lowest drop to be nearly 40 feet and the other two sections to add nearly another 30. In any case, this superior feature must be at least 70 feet high.

204 "Instant Falls"

A worthwhile fall is located on an unnamed stream on the west side of the Lamar River about one mile above the mouth of Flint Creek. The view of this falls gives one the impression that it springs forth from nowhere and drops immediately into the Lamar River. On our first visit this 25-foot plunge-and-fan-type falls appeared to occur nearly at the instant its subterranean waters reach the surface. On a second inspection, however, the water was found to flow inconspicuously from several hundred yards farther up the hill in a shallow, overgrown streambed. It is visible to hikers on the Lamar River Trail about one mile south of Flint Creek. We call it "Instant Falls."

"Jolie Creek"

Flowing from high atop the Thunderer, a mountain in the park's northeast section, is a beautiful, perennial stream that we call "Jolie Creek," using the French word for "pretty." This intimate little stream empties into Soda Butte Creek as it braids into the marshy meadow known as Round Prairie. Its flow is curious in that it is remarkably consistent. The water level seems hardly to vary from spring to autumn.

The lower reaches of the creek cannot be seen from the highway due to thick forest; however, these densely packed woods hide three lovely falls. Any hiker working his or her way up this stream soon discovers these interesting features that he or she would have never anticipated.

205-207   UNNAMED FALLS ON "JOLIE CREEK" "Mossy Falls," "Two-Lane Cascades," and "Swiftwater Cascade"

"Mossy Falls"

Mike Stevens

Closest to the mouth of "Jolie Creek" is what we call "Mossy Falls" (#205). A fan falls of classic shape, this 18-foot, steep cascade has a narrow brink but quickly fans out as it pours down the rock face below. It is in deep forest and difficult to see among dense spruce and fir. We suggest the name "Mossy Falls" for the unusually rich growth of moss in and around the falls.

"Two-Lane Cascade" (#206) is the second falls. Although a somewhat sloping feature, it loses at least 60 feet in elevation. It is in a deep, narrow canyon and is most visible from its northern side where relatively few trees are adjacent to the cascade itself. This long cascade seems to divide nicely into two even strips of water with a nearly dry center. We believe this phenomenon persists through most seasons, therefore "two-lane" seems appropriate.

The third feature is a 40-foot sliding cascade (#207) that moves swiftly down a steep canyon. "Swiftwater Cascade," as we call it, refers to the way the water flows in a reasonably smooth groove, free of impediments and able to shoot rapidly down the streambed. This leads us to "Jolie Creek's" grandest spectacle, "Recherché Falls."

208 UNNAMED FALLS ON "JOLIE CREEK"
"Recherché Falls"

LOCATION: 570912 4971934

FALL TYPE: Horsetail

HEIGHT: 75 feet

STREAM: "Jolie Creek"

MAP: Unmapped

ACCESS: Extremely strenuous off-trail hike.

A most exquisite gem of beauty is located on the south side of Round Prairie on the slopes of the mountain known as the Thunderer. The plunge-type falls is the fourth feature upstream on the unnamed southern tributary of Soda Butte Creek, which we call "Jolie Creek." The top portion of the falls is visible from the Mammoth-Cooke City Road.

As early as 1989, Paul Rubinstein noticed from the highway that this falls seemed permanent. He began referring to it under the geographical name "Round Prairie Falls." In 1996, Mike Stevens hiked to its base. He noted that the short trip is not easy. In addition to a ford of Soda Butte Creek, the hiker faces a forest full of deadfall, dense understory, and steep undulations. The canyons require sidehill walking and the uphill grade is severe.

Because he found the falls so worth the considerable effort it took him to reach it, Stevens searched for a word to describe that experience. A French-derived word serves the purpose well. We suggest the name "Recherché," meaning "sought out with care," "rare, exotic, or choice," or "worth the considerable effort required to be achieved." The word is pronounced "ray-SHARE-shay" or "ray-SHAR-shay."

Northeast Corner

209-210   UNNAMED FALLS WEST OF PEBBLE CREEK
"Zephyr Falls" and "Tempest Falls"

Photos by Mike Stevens

"Zephyr Falls"   *"Tempest Falls"*

Although these two waterfalls on Pyramid Mountain may be temporary, they are so spectacular that we include them here. Longtime backcountry ranger Bob Flather told us in 1998 of the existence of a very tall waterfall that "blows in the wind" on a mountain north of Trout Lake. Lee Whittlesey recognized the mountain as the subject of an 1870s stereo photo by Henry Bird Calfee that was captioned "Pyramid Mountain." Because no other name has supplanted that one, the mountain's historic name remains today.

Although we could see the top from a distance, we found it extremely difficult to reach. In fact, we failed to reach its base on all three attempts we made. However, we were finally successful in attaining a high point on an adjacent, eastern slope that enabled us to photograph it (#209) and a lower waterfall (#210) that we call "Tempest Falls."

Because this tall (300-plus foot), elegant falls is buffeted by the slightest wind, and because winds in this area are mostly west winds, we selected the name "Zephyr Falls."

#209 "ZEPHYR FALLS"

LOCATION: 567845 4974386

FALL TYPE: Plunge

HEIGHT: 300–400 feet

STREAM: Unnamed Tributary of Soda Butte Creek

MAP: Unmapped

ACCESS: Extremely strenuous off-trail hike.

#210 "TEMPEST FALLS"

LOCATION: 567886 4974195

FALL TYPE: Three-step Plunge

HEIGHT: 150 feet

STREAM: Unnamed Tributary of Soda Butte Creek

MAP: Unmapped

ACCESS: Extremely strenuous off-trail hike.

No. 127. Annie's Lake and Pyramid Mountain reflected.

"Zephyr Falls" is in the center of this historic stereoview

H.B. Calfee, Jack and Susan Davis Collection

In classical mythology, "zephyr" is a personification of the west wind. Moreover, the name connotes the wispy, delicate nature of the falls. Whenever the west wind blows, "Zephyr Falls" seems to behave much like a limp string in the wind. "Zephyr Falls" may not be permanent, but it persisted in 1998 into August in a summer that exhibited a brutally hot and dry July. It is even visible to auto travelers from the park's main road at Round Prairie.

For the lower 150-foot falls, we selected the name "Tempest Falls." A tempest is a violent and extensive wind, especially one that is accompanied by heavy rain, hail,

or snow. In contrast to the delicate, light-wind feel of a zephyr, one can directly experience "Tempest Falls" by reaching its base in a not-so-easy scramble. At that proximity, it seems to be a furious torrent. "Tempest" has an appropriate, contrasting sound and feel to the name "Zephyr" and it is meant to be so related.

"Zephyr Falls" (above) and "Tempest Falls" on Pyramid Mountain

Mike Stevens

211   UNNAMED FALLS ON ABIATHAR PEAK "Enchantress Falls"

LOCATION: 577437 4982315
FALL TYPE: Plunge
HEIGHT: 90 feet
STREAM: "Beauty Creek"
MAP: Abiathar Peak, Wyoming - 1989
ACCESS: Moderate to difficult off-trail hike.

Mike Stevens

This plunge-type waterfall is at least 90 feet high and world-class in setting and beauty. The only clue we had to its existence was the notation "falls" on the 1986 7½-minute map of Abiathar Peak. In 1997, our party crossed Soda Butte Creek and hiked up a steep, unnamed stream in an attempt to find the falls.

The payoff was intense. The falls was vertical and almost uninterrupted. It seemed to us that the water was falling out of a hole in the sky, behind which we could see the stunning, jagged outline of Abiathar Peak's summit.

We were entranced. We decided we needed a laudatory and significant name. The falls and its setting were a combination of two very different sorts of intense beauty. The cliff was rugged, strong, handsome, hard, and bold whereas the water seemed delicate, wispy, and fairy-like. Steep, rock walls surrounded the falls; indeed, part of the upper wall extended out over empty space. The walls gave the place an otherworldly feel. The name "Ethereal Falls" was our first choice, but that did not give proper shrift to the darkness of the place, with its somber grotto. We also considered "Hole in the Sky Falls," but decided it was too wordy and not magical enough for this very special place.

After much thinking, Lee Whittlesey became convinced that the place needed a name from folklore or mythology. The darkness of the place had an evil quality that seemed male, yet there was a light quality to the water that seemed female. He had visions of a dark yet beautiful female and so looked to the French tale written in 1757 that became *Beauty and the Beast* (*La Belle et la Bête* by Jeanne Marie Leprince de Beaumont).

In the tale, a beautiful yet wicked fairy changed a prince into a beast. After imprisoning a nearby merchant for stealing his roses, the beast suggested that the merchant's daughter come to his castle to dine in return for the man's freedom. They agreed and while dining the Beast appeared with a roar and drove the man from the castle, leaving Beauty there with him. Soon the Beast fell in love with Beauty and the two became fast friends. Beauty, in turn, came to know that he was very kind although ugly. When she professed her love for him the Beast changed into a handsome prince who thanked her for breaking the spell cast upon him long ago by the enchantress.

From this tale, we took the name "Enchantress Falls." Our suggested name for its creek is thus "Beauty Creek." For its more westerly branch, we propose "Beast Creek." Both are appropriate in Yellowstone, a place of great beauty and great beasts.

212 UNNAMED FALLS ON ABIATHAR PEAK "Fraternal Falls"

LOCATION: 577754 4981758

FALL TYPE: Two-tiered Plunge

HEIGHT: 60 feet

STREAM: "Beauty Creek"

MAP: Abiathar Peak, Wyoming - 1989

ACCESS: Moderate to difficult off-trail hike.

This dainty falls' two plunges on upper "Beauty Creek" are 32 feet (upper) and 28 feet (lower) in height, separated only by about 20 feet of stream.

Looking for this "falls" from notations on the 1989 7½-minute map of Abiathar Peak, we hiked up the steep gradient of "Beauty Creek," after fording Soda Butte Creek at the Warm Creek picnic area. After visiting "Enchantress Falls," we hiked another mile upstream to find this two-step falls, which we called "Fraternal Falls" from the fact that we envisioned the drops as brothers.

Mike Stevens

The Backcountry

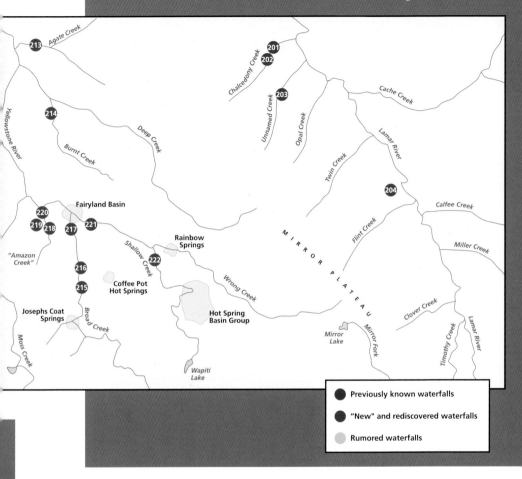

Legend:
- ● Previously known waterfalls
- ● "New" and rediscovered waterfalls
- ● Rumored waterfalls

213

UNNAMED FALLS ON AGATE CREEK
"Peterson Falls"

LOCATION: 550764 4966404

FALL TYPE: Two-tiered Plunge/Cascade

HEIGHT: 40 feet (total)

STREAM: Agate Creek

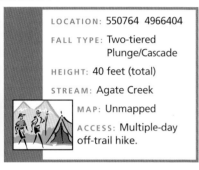

MAP: Unmapped

ACCESS: Multiple-day off-trail hike.

Mike Stevens

A plunge-type waterfall is located on Agate Creek about 300 yards above its mouth and tucked into a tiny niche. The falls, located in a partly covered grotto, drops 15 feet, then six feet, and then flows briefly to a cascade of 10 feet before finishing with successive drops of five and four feet. Its total height is thus 40 feet, and in the first three steps the water changes direction by nearly 180 degrees.

Mike Stevens, who hiked to this falls in 1997 after being advised of its existence by biologist Dan Mahony, calls it "so compact and so twisting that it cannot be seen all at once, let alone photographed."

We have long believed that something in the park needed to be named for the unhonored William Peterson of the 1869 Folsom-Cook-Peterson expedition. Peaks in the Washburn Range have been designated Folsom and Cook Peaks, but a peak just east of Folsom was named Prospect rather than Peterson. Thus we propose that this waterfall, in an area near the route of that expedition, be named Peterson Falls.

William Peterson (1834–1939) was the third and heretofore unhonored member of the 1869 Folsom expedition with Charles Cook and David Folsom. Born in Denmark, Peterson pursued a seafarer's life for a decade before traveling to California in 1860 and Idaho in 1862 to try his luck at mining. After a couple of unsuccessful years, he moved to Montana where he met Charles Cook. Peterson was a well-known employee of Cook's by 1869, at the time Cook and Folsom organized the expedition. That precursor to the 1870 Washburn expedition contributed a map and important information to the 1870 party, and its story is chronicled in Aubrey L. Haines's *Valley of the Upper Yellowstone*.[162] Peterson later became mayor of Salmon City, Idaho.

Burnt Creek

214 UNNAMED FALLS ON BURNT CREEK
"Palisade Falls"

LOCATION: 551944 4964345

FALL TYPE: Four-tiered Plunge

HEIGHT: 50 feet

STREAM: Burnt Creek

MAP: Unmapped

ACCESS: Dangerous off- trail hike, not recommended.

David Rothenburger

This plunge-type falls, height 50 feet in four steps, is located on Burnt Creek about 200 yards above its mouth in difficult canyon country. In 1997, Mike Stevens and David Rothenburger visited this beautiful falls in its amazing setting. They could not move around the falls because of the vertical canyon walls. Not only does it mark the absolute end of further travel, this topography creates difficulty for photography. There is no vantage point where one can get all four plunges into a single frame without the use of sophisticated lenses.

The steps of this falls are two of about five feet each, one of 30, and one more of about 10 feet. After discussion, we proposed the name "Palisade Falls," from the line of tall cliffs (actually a deep canyon) that surrounds it.

The canyon of Deep Creek, into which Burnt Creek flows, has walls at least 700 feet high. We do not recommend hiking in this area. Treks here are long and laborious as well as dangerous. Steep canyon walls and poor footing make for treacherous travel. Stevens and Rothenburger even found the carcass of a bighorn sheep on a narrow ledge near the bottom of the canyon. It underscored for them the danger of the area, because it was the final resting place of one of nature's most sure-footed creatures, which had apparently fallen to its death.

Broad Creek

For scenery, Broad Creek may be the most interesting backcountry stream in Yellowstone, not for its water level, but because of the varied and spectacular park landmarks through which it passes during its 23-mile journey. It begins at the outlet of White Lake and flows north for several miles as it passes through open meadows and many small thermal areas. It then arrives at Joseph's Coat Springs, one of the park's more colorful and diverse hot spring basins. Next it enters a densely forested canyon and passes numerous unmapped thermal features. Soon the canyon becomes more imposing. The sheer walls begin to rise and the forested banks give way to chutes and rapids, forcing the hiker to wade in the center of the stream. The rushing creek then begins to plummet over a series of waterfalls and cascades, and soon there is no place for the hiker to walk.

Exiting this intricate stretch of whitewater, the creek merges with Shallow Creek at the "Fairyland Basin," the site of one of the most astonishing and mysterious natural thermal formations of not only Yellowstone but the entire world. Here the canyon walls are over 1,000 feet high. The stream then turns west for its last section, another narrow stretch of canyon with huge boulders straddling its banks. By the time Broad Creek's waters empty into the Yellowstone River, its canyon's height and width are as large as the Grand Canyon of the Yellowstone.

The only documentation of the three major waterfalls in Broad Creek's canyon appears in an obscure USFWS document describing the creek in general. It reads: "Falls on the stream were identified by helicopter. Significant falls occur northeast of Joseph's Coat Hot Springs, northwest of Coffee Pot Hot Springs, and above Broad Creek's confluence with Shallow Creek. These falls prevented fish from penetrating upper Broad Creek historically."

We want to stress emphatically that Broad Creek Canyon is one of the most dangerous and confusing areas in the entire Yellowstone backcountry. We are aware of increased visitation here in recent years, yet many of these expeditions have gotten lost or been stopped by the country's geography and failed to achieve their goals. Sheer cliffs, swift water, and vast tracts of impenetrable deadfall make travel through this canyon extremely difficult.

215 UNNAMED FALLS ON BROAD CREEK
"Guardian Falls"

James Spanglet

LOCATION: **553872 4955118**

FALL TYPE: Plunge

HEIGHT: **30 feet**

STREAM: Broad Creek

MAP: Unmapped

ACCESS: Extremely
strenuous off-trail hike.

"Guardian Falls" is the first of three vertical water-falls in the Broad Creek Canyon below Joseph's Coat Springs. It is a wide plunge with massive rocky outcroppings on either side and it is the first major obstacle on Broad Creek when traveling downstream.

It was unknown to us until reported by park employee James Spanglet, who along with park employee Mike Jennings attempted a survey of the entire length of Broad Creek Canyon in September 1997. The name is used due to the waterfall's position at the head of the canyon. It "guards" the canyon's more difficult sections to navigate as well as the more imposing features downstream.

216 UNNAMED FALLS ON BROAD CREEK
"Halfway Falls"

James Spanglet

LOCATION: 553639 4956811

FALL TYPE: Plunge

HEIGHT: 20 feet

STREAM: Broad Creek

MAP: Unmapped

ACCESS: Dangerous off-trail hike, not recommended.

This waterfall was the second discovery of the Spanglet/Jennings survey of 1997, approximately three-quarters of a mile downstream from "Guardian Falls." Spanglet described the area: "Between Guardian and Halfway Falls there are numerous small falls and cascades. Because of the rocky terrain, it was much more difficult to navigate around this second falls than the first."

In Spanglet's opinion, "Halfway Falls" does appear to be located nearly equidistant from Joseph's Coat Springs and Broad Creek's confluence with Shallow Creek.

217 UNNAMED FALLS ON BROAD CREEK
"Impasse Falls"

LOCATION: 553234 4958367

FALL TYPE: Plunge

HEIGHT: 25 feet

STREAM: Broad Creek

MAP: Unmapped

ACCESS: Dangerous off-trail hike, not recommended.

Steve Wiechmann

The third waterfall of Broad Creek Canyon is an obstacle that prohibits travel in either direction on the stream. Any potential hikers of Broad Creek must make a wide and time-consuming detour around this falls. Furthermore, it is hidden inside one of the narrowest and deepest gorges in the entire park.

While Golden Fleece Falls on Shallow Creek represents an essentially impenetrable barrier to the magical place we call the "Fairyland Basin," "Impasse Falls" on lower Broad Creek represents the other "portal" (stream entrance) to the basin. It is not however, an entrance anyone would want to use. In this respect it is similar to Golden Fleece Falls; both are impenetrable natural barriers.

Until 1998 we knew of only two parties that had ever reached this falls. The 1997 Spanglet/Jennings party waded downstream and thermal expert Rocco Paperiello, while visiting the Fairyland Basin in 1993, trekked up the rocky canyon-side from below. Both were stopped cold by this waterfall and its treacherous gorge. Their impressions of this falls clearly illustrate the near impossibility of a complete Broad Creek Canyon survey. Spanglet says:

> Because we had to gingerly tread through the middle of Broad Creek, I only saw this falls from the brink. It was 5p.m. when we got there. [We had taken] 8 hours to go 3 miles! My best guess would be that it was 25 feet high. There was a sheer canyon wall on both sides of the creek, with no possible way to go around. From the brink I could see that after the falls, the creek cascaded down around the bend to the right, dropping at least another 20–30 feet but probably more. It was then with no physical way to continue that we decided to turn back. We called it "Impassable Falls."

Paperiello's impressions further describe the impenetrable natural barrier to travel:

> *The contour of this straight, steep-walled canyon was certainly not indicated by the 15-minute quadrangle map contours. Its walls could have been 1,000 feet or more straight down. I was amazed therefore to find this canyon. Unfortunately I couldn't get a look inside it because there seemed to be no way to climb up along the side of the falls. It was maybe 20–25 feet or so high . . . Not that big, but impossible to get around! It seemed impassable in spite of its relatively small size. I finally crossed to the southwest side of Broad Creek, climbed up onto the steep hillside, and got high enough to see inside the canyon. It looked totally "untravelable." The water appeared to go through it in a straight chute with no place to walk except perhaps in the creek itself. The rock on the straight, narrow canyon walls was of a dark color making the canyon itself extremely dark.*

In September 1998, park employees Kirk Hill and Michael Doran became the first party we know of to successfully navigate their way through "Impasse Falls." They did it by leaping off the 25-foot brink of the fall to the knee-deep plunge pool below. Bluntly put, these two men are lucky they didn't kill themselves, let alone break their legs. We do not suggest this course of action again for anyone looking to explore here. Take the extra time to circumvent this spot. The risks are simply not worth the gamble.

"Amazon Creek"

218–220

UNNAMED FALLS ON "AMAZON CREEK"
"Amazon Falls" and "Sojourner Falls

Photos by Tracey Jelly

Easterly branch of "Amazon Falls"   *"Sojourner Falls"*

At its deepest point, the canyon of Broad Creek rivals in size that of the Grand Canyon of the Yellowstone. Flowing into this 1,000-foot deep section of chasm from the south is a medium-sized creek. Its waters originate from springs and snowmelt on the north face of a peak labeled 8895 on USGS topographic maps, some seven air miles east/northeast of Canyon Village. In its short span of not more than two miles, this stream falls over three waterfalls of substance.

The creek was surveyed and photographed by Wyoming residents Bill Dooley, David Frahm, and Tracey Jelly on July 6, 1998. Their observations matched almost completely those of a second survey by park employees Marek Hrebicek and Steve Wiechmann on August 16 of the same year. Wiechmann referred to the creek as "Amazon Creek" for its moist and dense vegetation. The area apparently receives

#218–#219 "AMAZON FALLS"

LOCATION: 552336 4959000

FALL TYPE: Segmented Plunge

HEIGHT: 60 feet

STREAM: "Amazon Creek"

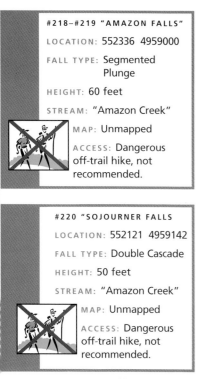

MAP: Unmapped

ACCESS: Dangerous off-trail hike, not recommended.

#220 "SOJOURNER FALLS"

LOCATION: 552121 4959142

FALL TYPE: Double Cascade

HEIGHT: 50 feet

STREAM: "Amazon Creek"

MAP: Unmapped

ACCESS: Dangerous off-trail hike, not recommended.

more moisture than the surrounding terrain and thus contains thick plant growth and groundcover creating a jungle-like environment. As it begins its descent into the canyon of Broad Creek, the stream sinks beneath the ground and disappears for at least 50 yards. During its subterranean flow the stream apparently splits. When it emerges again it falls (#218–#219) over two 60-foot falls on twin streams that are parallel to each other and separated by not more than 30 yards. Because of the low water levels of the creek, the westerly of these twin falls (#219) is seasonal only, drying up in August. Below these falls, which we have named "Amazon Falls," the waters of the two streams reunite.

Several hundred yards below "Amazon Falls" and after the waters have converged, the stream begins another drop in its final descent towards Broad Creek. Here the two surveys of 1998 differ. Bill Dooley's group reported a single 50–60 foot falls that cascades in a two-step drop and slide. Wiechmann and Hrebicek, a month later and in much lower water, saw this as two separate falls. We refer to this double fall as "Sojourner Falls" (#220) in an effort to honor those parties that have made the difficult bushwhack to this disorienting and complex stretch of land.

221 GOLDEN FLEECE FALLS

LOCATION: 553616 4958665

FALL TYPE: Two-step Plunge/Fan

HEIGHT: 100 feet

STREAM: Shallow Creek

MAP: Unmapped

ACCESS: Dangerous off-trail hike, not recommended.

Lee Whittlesey

Golden Fleece Falls is located on Shallow Creek about one-third mile above its mouth in the midst of impenetrable natural barriers. It is at least 100 feet high with a spectacular twist in its middle. This is an area that is extremely difficult to reach; because of the high potential for injury in this remote canyon country, we recommend against traveling to this spot.

Golden Fleece Falls was named by park geologist Rick Hutchinson after he "discovered" it in November 1976. He went there to look at the remarkable thermal formations that cover the area at the confluence of Shallow Creek with Broad Creek, a place that has since been called "Fairyland Basin." Hutchinson told Lee Whittlesey that he suggested the name of the falls from "golden thermal cyanobacteria," which twine through and around the falls and that grow on the canyon walls. (Sadly, Hutchinson was killed in an avalanche near Heart Lake in March, 1997.)

The name Golden Fleece also has a wonderful folklorean link with Greek mythology. Nephele the queen of Thessaly placed her children on the back of a ram with golden fleece to protect them from their evil stepmother. When the ram arrived in the country of Colchis, delivering the boy-child Phryxus, the boy killed it and gave the Golden Fleece to King Aeetes, who placed it in a consecrated grove under the care of a sleepless dragon. When Jason, the son of a neighboring king, grew up and demanded the crown from his Uncle Pelias, Pelias suggested to Jason the glorious adventure of going in quest of the Golden Fleece through a land of impenetrable barriers (just as exist around

Golden Fleece Falls). Jason prepared for the expedition by building a gigantic vessel known as the "Argo" on which he placed the great men of Greece including Hercules. Then he and his lover, the sorceress Medea, stood before the altar of Hecate and vowed to find the Fleece. The story of how he ultimately obtained the Golden Fleece, guarded by the sleepless dragon and two fire-breathing bulls, is called "Jason and the Argonauts."

222 UNNAMED FALLS ON SHALLOW CREEK "Vest Falls"

LOCATION: 557253 4956858

FALL TYPE: Horsetail/Plunge/Cascade

HEIGHT: 150 feet

STREAM: Shallow Creek

MAP: Unmapped

ACCESS: Multiple-day off-trail hike.

Much of this falls on the Mirror Plateau's remote Shallow Creek is vertical in nature; its total drop is 150 feet in a combination plunge-horsetail-cascade.

"Vest Falls" is first known to have been visited in 1976 by park geologist Rick Hutchinson who learned of it from a park fly-over. In 1979, Rick Hutchinson again entered the area with a party of five that included Lee Whittlesey. Amazed by its height and isolation, Whittlesey proposed the name "Vest Falls" for Senator George Graham Vest, the U.S. Senator from Missouri who fought so hard for the preservation of Yellowstone in the 1880s. Vest successfully blocked legislation on at least three occasions that would have abolished Yellowstone National Park. Without Vest, the national park might have been eliminated and the area thrown open to private settlement.

To underscore the locating of this beautiful falls and its proposed name, the manuscript "Discovery of a Waterfall" (1980) was reposited at that time in the park's research library. In that manuscript, Whittlesey noted: "I will never forget the way I felt upon first gazing at 'Vest Falls'—how marvelous for humankind that there are still places on earth where an exquisite gem of nature such as this could have remained unheralded and unsung for so long!"[163]

The Backcountry

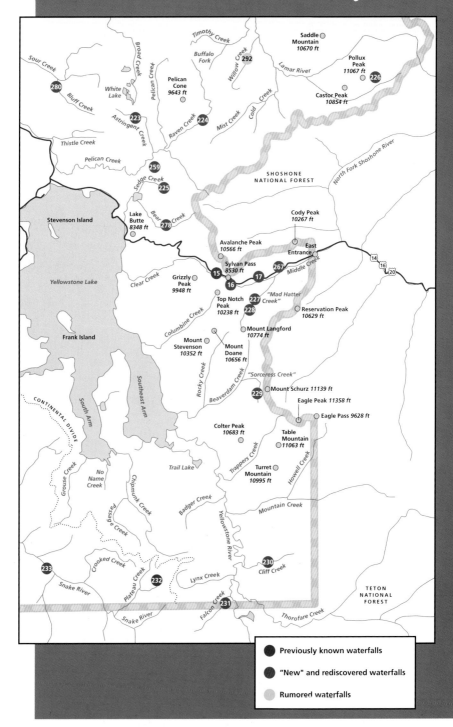

Previously known waterfalls

"New" and rediscovered waterfalls

Rumored waterfalls

223 UNNAMED FALLS ON ASTRINGENT CREEK "Thermal Falls"

Mike Stevens

LOCATION: **558308 4941214**

FALL TYPE: **Segmented Plunge**

HEIGHT: **35 feet**

STREAM: **Astringent Creek**

MAP: **Unmapped**

ACCESS: **Moderate to difficult off-trail hike.**

The waters of Astringent Creek begin in a massive unnamed thermal area in the Sour Creek Dome region of Yellowstone. It is thought to be one of the newest geologically thermal regions in the park, with several features present for only a few years. By mid-July after the snows have melted, nearly 100 percent of this stream's flow has thermal origins.

You can find one of the more unusual waterfalls in Yellowstone near the headwaters of this creek roughly two miles north/northwest of Pelican Valley. What makes it so distinctive is not only the shape of its cascading water, but also the presence of a large, active thermal feature in the waterfall itself. This feature, known as a "frying pan," steams and gurgles at the waterfall's base. Although the water from the falls does not mix with the frying pan, this is imperceptible when one views it from the front. Heavy concentrations of sulphur in the rock give the water a golden appearance, and its cliffs are roughly formed. As the waters labor over this falls, the beads of white intermingle with each other. In late season, a time of low water, the stream still finds ways to descend through the jutting rocks.

This falls' only documented history came from a dusty, cracked notebook in the park's archives. In this forgotten collection of ranger logs, Paul Rubinstein found the following passage. Dated July 29, 1947, it reads: "Chief park Naturalist Condon and Senior park Ranger Naturalist Lowell Biddulph to examine thermal area at head of Astringent Creek, found 'pretty' 35-foot falls on stream." With only that cryptic entry, the authors were able to locate and photograph this obscure locale.[164]

The low water of late August makes the falls difficult to photograph. However, its strange, unique structure and its water's unusual source more than make up for its small flow and lack of photogenic quality. July is the best month in which to view it.

224 UNNAMED FALLS ON RAVEN CREEK "Iddings Falls"

Mike Stevens

LOCATION: 566173 4941272

FALL TYPE: Segmented Plunge

HEIGHT: 22 feet

STREAM: Raven Creek

MAP: Mount Chittenden, Wyoming - 1989

ACCESS: Moderate to difficult off-trail hike.

The picturesque spot that contains this waterfall of Raven Creek is located about two miles southeast of Pelican Cone. It was discovered in 1871 by members of the first Hayden Survey. They wrote: "Ten miles up the creek is a pretty little cascade, where the waters pour over a descent of fifteen feet."[165]

Both Hayden and later geologist Arnold Hague documented the height of this falls as 15 feet. Hague studied it in 1888[166] and appears to have mentioned it to his compatriots, J.P. Iddings and L.V. Pirsson, because they visited it the following year. Iddings described the andesitic geology "near the falls on Raven Creek" in Hague's large monograph on the park's geology,[167] and for that early visit and description, we propose that the falls be named for him.

A party of USFWS surveyors studied the area in 1977 and measured the height of the falls as 22 feet.[168] They no doubt used a nearby, well-worn buffalo trail to reach this pretty spot from Pelican Valley.

"Iddings Falls" is a segmented falls with a wide separation of 50 feet or so. The portion of the falls to the left (northeast) is only three or four feet wide while the portion to the right (southwest) is some 40 feet wide.

225 UNNAMED FALLS ON SEDGE CREEK "Thistle Falls"

LOCATION: 563124 4932780

FALL TYPE: Cascade

HEIGHT: 15 feet

STREAM: Sedge Creek

MAP: USFWS Map of Upper Sedge Creek - 1979

ACCESS: Extremely strenuous off-trail hike.

High on the slopes of Mt. Chittenden on the wild, upper reaches of Sedge Creek is "Thistle Falls." This wide, steep, cascade-type falls flows in an area comprised of an endless combination of swampy muck, stacked deadfall, steep hills and cliffs, and thick, dense under-story. Just downstream from this little-known waterfall is a separate, gently-sloping cascade that descends over 30 feet. We propose the name "Thistle Falls" based on an unusual concentration of the mountain plant in the immediate area around the falls.

Sedge Creek has actually been surveyed twice by the USFWS, once by air in 1977 and a second time on foot in 1978. "Thistle Falls" was noted on each exploration. The first described it only as a "long cascade, probable barrier." The ground survey, however, was more detailed, calling it "a definite barrier falls, 9.14 meters high and a series of cascades 24.38 meters in length flowing through large boulders with much rubble and some gravels." This last description refers to the downstream drop (not pictured). The two drops are close to each other. The photogenic upper falls (the one we call "Thistle Falls") is only about 15 feet high while the lower "messier" one drops about 30 feet in its own confused way and then continues in a long series of cascades.

With the current bear management restrictions in Pelican Valley, the entire area can only be accessed between the hours of 9 a.m. and 7 p.m. and only after July 4. The area around Turbid Lake also has a permanent bear closure. A trek to "Thistle Falls" will test the limits of even the strongest hiker, as there are only so many hours of light in a day.

The Absarokas

226 UNNAMED FALLS ON THE SLOPES OF POLLUX PEAK "Pollux Peak Falls"

Darla Choquette

LOCATION: 585745 4946793

FALL TYPE: Horsetail

HEIGHT: 100–200 feet

STREAM: Little Lamar River

MAP: Unmapped

ACCESS: Extremely strenuous off-trail hike.

A dainty, horsetail falls is located on the Little Lamar River some three miles west of Lamar Mountain. It is apparently a permanent falls, flowing from what the 1989 Pollux Peak 7½-minute quadrangle shows as a 10,000-foot glacial area. Its brink at that elevation makes it elevationally the highest waterfall we found in Yellowstone.

Park employees Mike Yochim and Darla Choquette visited "Pollux Peak Falls" in 1994. They derived the name from the mountain from which it flows, Pollux Peak. In Greek mythology, Pollux and Castor were "the twins" as well as gods and protectors of travelers, significant in Yellowstone where there are so many travelers.

Middle Creek

227–228 UNNAMED FALLS ON UNNAMED TRIBUTARY OF MIDDLE CREEK "Looking Glass Falls"

LOCATION: 572003 4920507

FALL TYPE: Three-tiered Plunge

HEIGHT: 75 feet (including the upper drop)

STREAM: "Mad Hatter Creek"

MAP: Plenty Coups Peak, Wyoming -1989

ACCESS: Extremely strenuous off-trail hike.

Mike Stevens

"Looking Glass Falls" (#227) seems to have escaped notice by even east-entrance residents until the 1986 7½-minute quadrangles were released. Located on a south branch of Middle Creek, it is difficult to reach. Severe "sidehilling" is necessary and the area is loaded with alder thickets, swamps, and soft muck. Your hiking companions may hate you if you take them there.

The falls contains a series of drops: a 15–20 feet section at the top, with a 25–30 foot middle section, followed by two more drops of less than 10 feet each. A separate drop of 12 feet is located above the topmost falls at a distance of less than 100 yards (#228). The total drop is more than 70 feet.

We propose the name based upon Lewis Carroll's *Alice's Adventures in Wonderland* (1865) and its companion volume *Through the Looking Glass* (1872). These books were published just before Yellowstone's final discovery; thus, they loaned a name and image to the park. By 1871, the popular press referred to Yellowstone as "Wonderland."

Says Mike Stevens: "The vicinity of the falls seemed to be a little wonderland. I thought for a moment that 'Wonderland Falls' might be a good name for it. It hit me that that name would be too presumptuous since Wonderland is an alternate name for the whole of Yellowstone. That is when I hit upon the name 'Looking Glass' as the perfect alternative." (Later Stevens realized that Looking Glass was also the name of one of the Nez Perce leaders who fled through the park in 1877. Their party passed not far from this falls during their escape from the U.S. Cavalry.)

The difficulty of the terrain in the area, with its spruce deadfall, high understory, and poor footing, as well as the turmoil of the stream itself, led us to propose the name "Mad Hatter Creek" for the stream, a name which is also taken from *Alice in Wonderland*. In the story, the Mad Hatter attends a bizarre tea party with Alice and the White Rabbit. Hatters during the nineteenth century sometimes went crazy due to their constant inhalation of mercury fumes used during the hat-making process.

The Thorofare

The Thorofare Region of southeastern Yellowstone comprises an area of over 200 square miles with few trails and even fewer people. It is possibly the most remote wilderness left in the lower 48 states. Many of its streams and tributaries have never been officially surveyed. Wildlife thrives here; the Thorofare is a haven for elk, moose, and particularly the grizzly bear. A large population of healthy bears makes their home in the high meadows of the Absarokas during late summer for the annual hatching of the army-cutworm moth.[169] Because bears are extremely sensitive and easily disturbed, the pristine country of Thorofare provides a perfect habitat for them.

In addition its most remote locales are dotted with archeological sites. Some of these sites are untouched to this day, providing a veritable treasure trove of information for scientists on the life of our predecessors. Perhaps the Thorofare's only downfall is the continued problem of poaching. Because it is bounded on two sides by national forest, hunting season brings with it scores of armed outdoorsmen, some just itching to cross over the border for that trophy elk. Each autumn a handful of dedicated rangers vigorously patrols these boundary lines, but unfortunately they can have only so much effect. This is to be expected with such a huge and remote area to cover.

Naturally there has been much concern among the rangers who patrol here about any publicity. Many of them are strongly opposed to the prospect of losing the "secrets" of the Thorofare. For years, unofficial policy in the region has been to limit information about the details of this land. In their views, the fewer people to visit the Thorofare the better. They feel that if the true wonders of this region were extensively written of and photographed, then the Thorofare as we know it would disappear. This may be an overreaction, but the feeling is understandable.

For these reasons we are choosing to present only four waterfalls in the entire Thorofare region, although there are surely many more. Two of these falls, "Rapunzel Falls" and Plateau Falls, have been mapped by the USGS and thus warranted inclusion. The other two, "Mist of the Trident Falls" and "Isolation Falls," are both spectacular and have been mentioned often in ranger logs, firefighting records, and backcountry reports. We felt that they were too important not to include.

229 UNNAMED FALLS ON THE NORTH SLOPES OF MT. SCHURZ "Rapunzel Falls"

LOCATION: 571736 4911166

FALL TYPE: Multi-tiered Plunge/Horsetail

HEIGHT: 400–500 feet

STREAM: "Sorceress Creek"

MAP: Eagle Peak, Wyo. - 1989

ACCESS: Dangerous off-trail hike, not recommended.

This rarely photographed water-fall is one of the park's tallest at 400–500 feet. It is located on what we call "Sorceress Creek," a southerly branch of Beaverdam Creek, which flows north then west from Glade Lake on Mount Schurz.

More than 20 years ago, Lee Whittlesey learned of the possible existence of this falls from his friend Tom Carter, author of *Dayhiking Yellowstone.* Carter had walked the rim of the Absaroka Range nearby and photographed a spot where he believed there was a very high waterfall. His photos of the area and his belief in the falls' existence intrigued us. In the summer of 1997, our party of five hiked up the highest southerly branch of Beaverdam Creek's headwaters to emerge in a beautiful valley, walled in by sheer ramparts of the Absaroka Range. There, dropping "mistfully" for hundreds of feet into the valley, was this narrow, horsetail ribbon of water.

Captivated by the beauty of this falls and by its spectacular alpine surroundings, we searched for a name. One party member mentioned that it reminded him of maiden's hair, and party member Chris Benden remembered a fairytale where a woman unfurled her hair to be climbed by her lover. Other party members responded, "Rapunzel!" as they remembered the mythical character's long hair. The rest of us agreed, recalling the 1812 fairytale from the Brothers Grimm.

A beautiful, almost magical place such as this walled-in valley on a tributary of upper Beaverdam Creek deserves to have mystical, folklorean place names such as "Rapunzel Falls" and "Sorceress Creek."

Joanne Sides

230   UNNAMED FALLS ON CLIFF CREEK
"Mist of the Trident Falls"

LOCATION: 572609 4891292

FALL TYPE: Three-step Plunge

HEIGHT: 120–140 feet

STREAM: Cliff Creek

MAP: Unmapped

ACCESS: Multiple-day off-trail hike.

Patrick Wherritt, Jr.

Because this waterfall in Thorofare country is relatively close to the main trail, it has probably been seen by more people than the other waterfalls of this region. "Mist of the Trident Falls" is located one to two miles above the mouth of Cliff Creek. Our friend Patrick Wherritt, a knowledge-able Yellowstone photographer, estimated its height at 120–140 feet in three drops when he took these photos in late 1998.

We learned of this water-fall from an entry that ranger Bob Jackson made in the Thorofare logbook on July 3, 1980: "Came back on open meadows to Cliff Creek and checked out the falls that one always sees from out in the open [meadows of the upper Yellowstone River]. [They are] Beautiful, 60–70 feet high. One can go around behind them." Jackson was apparently referring only to the main plunge of the falls and not to its upper and lower portions. "Mist of the Trident Falls" sits deep within one of the two notches of The Trident, a nearly 11,000 foot, three-pronged mountain of the Absaroka Range that encompasses a large percentage of the park's southeast corner.

231 UNNAMED FALLS ON FALCON CREEK
"Isolation Falls"

LOCATION: 569502 4887213

FALL TYPE: Plunge

HEIGHT: 50 feet

STREAM: Falcon Creek

MAP: Unmapped

ACCESS: Multiple-day off-trail hike.

Reagan Grau

At well over 30 miles from any road, "Isolation Falls" is the most remote waterfall in all of Yellowstone, if not the entire contiguous United States. Found deep in the Thorofare, it is located on Falcon Creek less than a quarter mile from the park's south boundary. "Isolation Falls" breaks over a rock ledge and thunders straight down for 50 feet. Behind the falls you can negotiate a deep cave on foot for an extremely intimate and exciting view.

We first learned of this falls from ranger John Lounsbury who had seen it while patrolling the area on horseback. In an effort to see and photograph this falls, Paul Rubinstein set out in September 1995 with park employees Tom Mazzarisi and James Spanglet on an eight-day, 80-mile odyssey. Ironically, three days into the journey a record-setting September cold front dumped considerable snowfall and dropped temperatures into the single digits just hours before the men were to reach their goal. After a ford of the Yellowstone River in the bone-chilling cold and with the first signs of hypothermia beginning to set in, they decided to bypass Falcon Creek altogether.

For this reason, the authors mention the efforts of Reagan Grau of Lubbock, Texas, who one year later hiked alone for a distance of 75 miles in six days in order to take the only known published photograph of this incredible waterfall. In gratitude for his success, we have included his notes of that day and extended the privilege of suggesting a name for it. Here is his description:

> In choosing a name for this falls, I remember considering several words. At the time, I applied various feelings I was having while observing the falls as I reflected on how I had gotten there. Words such as independence, lonesome, and solo passed through my mind until I got out my map and looked once again at where I had come. As I sat alone, I was for a brief moment, a sojourner in this waterfall's reality. In contemplating this falls, I became duly aware of a distinct sense of isolation as the reality of this lonely, and beautiful falls became obvious. So, I looked at the falls again and thought Isolation Falls.

232   PLATEAU FALLS

LOCATION: 561149 4889618

FALL TYPE: Four-serial Plunge

HEIGHT: 80 feet

STREAM: Plateau Creek

MAP: Badger Creek, Wyoming - 1989

ACCESS: Multiple-day off-trail hike.

Paul Rubinstein

This extremely remote waterfall was named in approximately 1896 by members of the Hague parties of the USGS. Located high on the Two Ocean Plateau in the Thorofare region, it is Yellowstone's most distant, officially named waterfall.

Plateau Falls plunges in four vertical steps of 10, 15, 20, and 35 feet as Plateau Creek makes a turn of 45 degrees from northwest to due north. Although it is a minimum three days' hike from any park trailhead, it was visited in September 1995 by Paul Rubinstein who noted: "Its north-facing quality and forested surroundings make it nearly impossible to photograph in good light. Shadowing is a definite problem for the serious photographer here."

233 PREVIOUSLY MAPPED FALLS EAST OF MT. HANCOCK

During our research we encountered a perplexing map mystery: an 80-foot waterfall that repeatedly appeared from 1872 through 1885. It was located on what (at the time) was referred to as "Barlow's Fork" but what is today the upper reaches of the Snake River. The canyon in which the crude early maps showed this falls was just east of Mt. Hancock. Also, the heights for this falls were never consistent. Measurements of 30, 40, and 80 feet were common.

We wrestled with the possibility that the falls was actually Plateau Falls. This would have explained its disappearance from maps around the time that Plateau Falls was discovered and named. Yet none of these early maps showed this falls that far to the east. They all marked it some 10 miles west of Plateau Creek and put it directly on the Snake River (Barlow's Fork).

Further evidence of this new falls was furnished to us by veteran ranger Jerry Mernin. He vaguely remembered a waterfall in the upper section of the Snake River, but he could not recall any specific details about it.

The matter was put to rest when we unearthed a quote by Dr. Frank Bradley of the second Hayden Survey. In describing a sloping cascade-type fall on the upper Snake River he wrote:

> The lower slopes of Mt. Hancock on the west and those of an
> unnamed peak of nearly equal height on the east, soon close in upon
> the stream, forming a deep and narrow canon. To avoid traveling in
> the bed of the stream, we followed some of the numerous game-trails,
> which led us to from 300 to 400 feet above its level, but finally
> brought us down again about ten miles from Heart River, and just
> below some small falls and rapids, where the stream descends about
> 30 feet in about 200...At the falls, the rock is heavy-bedded.[170]

Rubinstein believes the mapping errors resulted from difficult-to-read markings on the initial map showing this falls. He theorizes that the 1872 notation "Falls30," which accurately represented the falls described by Bradley, was subsequently changed to "Falls80" on later maps because the number "30" could not be properly deciphered. It is possible that once other surveys began visiting the area, and no falls of 80 feet was seen, that subsequent maps omitted this very real 30-foot feature.

The Backcountry

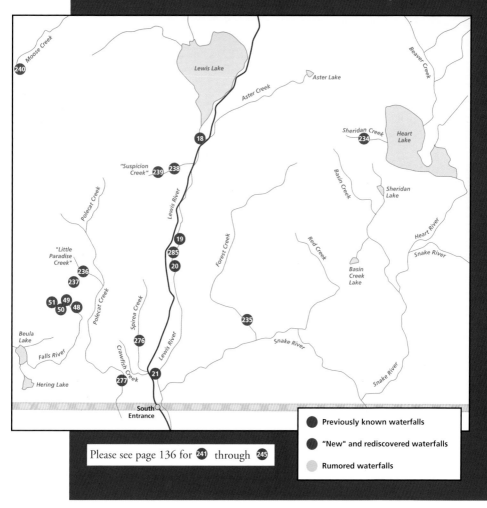

Moose Creek

240

Lewis Lake

Aster Lake

Aster Creek

Beaver Creek

Sheridan Creek

234

Heart Lake

18

"Suspicion Creek" 239 238

Basin Creek

Sheridan Lake

Polecat Creek

Lewis River

Heart River

19

Forest Creek

Red Creek

Snake River

"Little Paradise Creek"

285

20

Basin Creek Lake

236

237

51 49
50 48

Polecat Creek

Spirea Creek

235

Beula Lake

Falls River

Lewis River

Snake River

276

Crawfish Creek

Snake River

Hering Lake

277 21

South Entrance

● Previously known waterfalls

◍ "New" and rediscovered waterfalls

○ Rumored waterfalls

Please see page 136 for 241 through 245

234 UNNAMED FALLS ON SHERIDAN CREEK
"Whortleberry Falls"

LOCATION: 539024 4901718

FALL TYPE: Two-tiered Fan/ Cascades

HEIGHT: 40 feet (in two steps)

STREAM: Sheridan Creek

MAP: Unmapped

ACCESS: Moderate to difficult off-trail hike.

Bob Berry

This double waterfall on the east slopes of Mount Sheridan is visible from Heart Lake. It makes two descents separated by about 50 feet; the upper is about 20 feet and the lower is about 15 feet. The falls is located on completely open slopes with no large trees of any kind around it.

We propose the name "Whortleberry Falls," an idea suggested by park employee Barbara Totschek, for the small, delicate green plants which grow so prolifically in lodgepole forests throughout the park. The red berries are sweet and delicious, if tiny and sometimes unnoticed.

235 UNNAMED FALLS ON FOREST CREEK "Forbidding Falls"

LOCATION: 531843 4891357

FALL TYPE: Two-tiered Plunge

HEIGHT: 25 and 15 feet

STREAM: Forest Creek

MAP: Snake Hot Springs, Wyoming - 1989

ACCESS: Moderate to extremely strenuous off-trail hike (depending on the river depth).

A most engaging waterfall on Forest Creek was unknown to us until it appeared on the 1989 7½-minute map of Snake Hot Springs, about a half-mile upstream from where Forest Creek enters the Snake River.

In July 1995, with his hiking partners waiting downstream, Mike Stevens made his first journey, solo, to the falls, a difficult ordeal. The Snake River had been barely fordable and the approach to the falls was hazardous because of an extremely narrow canyon on Forest Creek. The canyon was only 15 feet wide in places and the walls became vertical or even overhanging, so the only travel possible was in the stream. The waist-deep creek had a strong current and slippery footing. The setting reminded Stevens of The Narrows in Zion National Park in that the canyon walls came directly (vertically) into the creek. After such an effort, however, he found the falls "very rewarding."

Stevens thought for several days before settling on the proposed name "Forbidding Falls." The name is alliterative, but it was also chosen to describe the arduous approach he endured to see the falls and the ominous feeling the canyon's walls gave him.

Surely others must have seen the falls at some time. We launched a dedicated effort to find out. We spoke to Jerry Mernin, the long-time district ranger in the area. He knew of the falls and had himself seen it from the air. He had never actually been there, but he remembered that NPS employee Kristin Legg had led a reconnaissance effort along Forest Creek a few years earlier. As Legg recounted, in 1991 the Resource Management Division sent her to survey Forest Creek in the interest of research on bighorn sheep. She and a partner traveled down Forest Creek from its source. Near the falls, the steep terrain forced her to the high ground at the canyon's edge. She was able to look down and observe the falls from high above it, and she noted that it was a double falls.

Legg's report of an additional upper fall inspired the three of us to mount a return trip along with park employee Doug Hatfield in August 1996. Because it was late in the season, the critical, last quarter mile to the falls was infinitely easier to travel than it had been for Stevens. The level of water in the narrow, constricted canyon had dropped nearly three feet and the current had slowed considerably. Once at the falls, we were able to scramble up a sidewall high enough to see the second (upper) falls.

Both falls are plunge-type falls. The lower is at least 25 feet in height, while the upper falls is 15 feet.

"Forbidding Falls;" Photo by Paul Rubinstein

236 UNNAMED FALLS ON "LITTLE PARADISE CREEK" "Serendipity Falls"

Mike Stevens

LOCATION: 523856 4894317

FALL TYPE: Segmented

HEIGHT: 30 feet

STREAM: "Little Paradise Creek"

MAP: Unmapped

ACCESS: Moderate to difficult off-trail hike.

In 1997, four of us hiked into the trailless country west of Lewis Canyon in a sea of mosquitoes. Mike Stevens, Lee Whittlesey, Joanne Sides, and Mike Yochim arrived on upper Polecat Creek to find a dry canyon. Walking downstream, we began to see many small streams gushing from the southeast side of Pitchstone Plateau. Within a quarter mile we noticed a stream coming into Polecat from the north. We decided to investigate. As we moved upstream, Stevens spotted a distant iota of whitewater disappearing into a snow bank that warranted further investigation. It turned out not to be a falls, but from this new vantage point, he noticed another speck on the horizon. The second exploration yielded a beautiful segmented falls with drops of 25 and 30 feet, respectively. All of us were excited; this seemed like the kind of place where we might literally be the first Euro-American visitors.

We suggest the name "Serendipity Falls" for our accidental, fortuitous discovery. Serendipity means "an apparent aptitude for making fortunate discoveries accidentally." This falls is on an unmapped stream that we had not come to search. Sides suggested "Little Paradise Falls." Eventually we decided to transfer her suggestion to the stream itself, essentially the highest tributary of Polecat Creek, hence "Little Paradise Creek."

237 UNNAMED FALLS ON A TRIBUTARY OF POLECAT CREEK "Rocky Top Falls"

LOCATION: 523404 4894305

FALL TYPE: Segmented Plunge

HEIGHT: 30 feet

STREAM: Unnamed Tributary of Polecat Creek

MAP: Unmapped

ACCESS: Moderate to difficult off-trail hike.

Mike Stevens

Located on an unnamed western branch of Polecat Creek, which is the next branch south of "Little Paradise Creek," this plunge-type falls is 30 feet high, with perhaps 200 feet of furious cascades trailing below it. It originates from the Pitchstone Plateau, and its top is made of huge, dark, rocky boulders, hence the proposed name. The name came to us all instantaneously when we first saw this falls.

"Suspicion Creek"

Less than a mile north of the trailhead to Pitchstone Plateau, an unnamed permanent stream crosses the South Entrance Road from the west. Although it has no official name it does contain a rather significant amount of water for its relative anonymity. In the summer of 1969, Lee Whittlesey first took note of this stream. Even then he believed it was an intriguing watercourse and suspected it contained a waterfall.

Twenty-eight years later, in the summer of 1997, Mike Stevens surveyed a portion of this stream. He found it to be more complex than park maps showed. Only one-half mile upstream he found an area where at least three small creeks converged in a swampy meadow. He chose to follow the largest of the three tributaries, but found no falls or cascades of any kind. Instead, the stream's origin was another of the familiar numerous cold-water springs pouring from the base of a steep hillside.

In 1999, we decided another survey was needed to determine if the other smaller tributaries contained falls and if so, were they permanent features. In June, in one of the last surveys for this book, we researched the area again. This time we were rewarded with the discovery of two elegant falls: one a permanent 20-foot double falls and the other a magnificent 75-foot waterfall that, although seasonal, is undoubtedly one of the finest Yellowstone has to offer. Thus, Whittlesey's suspicions that the seemingly insignificant creek had waterfalls proved to be correct. For this reason we call the stream "Suspicion Creek."

238 UNNAMED FALLS ON "SUSPICION CREEK" "Premonition Falls"

LOCATION: 526985 4900530

FALL TYPE: Two-step Plunge

HEIGHT: 20 feet

STREAM: "Suspicion Creek"

MAP: Unmapped

ACCESS: Moderate to difficult off-trail hike.

Paul Rubinstein

One mile upstream from where "Suspicion Creek" crosses the South Entrance Road, a green, marshy meadow contains three main tributaries that form the majority of the stream. By continuing another half-mile up the middle tributary, the hiker enters a small canyon and almost immediately encounters a 20-foot, two-step drop that we call "Premonition Falls." This feature is formed where the stream makes a sharp twist from an easterly to southerly and then back to easterly course. This portion of the stream appears permanent.

It was Lee Whittlesey's 30-year premonition of falls on this stream that inspired our suggested name for this waterfall.

239 UNNAMED FALLS ON "SUSPICION CREEK" "Confirmation Falls"

LOCATION: 526880 4900553

FALL TYPE: Plunge

HEIGHT: 75–90 feet

STREAM: "Suspicion Creek"

MAP: Unmapped

ACCESS: Moderate to difficult off-trail hike.

Mike Stevens

Only one-quarter mile upstream from "Premonition Falls" is a stunning and massive waterfall. A 75- to 90-foot giant, it is a true waterfall if ever there was one. Here the waters of "Suspicion Creek" crash down a vertical cliff face, splitting into multiple bands of white foam. During peak snowmelt, this gem of the eastern Pitchstone Plateau qualifies as one of the most beautiful waterfalls in all of Yellowstone.

Its proximity to the highway makes this grand spectacle one of the more accessible "new" waterfalls that we encountered. For the adventurous waterfall lover, we highly recommend this two-hour walk. It is well worth the effort. Unfortunately, this phenomenal hidden treasure is not a permanent feature, so the spectacle is short lived. We hoped this portion of "Suspicion Creek" would contain at least some water in late summer. In reality, our research determined that the stream duplicates what is happening on so much of the Pitchstone Plateau during mid to late summer. The waters seep into the porous rock and then gush forth from the base of the cliff instead of flowing over it. By late July, "Confirmation Falls" is nothing more than a giant cliff-wall with a small brook flowing from its base. For Whittlesey, its discovery was "confirmation" that a granddaddy of a waterfall had indeed been hiding up this most suspicious stream. At last a 30-year mystery was put to rest.

240 UNNAMED FALLS ON MOOSE CREEK
"Orchid Falls"

LOCATION: 518234 4905245

FALL TYPE: Cascade

HEIGHT: 100 feet

STREAM: Moose Creek

MAP: Unmapped

ACCESS: Multiple-day off-trail hike.

Mike Stevens

Falling from Pitchstone Plateau, Moose Creek forms a beautiful, 100-plus-foot cascade near its headwaters. A backcountry ranger "let it slip" to us that this feature might exist, and so in 1998 we undertook a 25-mile roundtrip to search for it.

We were struck by how the stream seemed to go on forever through large meadows near its head. Striking, white bog orchids (Habenaria sp.) grew in the marshes most of the way to the falls, hence our name proposal of "Orchid Falls."

The falls is a much steeper entity than it appears in photographs. Its ferocious waters and jumbled character are imposing when viewed up close. Situated on one of the lower tiers of the Pitchstone Plateau, we believe it is a permanent feature. From the brink, one can see more steps upstream in the distance.

Unfortunately, time constraints prevented further exploration of Moose Creek. We do believe the possibility exists for more falls upstream, but they would require a multiple-day exploration and lengthy off-trail travel.

Shoshone Geyser Basin

241 UNNAMED FALLS ON FALL CREEK
"Tawny Falls"

LOCATION: 515552 4910454

FALL TYPE: Cascade

HEIGHT: 17 feet

STREAM: Fall Creek

MAP: Unmapped

ACCESS: Moderate to difficult off-trail hike.

Fall Creek flows into the southwestern side of the Shoshone Geyser Basin. A short distance upstream from the extensive thermal area, we have named a picturesque waterfall "Tawny Falls." Its pleasing waters first slide down a streambed ramp before rushing over a rounded edge. The cascade appears to step down in three or four segments.

Our suggested name comes from the unusual color of the steep hill that borders the waterfall's southern side and from the golden rocks in the creek, even though we feared confusion might occur if readers assumed we were referring to the color of the water and not the rock. We eventually settled on Tawny because the word means a brownish-orange shade and it seemed an accurate representation of the unique coloration of the cliffs here.

Perhaps 30–40 yards up Fall Creek from "Tawny Falls," a dilapidated bridge crosses the stream. This is part of the loop trail that bypasses the Shoshone Geyser Basin.

242-243 TWO SMALL FALLS NEAR SHOSHONE GEYSER BASIN

A complex little falls can be found southwest of Shoshone Geyser Basin on a spring-fed tributary to the north fork of Fall Creek, about one-half mile above its split. The water here flows from a hanging valley between an array of protruding ledges. It drops vertically for its first 25 feet, then cascades through a mixture of small boulders and dense pines for another 30. The stream here tends to be hidden in its narrow channel by knee-high, bushy groundcover. We call it "Chaos Falls" (#242) from the jumbled nature of the water's descent.

The Shoshone Geyser Basin yields yet another small cascade-type falls (#243). Mapped at 15 feet by Gustavus Bechler in 1872, it is located just south of what his map of that year shows as Grand Boiling Spring on a stream he called "Quick Run" [Fall Creek]. It hardly passes as a falls, however, appearing more like a short section of rapids.

"Tawny Falls;" Photo by Mike Stevens

244-245

UNNAMED DOUBLE FALLS ON TRIBUTARY OF SHOSHONE CREEK "Forks of Shoshone Falls"

Mike Stevens

LOCATION: 513463 4912429

FALL TYPE: Cascade/Double Plunge

HEIGHT: 30 & 30 feet

STREAM: Unnamed Tributary of Shoshone Creek

MAP: Unmapped

ACCESS: Moderate to difficult off-trail hike.

On the largest unnamed tributary of Shoshone Creek two small waterfalls (#244, #245) have the distinction of being Yellowstone's only double falls we know of. What do we mean by double falls? A place where two separate waterfalls on two separate streams are so close together they can be photographed in a single shot. (While "Bride Falls" and "Groom Falls" can be photographed in one shot, they are located on the same stream that splits around an island.)

These two falls are right at the mouths of their respective streams. Facing the two features, the left (southwesterly) is a 30-foot steep cascade while the right (northwesterly) is a two-step, 30-foot double plunge. Maps indicate that the former is probably seasonal while the latter exists (at least to some degree) year-round.

Our proposed name, "Forks of Shoshone Falls," is geographical, since these features occur at a natural fork in the Shoshone Creek drainage. These waterfalls also have the distinction of being the only feature we found during our research while genuinely lost in the backcountry. Navigating in heavy snow cover, we missed our trail during this particular survey. Stumbling upon these falls while approaching from the southwest, we were not sure which drainage we were actually in for at least an hour after finding these falls.

We recommend viewing the falls before the end of July in order to capture the full effect of the two streams merging with two falls at their mouths. Leaving from the Lone Star Geyser trailhead, follow the Old Faithful-Bechler River Trail to the southwest for at least five miles until just beyond the junction with the Shoshone Lake Trail. The unnamed tributary is one-quarter mile beyond this junction. The trail crosses it with an easy ford (sometimes there are logs). Here leave the trail and proceed upstream. The two falls are approximately one mile from the trail in a rather steep, narrow canyon. The off-trail travel is somewhat marshy but not difficult if a route in the canyon is followed.

The Backcountry

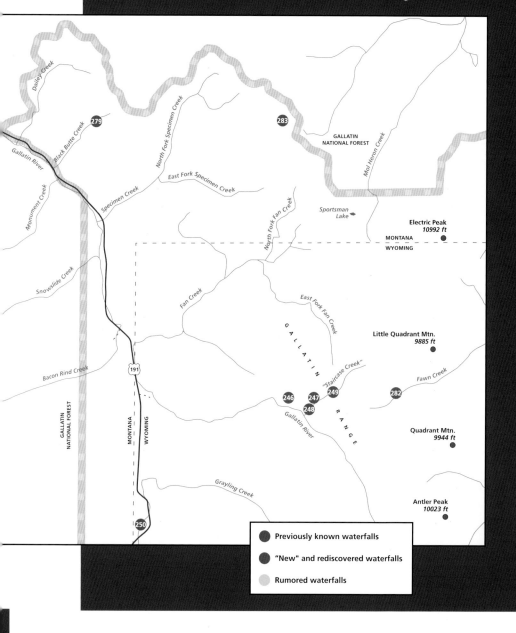

Previously known waterfalls

"New" and rediscovered waterfalls

Rumored waterfalls

246 "BIGHORN SPRINGS CASCADES"

About two miles west of Bighorn Pass in the Gallatin Range lies an unusual set of cascades. Their waters flow south from a series of large, hillside springs. These perennial springs start abruptly and are quite audible from the Bighorn Pass Trail. There are no less than a dozen of these spring-born cascades ranging in height from 20 to 200 feet.

The largest cascade braids and twists within itself as it descends a steep, open hillside. The complexity of this intertwining descent lines the slopes of the lush meadows with ribbons of white. Although not visible from the Bighorn Pass Trail, a bushwhack of only a few hundred yards to the north brings it into view. The fact that so many separate, spring-fed cascades exist in such close proximity to each other makes "Bighorn Springs Cascades" another worthwhile destination in Yellowstone.

Paul Rubinstein

247-248   UNNAMED FALLS ON LOWER "STAIRCASE CREEK" "Gilded Falls" and "Stone Hollow Falls"

"Gilded Falls" (upper)

"Gilded Falls" (lower)

#247 "GILDED FALLS"

LOCATION: 505385 4973846

FALL TYPE: Cascade & Plunge

HEIGHT: 25 & 50 feet

STREAM: "Staircase Creek"

MAP: Unmapped

ACCESS: Moderate to difficult off-trail hike.

Several miles west of Bighorn Pass on the north side of the valley cut by the Gallatin River stands a formidable ridge of cliffs. Snaking through them almost unnoticed, a good-sized creek slips and steps methodically down a complex series of ledges and walls. We refer to this stream as "Staircase Creek." It begins high in the Gallatins in an alpine pond near Fawn Pass. Its name, originally conceived by park employee Steve Wiechmann, is for the stream's multi-step nature. With the help of many springs and seeps, its step-down flow is quite full by the time its waters reach the Gallatin River.

Two large waterfalls are present on the lower reaches of the stream. The first is a two-step combination cascade and falls (**#247**) whose total drop is about 80 feet. The

#248 "STONE HOLLOW FALLS"

LOCATION: 505296 4973718

FALL TYPE: Plunge

HEIGHT: 40 feet

STREAM: "Staircase Creek"

MAP: Unmapped

ACCESS: Moderate to difficult off-trail hike.

most distinguishing characteristic is the yellow-stained coloring of its rocky streambed. From its upper end the falls is made up of a 30-foot section of cascade that shoots and rolls through a heavily forested, submerged trench before leaping into the open in a 50-foot free fall. The consistent coloring of its rocky sidewalls and the illusion of golden-colored water were the inspiration for our friend Katarina Gvozdić to propose the name, "Gilded Falls."

Below "Gilded Falls" the creek enters an extremely treacherous gorge. After dropping over a small, fan-shaped cascade, the stream comes to a place so incredible and bizarre that neither photographs nor words do it justice. Can you imagine a waterfall that, rather than flowing from a cliff overhang, pours through it? This is the case at the most downstream falls **(#248)** of "Staircase Creek." Moments before reaching the precipice, its waters plummet through the ledge of its overhanging brink and free-fall some 35 feet to the rocks below. In the high water of springtime, a portion of the stream does manage to flow over the lip as well, creating a double parallel fall that seems to defy the laws of nature.

Paul Rubinstein first learned of this falls in 1994 from park employee Bruno Picinich, who stumbled upon

"Stone Hollow Falls,: a geologic wonder.   Paul Rubinstein

it accidentally while searching for the aforementioned "Bighorn Springs Cascades." We then received confirmation of this falls in July 1998 when employees Steve Wiechmann and Marek Hrebicek caught a glimpse of "white" from the Bighorn Pass Trail and ventured up the stream. Inspired by a photograph of this remarkable falls in October 1998, park employee Barbara Totschek offered the designation, "Stone Hollow Falls." The name has since become entrenched among those of us who have traveled to it.

249   UNNAMED FALLS ON UPPER "STAIRCASE CREEK" "Sublimity Falls"

LOCATION: 505722 4974076

FALL TYPE: Plunge

HEIGHT: 15 feet

STREAM: "Staircase Creek"

MAP: Unmapped

ACCESS: Multiple-day off-trail hike.

Steve Wiechmann

Approximately half a mile upstream from "Gilded Falls" is a hidden, rarely visited gem. Set amidst the isolated alpine forest of the western Gallatins, the peaceful isolation of this locale was the inspiration for the name "Sublimity Falls." Meaning that which causes awe, reverence, or a sense of vastness especially when it is combined with danger, "Sublimity" seemed to capture the mood here.

This portion of the stream was surveyed in August 1998 by park employees Marek Hrebicek and Steve Wiechmann, who followed it to its source. They report that its waters originate at the base of a 100-foot wall in a meadow of mucky seeps southwest of Fawn Lake. Wiechmann is convinced that during early season snowmelt, the vertical cliff undoubtedly contains a superb 100-foot seasonal falls as evidenced by the dry streambed they encountered upon scaling the precarious precipice to its brink.

250 GRAYLING FALLS

Mike Stevens

LOCATION: 496061 4967605

FALL TYPE: Plunge

HEIGHT: 6 feet

STREAM: Grayling Creek

MAP: USFWS Map of Grayling Creek - 1983

ACCESS: Easy to moderate off-trail hike.

Although only 300 yards west of U.S. Highway 191 at Horseshoe Hill, this small, six-foot drop of Grayling Creek can be one of the trickier waterfalls to reach in Yellowstone. Unless one wants to wade through the unpredictable waters of Grayling Creek itself, there seems to be no good way to navigate directly to the base of this falls from the highway. A precarious 70-degree slope lines the eastern side of this falls from a quarter-mile upstream to a half-mile below. There is an easy alternative, however. Approach this hidden oasis from the opposite side. Follow the old U.S. 191 roadbed up the creek's western side for a relatively easy three-quarter mile walk.

Grayling Falls appears much larger than its height suggests. This is a fine example of a waterfall that is more impressive in the low water of September than in the swollen flows of the June runoff. The name Grayling Falls has been in local usage by area fishermen for years. We include it here not for its height, but because it is a previously documented and named waterfall, appearing in the USFWS *Annual Project Report* for 1982 and in Lee Whittlesey's *Wonderland Nomenclature*.

APPENDIX A

Best of the Rest

One of the most difficult tasks in the creation and editing of this book was determining what to do about the many notable waterfalls and cascades that did not quite meet our criteria for individual entries in the main text, yet had previous documentation or have undoubtedly been seen by backcountry hikers. The reasons they were omitted fell into a variety of categories. Some were too small, others were seasonal only, and in a few cases, they had been reported but we could not confirm that they existed at all.

The authors have seen most of the waterfalls that didn't make the cut. We have listed them in four categories. It will be left up to those readers who venture to them to determine whether or not they are worthy of true Yellowstone waterfall status.

ON-TRAIL OR ROADSIDE WATERFALLS

Boundary Creek—A sightly 20-foot cascade **(#252)** can be found on upper Boundary Creek roughly two and a quarter miles above Dunanda Falls. The name "Paintbrush Cascade" was suggested in 1997 from the profusion of crimson Indian paintbrush (*Castilleja sp.*) growing in the area.

Another beautiful 10-foot vertical falls **(#251)** on Boundary Creek can be seen from the Boundary Creek Trail between Dunanda Falls and "Paintbrush Cascade." We mention it here for its outstanding scenic beauty.

"Campsite Falls"—This pretty 12-foot plunge **(#253)** is found at campsite OG2 on an unnamed tributary of Sentinel Creek. It is a seasonal falls that is undoubtedly seen by those overnight campers who explore the area in the first half of summer.

"Continental Divide Falls"—Almost precisely at the Continental Divide on the Bechler River Trail and south of Shoshone Creek, this extraordinary waterfall **(#254)** can be heard from the trail but not seen. A quarter mile east of the trail, the 25-foot, cascade-type falls pours from the top of a hill. There is no stream leading to it; it is 100 percent spring fed. The stream created by this cold mountain spring eventually enters the Little's Fork drainage.

"Culvert Falls"—This overlooked little falls **(#255)** makes a 20-foot tumble moments after its unnamed stream passes through a large, steel culvert beneath the South Entrance Road adjacent to Lewis Canyon. The falls splits at its brink and plunges in two parallel sections down the hillside and eventually into the Lewis River. In drier years it disappears by August.

East Entrance Road—Numerous temporary falls along the East Entrance Road tumble down to the roadside east of Sylvan Pass. The most notable is some 35 feet in height, located about three miles east of the pass **(#267)**. However, current plans are to reroute the highway in this area. What impact it will have on these waterfalls is not known, but it is likely that several of the falls here will be altered to some degree.

Elk Creek—Elk Creek contains a 20- to 30-foot cascade **(#256)**. It can be seen along the Garnet Loop Trail just west of Garnet Hill.

"Embowered Falls"—This falls **(#257)** can be found just below the Grand Loop Road about one-half mile north of Dunraven Pass. It is 100 yards west of the highway down a steep slope. Surprisingly, this 25-foot plunge is a perennial, snowmelt and spring-fed waterfall. We refer to it as "Embowered Falls" for its multi-flowered surroundings during most of the summer. North of "Embowered Falls" on a separate parallel stream, a four-step cascade of nearly 100 feet is seasonal.

"Embowered Falls;" Photo by Mike Stevens

Glen Creek—Located below Rustic Falls on Glen Creek a short distance above the place where the old Bunsen Peak loop drive crosses it, is a roiling and turbulent 18-foot waterfall **(#258)**. It is curious why this waterfall has never been mentioned or named in the past. Its visibility from the old auto road and its close proximity to Mammoth employee housing are a strong indication that it has been seen by scores of people over the years.

"Idyllic Falls"—Although scarcely 10 feet high, this falls **(#259)** in Pelican Valley is seated in a charmingly pastoral and poetic setting. The pretty falls is located on Sage Creek, the more southerly of two long streams that flow northwest from Mount Chittenden to Pelican Creek, where the trail to Pelican Springs crosses that stream.

Iron Cañon Cascades—This small series of cascades **(#260)** in Gibbon River Canyon above Gibbon Falls was named sometime between 1871 and 1874 by Bozeman photographer Joshua Crissman. All of Crissman's photographs were subsequently purchased by prospector William Isaac Marshall and released under his copyright in 1876. One of these photos, labeled #4 in Marshall's "Firehole and Gibbon River Series," was released as a stereoview entitled "Iron Cañon Cascades."

Lost Lake Trail—Behind Roosevelt Lodge and along a switchback of the Lost Lake Trail is a fine 40-foot cascade **(#261)**. This cascade is often confused with Lost Creek Falls by hikers who mistakenly take the wrong fork on the trail. The feature described here is about a half-mile north/northeast of Lost Creek Falls.

Mountain Ash Creek Trail—Two separate, 15-foot seasonal waterfalls **(#262, #263)** can be seen through July along the Mountain Ash Creek Trail. Both are on an unnamed tributary of Proposition Creek, just west of the trail where it makes its steep descent from the Birch Hills.

Observation Point—In the immediate Old Faithful area, a seasonal 40-foot cascade **(#264)** is quite prominent while it flows. It drops from the ridge directly north of Old Faithful Geyser, and can be seen from the trail between Observation Point and Solitary Geyser. Unfortunately its life is short; it lasts only about two weeks each year, usually in June.

Pipeline Creek—There are actually two waterfalls that should be mentioned here. The first is a 10–12 foot cascade-type falls **(#265)** on Pipeline Creek that we call "Pipeline Creek Falls." It is just downstream from where the Mallard Lake trail crosses the creek, about three-quarters of a mile east of the Old Faithful Lodge. The second is an 80-foot, rope-like falls **(#266)** that plummets into Pipeline Creek from the north, just a few yards from the smaller "Pipeline Creek Falls."

Upper Gregg Fork—A series of small cascades **(#268)** on the upper reaches of the Gregg Fork total 17 feet in a group of five bunched but independent falls. They can be heard but not seen from the Bechler Trail between Douglas Knob and Twister Falls.

Washboard Cascade—In Charles Maynard's 1996 book *Waterfalls of Yellowstone* there is an entry labeled Washboard Cascade **(#269)**. It is found where the Bechler River divides around Treasure Island, not far upstream from Iris Falls. Unofficially named by his chief photographer David Morris, the two felt it was too beautiful a stretch of whitewater not to include in their book.

OFF-TRAIL WATERFALLS

"Bonus Falls"—This thin, wiry, 60-foot (and probably seasonal) falls **(#270)** flows south from the hills of the Central/Solfatara Plateau on an unnamed stream into Otter Creek about three-quarters of a mile above "Bear Feeding Falls." The name was proposed by one of our party, Michelle M. Serio, from the fact that we had no inclination that we would find a falls there.

"Check Falls" and "Geode Falls"—A 16-foot, cascade-type falls **(#271)** is located on Geode Creek about one and one-half miles below its crossing of the Grand Loop Road. The name that we use refers to its physical shape: that of a classic check mark. (Its appearance undoubtedly varies with the season.)

Just upstream from "Check Falls" another small waterfall cascades **(#272)** with five countable steps that give a total vertical drop of about 25 feet. Ranger David Rothenburger originally dubbed it "Geode Falls."

"Dancing Water Cascade" and "Terminal Falls"—"Dancing Water Cascade" **(#273)** is found on the Gardner River about a mile below the Sheepeater Cliff parking area and about one-half mile below our "Tukuarika Falls." Its vertical drop stretches across the entire river, perhaps 40 yards. The eight- to 12-foot drop is augmented by an even descent of water that drops rapidly away from the base of the falls.

A dozen yards upstream from the brink of this cascade another feature **(#274)** bears mentioning. We call it "Terminal Falls." It is on a spring-fed stream that pours out of the hillside and immediately rushes hundreds of feet as a ribbon of white until it finally drops over a legitimate falls of about 25 feet, falling almost directly into the Gardner River at its base.

"Silent Gorge Falls"—On Buffalo Creek about three-quarters of a mile from the park's north Boundary is a marvelous little waterfall **(#275)** we call "Silent Gorge Falls." It is set in an extremely narrow notch. Viewed from above, the water disappears as if it has been captured by the towering granite outcroppings. Deep in this silent chasm the creek makes a 10-foot vertical plunge.

Spirea and Polecat Creeks—At the mouth of a large tributary of Spirea Creek, about four miles north/northwest of the park's south entrance, is a charming, step-down cascade **(#276)**. Our best estimate is that this forested cascade drops around 45 feet in total vertical descent.

The authors have also heard from park visitor Chuck Mohr of a 50-foot waterfall **(#277)** on Polecat Creek about a half-mile upstream from the park's south boundary. He described it as quite scenic.

WATERFALLS FROM THE U.S. FISH AND WILDLIFE SERVICE SURVEYS

Bear Creek—Unknown cascades **(#278)** were reported in a small gorge on Bear Creek about two miles upstream from where the stream crosses the East Entrance Road. They prevented fish from migrating upstream and were described as "very hard to see."

Black Butte Creek—A 12-foot falls **(#279)** was reported as being about three miles upstream from the outlet of Black Butte Creek in the park's northwest corner. This creek flows southwest from high in the Gallatins near the Skyline Trail.

Bluff Creek—A cascade **(#280)** of unknown dimensions was reported on the upper reaches of this creek east of the Hayden Valley.

Cutoff Creek—A cascade barrier of unknown height is on this stream in the park's northeast corner. The authors have heard of a "Silver Tip Falls" **(#281)** in this area.

Fawn Pass—A 15-foot seasonal falls **(#282)** located one-quarter mile southeast of Pass Lake at Fawn Pass can be seen from the Fawn Pass trail.

High Lake—A 10-foot falls **(#283)** is on an unnamed creek 200 yards upstream from High Lake in the park's northwest corner.

Hornaday Creek—A 15-foot waterfall **(#284)** is located on Hornaday Creek less than a mile from where it flows into upper Slough Creek.

"Narrow Cascades"—Mike Stevens proposed this name for a 100-foot, sloping cascade **(#285)** on Reese Creek about a third of a mile west of Cache Lake. This feature was extensively surveyed by USFWS as part of perhaps their most complex study of fish migration ever undertaken in Yellowstone. This cascade is impossible to photograph in its entirety due to the heavy forest canopy around it.

Spruce Creek—Although only six feet in height, this cascade **(#286)** on Spruce Creek is noteworthy. A 1977 USFWS survey team believed that there were more waterfalls upstream from it. They strongly suggested that Spruce Creek be further studied upstream. In 1998 the authors surveyed an uncharted portion of upper Spruce Creek but found no falls. Time did not permit a complete survey. The possibility remains that a large waterfall is hidden on its uppermost reaches.

RUMORED WATERFALLS AND MYSTERIES ON THE MAP

Cowan Creek—The 1986 Norris Junction 7½-minute quadrangle shows the word "falls" on upper Cowan Creek. Author Mike Stevens and archivist volunteer Joanne Sides surveyed the area in 1997 and found no waterfall. They did find a section of whitewater **(#290)** that Mike described as "a long flat cascade much like Wraith Falls." They theorized that it probably appeared as a waterfall to aerial surveyors.

Dry Creek Falls—In 1998, the authors received a postcard from AmFac Information Specialist Leslie Quinn entitled "Dry Creek Falls" **(#291)**. On it was an obscure photograph copyrighted 1908 by F. E. Van Toast of Townsend, Montana. The card was postmarked in Yellowstone on July 7, 1907, and addressed to Miss M. Pratchen at Mammoth Hot Springs Hotel. Yet we cannot confirm that this is a Yellowstone waterfall. It will probably always remain a mystery.

Miller Creek—Two waterfalls **(#287, #288)** may exist in a canyon on upper Miller Creek. Nez Perce expert Stan Hoggatt, in an effort to retrace the path of the Nez Perce's 1877 trip through the park, painstakingly explored this area of east central Yellowstone. He reported two cascades 20 feet high.

The other "Morning Falls"—A seasonal Bechler ranger passed along an intriguing story to us. A local Idaho resident whose family had been visiting the Cave Falls area for decades told this ranger that they called an area falls **(#289)** "Morning Falls." The man was adamant that this falls is not the Morning Falls in the Mountain Ash Creek drainage, but rather was within four miles of Cave Falls on a tributary of the Falls River. We were never able to find any waterfalls in the area in question.

Willow Creek—We have received two independent reports of a large waterfall **(#292)** on Willow Creek on the east side of the Mirror Plateau. The reports we received were from very reputable sources, yet we were unable to find any waterfall. We do believe that a large falls is in the area, but probably on a tributary rather than on Willow Creek itself.

An Unnamed Fall on the East Entrance Road; Photo by Mike Stevens

Where to Find More Waterfalls

Although this book makes reference to nearly 300 different park waterfalls, there are undoubt-edly many more in the seemingly endless Yellowstone backcountry. It would be ludicrous for us to assume we have found them all. In fact, there are likely scores of them out there yet to be seen. Research for this book could have gone on for another 20 years and still not covered it all. Such is the mystique of Yellowstone.

There is some disagreement among the three of us as to exactly how many are left, but it is safe to say the number is high. Based on the percentages of Yellowstone streams that have been surveyed to date, and from our extensive Yellowstone map and field research, we strongly believe there is still much opportunity for those who want to seek out unknown waterfalls.

Paul Rubinstein believes there are so many left that someone could do a follow-up waterfall book entitled *Waterfalls of Yellowstone That Those Three Guys Didn't Find* and still have a publication comparable to this one. He bases that theory on several factors:

• He estimates that, for this book, we surveyed less than a quarter of the park's creeks and rivers.

• The USFWS surveys from the 1960s through the 1980s covered only about 30 percent of the park's creeks.

• The park trail system follows less than one percent of the watercourses in the backcountry.

• Early explorers saw a limited number of streams, following instead existing Native American or game trails, and limited their off-trail travel to a minimum.

If we are to accept that there are still numerous unknown falls in the park, then where are they? Some of the most intriguing—and essentially unsurveyed—possible places are:

1. **The Thorofare**—Much of this region (the size of a small state) is still essentially unexplored. Tributaries draining the Absarokas and Two Ocean Plateau are likely to be littered with waterfalls.

2. **The Northeast Corner**—The mountain geography here suggests dozens if not hundreds more falls. Late snowmelt, extensive springs, amphitheater-shaped valleys, and jagged peaks all add up to possible waterfalls. Four of our most spectacular finds were in this area and it is a safe bet that this was just the tip of the iceberg.

3. **The east side of the Mirror Plateau**—Over a dozen streams flow into the Lamar River from the far side of the Mirror Plateau. Each of these streams has multiple small tributaries. Plateau country by its very nature contains falls. Rumors still exist of at least one hidden giant in this remote area.

4. **The Gallatins**—Although probably smaller or more cascade-like, the yet-to-be-discovered waterfalls of the Gallatins should not be overlooked. "Stone Hollow Falls" and "Gilded Falls" are two superb examples of a seemingly eroded area that still created some magnifi-cent features.

5. **The North Boundary**—Many of the streams flowing from north of the park into the Yellowstone River have little or no documented history and are just waiting to be explored. In particular are those stretches nearest to the north boundary and away from trails.

6. **The remote Bechler high country**—Although we have presented more than 80 waterfalls in this region, it is likely that many more falls are present here. They are probably far up streams and away from any trails or named creeks. Tributaries of Boundary Creek, Mountain Ash Creek, and the area north of Rainbow Falls would be good places to look.

7. Burnt Creek—One stream in Yellowstone that we wanted to survey extensively but were not able to reach was the middle section of Burnt Creek. Little is known about this stream above the multi-step falls at its mouth ("Palisade Falls") and below the large meadow at its headwaters. We are confident that at least one and perhaps two large waterfalls or cascades are between these seemingly impassable barriers.

We have left many waterfalls to be discovered, of that there is little doubt. But those still unknown are that way for a reason. Most are probably quite distant and likely to require multi-day trips to view. If they have stayed secret, they certainly require difficult or lengthy off-trail travel. Adventurers looking for undiscovered Yellowstone waterfalls must be in prime physical and mental condition and possess excellent navigation skills. Expect steep grades, unstable footing, thick foliage, and terrible downfall. However, if you are up to the task, you may be rewarded with a feeling that is indescribable—the knowledge that you have found something previously unknown and have thus gained the title of true "explorer."

Yellowstone is waterfall country. They are everywhere.

Gibbon Falls; Photo by Paul Rubinstein

Notes

FOREWORD:

1. Killian, "Mythical Shangri-La Found."
2. Stanley, *Rambles in Wonderland*, 76.

INTRODUCTION:

3. Brower, *Gentle Wilderness*, 88.
4. *Ibid.*, back cover.
5. Langford, *The Discovery of Yellowstone Park*, 21.
6. Hayden, *USGS 5th Annual Report*, 8.
7. Brilliant, *Abandoned My Search for Truth.*
8. Thwaites, *Journals of Lewis and Clark*, 149–50.

PART I: THE FRONTCOUNTRY
Lower Loop:

9. Bonney, *Battle Drums and Geysers*, 340.
10. Thayer, *Marvels of the New West*, 72.
11. Saltus, *Week in Yellowstone*, 53.
12. Barlow, "Reconnaissance of the Basin of the Upper Yellowstone," 25-6.
13. Wheat, *Mapping the Transmississippi West*, vol. 5, part II, (opposite) 347.
14. Hayden, *USGS 6th Annual Report*, 231.
15. Wineman, "Through Yellowstone National Park," 38.
16. Hayden, *USGS 6th Annual Report*, 159, 231.
17. Ibid., 160; Norris, Report to the Secretary of the Interior, 844.
18. Chittenden, *Yellowstone National Park 1895*, 222.
19. Hayden, *USGS 6th Annual Report*, 160.
20. "Climbing a Height."
21. Bumpus, *Trailside Notes*, 20; Haynes, Haynes Guide—1939, 64.
22. Hague, 1896 Letter to Chittenden, Hague papers.
23. Henderson, G.L. *Yellowstone Park Manual and Guide*, 2.
24. Pierce, Letter to mother, 1.
25. Bonney, *Battle Drums and Geysers*, 173.
26. Whittlesey, *Nomenclature*, 1010.
27. Wheeler, "The Late James Gemmell," 32; Haines, *Yellowstone Story*, 22, 188.
28. Haines, *Yellowstone Story*, 38.
29. *Ibid.*, 193.
30. Peale, Diary, 14.
31. O'Neill, "The Falls of the Yellowstone," 223.
32. Stanley, *Rambles in Wonderland*, 77.
33. T.E.S., "Across the Continent," 37–8.
34. *Livingston Enterprise*, Oct. 16, 1886.
35. *Ibid.*
36. Cook, "Valley of the Upper Yellowstone," 64.
37. Norris, "Meanderings of a Mountaineer," Letter #22.
38. Smith, *Book of a Hundred Bears*, 170.
39. Atwood, *Yellowstone Park in 1898*, 25.
40. Henderson, "Park Notes."
41. Turrill, *Tale of the Yellowstone*, 69.
42. Wineman, "Through Yellowstone National Park," 83.
43. Hauser, Diary, 12.
44. Wheeler, "James Gemmell," 331–6.
45. Davis, "Yellowstone Park—An Interview."
46. Langford, *Diary of the Washburn Expedition*, 34.
47. Hedges, "Great Falls of the Yellowstone."
48. Gunnison, *Rambles Overland*, 57.
49. Langford, "Wonders of Yellowstone," 11–12.
50. Barlow, "Reconnaissance," 14.
51. Hayden, *USGS 6th Annual Report*, 133.
52. Norris, "Meanderings of a Mountaineer," Letter #22.
53. Norris, *Calumet*, 132–134.
54. Norris, *Calumet*, 71.
55. Bornstein and Wexler, *Hiking Through the Wonders of the World*, 23–4.
56. Chittenden, *Yellowstone National Park 1903*, 343. (Crecelius's reports appended to Chittenden's in various Chief of Engineer's reports.)
57. Hayden, *USGS 6th Annual Report*, 256.
58. Chittenden, *Yellowstone—1895*, 324.
59. Hayden, *USGS 6th Annual Report*, 257.
60. Evermann, "Reconnaissance of Streams and Lakes," 21; Smith and Kendall, "Fishes of Yellowstone," 84.

Upper Loop:

61. Whittlesey, *Nomenclature*, 1541.
62. Barlow, "Reconnaissance," 10.
63. Henderson, *Yellowstone Park Manual*, 2.

64. Whittlesey, *Nomenclature,* 696, 894, 1541.
65. Jones, "Reconnaissance of Northwestern Wyoming," 29.
66. Smith, *Book of a Hundred Bears,* 214.
67. Chittenden, *Yellowstone—1895,* 325.
68. Haines, *Yellowstone National Park,* 189.
69. Langford, "Wonders of Yellowstone," 9; Cramton, *Early History of Yellowstone,* 93; Hauser, Diary, 6.
70. Henderson, Diary, 47; Strahorn, *Enchanted Land,* 30; Wineman, "Through Yellowstone," 88; Langford, "Wonders of Yellowstone," 8-9.
71. Bonney, *Battle Drums,* 254.
72. Langford, *Discovery of Yellowstone,* 79–80.
73. Trumbull, "Washburn Expedition," 433.
74. Cramton, *Early History of Yellowstone,* 93.
75. Hayden, "More About the Yellowstone," 392.
76. Gunnison, *Rambles Overland,* 77.
77. Chittenden, *Yellowstone—1903,* 333–4.
78. Hayden, *USGS 12th Annual Report,* 44.
79. Smith and Kendall, "Fishes of Yellowstone," 19.

PART II: THE BACKCOUNTRY
Cascade Corner:
80. Russell, *Journal of a Trapper, 92.*
81. Hayden, *USGS 12th Annual Report,* 468; Hayden, *USGS 6th Annual Report,* 93, 213, 258; *USFWS Annual Project Report 1978,* 167, 178.
82. Gregg, "Cornering Cascades," 83.
83. Hague, *Geology of Yellowstone,* 377.
84. Haynes photo 21125, *Haynes Bulletin.*
85. Chittenden, *Yellowstone—1895,* 325.
86. *Ibid.*
87. Gregg, "Cascade Corner," 476.
88. C.S. Sloan letter to Haynes, March 8, 1922 in Haynes Personal Files.
89. Hayden, *USGS 6th Annual Report,* 93.
90. *Ibid.,* 258.
91. Haynes, *Haynes Guide—1922,* 158.
92. Bach, *Exploring Yellowstone Backcountry,* 86.
93. Haynes, *Haynes Bulletin,* 1; YCF.
94. Hayden, *USGS 6th Annual Report,* 258.
95. Beal, *Story of Man in Yellowstone,* 25.
96. Frazer, "The Land of the Whopper," 44.
97. Hayden, *USGS 6th Annual Report,* 257.
98. Iddings, "USGS Field Notebooks," box 53, Iddings notebook, vol. 21, 1886, #3893-R, 42.
99. C.S. Sloan letter to Haynes, March 8, 1922 in Haynes Personal Files.
100. Carter, *Yellowstone Backcountry Basics and Trail Guide,* 84.
101. "Topographic Map of Yellowstone National Park," 1922.
102. Chittenden, *Yellowstone—1895,* 324.
103. *Ibid.*
104. Gregg, "Cornering Cascades," 78.
105. Manns, 1987 Memo to Superintendent, 1.
106. Whittlesey, *Nomenclature,* 15; Albright, *Birth of the National Park Service,* see generally.
107. Gregg, "Cascade Corner," 471; Haynes photo 21081 in *Haynes Bulletin.*
108. Gregg, "Cascade Corner," 476; Haynes photo 21081 and 21083 in *Haynes Bulletin.*
109. USBGN Folder File for "Gregg, Fork;" Haynes personal files.
110. Gregg, "Cascade Corner," 475.
111. Rees, *Idaho: Chronology, Nomenclature, Bibliography,* 115; Crowder, *Tendoy,* 41.
112. Pickett, *Hunting at High Altitudes,* 280.
113. Haynes, *Haynes Guide—1924,* 169; YCF; Bauer, "Place Names of Yellowstone," 43; Haynes, *Haynes Bulletin.*
114. C.S. Sloan letter to Haynes, March 8, 1922 in Haynes Personal Files; USBGN to Haynes, March 3, 1922, YCF under Wahhi Falls; Wesley L. Kosin to Lee Whittlesey, Jan. 11, 1979, Wyo.; Haynes photos 21063 and 21065, *Haynes Bulletin.*
115. YCF under Phillips Fork Fall; Haynes, *Haynes Guide—1939,* 187; Haynes photo 21055 in Personal Files; an attempt to place the name on maps is David Condon to J.M. Lawson, October 8, 1958, USGS memorandum K3827, USGS files, Denver, Colorado.
116. "Topographic Map of YNP," 1922; Haynes, *Haynes Bulletin.*
117. Whittlesey, *Nomenclature,* 823.
118. Whittlesey, *Death in Yellowstone,* 190–1.
119. Bauer, "Place Names of Yellowstone," 96; YCF, Twister Falls; Birdseye, "Map of Cascade Corner of Yellowstone National Park," 1922; *USFWS Annual Project Report 1979,* 175.
120. Hayden, *USGS 6th Annual Report,* 243–4.
121. Chapman, *Yellowstone Back Country,* 6.
122. Gregg, "Cornering Cascades," 78.

123. Gregg, "Cascade Corner," 470.
124. Haynes, *Haynes Bulletin.*
125. USFWS *Annual Project Report 1978,* 178–9.

Madison Plateau and Vicinity:

126. *USFWS Annual Project Report 1977,* 140.
127. Hayden, *USGS 6th Annual Report,* 242.
128. *USFWS Annual Project Report 1977,* 148.
129. Wingate, *Through the Yellowstone,* 1882 map in book pocket.
130. *USFWS Annual Project Report 1977,* 131.
131. Hayden, *USGS 6th Annual Report,* map opposite p. 254.
132. *USFWS Annual Project Report 1977,* 141.
133. Barlow, "Reconnaissance," 23; Hayden, *USGS 5th Annual Report,* 112; Baldwin, *Enchanted Enclosure,* 30.
134. "Leatherman's Lost Falls."
135. Jackson, *Autobiography of William Henry Jackson,* 203; Haines, *Yellowstone Story,* 153; Barlow, "Reconnaissance," 34–5.
136. Barlow, "Reconnaissance," 23.

Central Yellowstone:

137. Strahorn, *Enchanted Land,* 32.
138. Whittlesey, *Nomenclature,* 876.
139. Smith and Kendall, "Fishes of Yellowstone," 19.
140. Whittlesey conversation with John Varley, USFWS, various 1978-80, citing *Master Domestic Water Systems Study,* 1972, Casper, Wyoming; *USFWS Annual Project Report 1973,* 60–3; *USFWS Annual Project Report 1975,* 52.
141. Whittlesey, *Nomenclature,* 1937.
142. Smith and Kendall, "Fishes of Yellowstone," 13; Seamans, "Survey of Trout Streams," 18; *USFWS Annual Project Report 1973,* 45–7; *USFWS Annual Project Report 1975,* 52.

Grand Canyon and Vicinity:

143. Toll, *Annual Report,* 13.
144. Wheeler, *Wonderland '97,* 58.
145. Langford, "Wonders of Yellowstone," 12.
146. Hedges, "Great Falls of Yellowstone."
147. Whittlesey, *Nomenclature,* 1609.
148. Norris, *5th Annual Report,* 11 and map.

149. Wylie, *Yellowstone National Park,* 63; Haupt, *The Yellowstone National Park,* 147.
150. Haupt, *The Yellowstone National Park,* 147.
151. See note 148 above.
152. *Ibid.*
153. Norris, *5th Annual Report,* 12, 66.
154. Wister, *Owen Wister Out West,* 127–8.
155. Robinson and Wilson, *Myths and Legends,* 376.
156. Herzberg, *Myths and Their Meaning,* 366.

Northern Yellowstone:

157. Dominic, "The Sheepeaters," 131–68.
158. Wingate, "Through the Yellowstone," 79–80.
159. Barber, *Ribbons of Water,* 47.
160. Bonney, *Battle Drums,* 470; YCF, Knowles Falls, "Type Map, 1931."

Northeastern Yellowstone:

161. Haupt, *The Yellowstone National Park,* 158; Chittenden, *Yellowstone—1895,* 343.

Mirror Plateau:

162. Haines, *Valley of the Upper Yellowstone,* 57–8.
163. Whittlesey, "Discovery of a Waterfall," 3.

Southeastern Yellowstone:

164. NPS, *Monthly Report of the Superintendent,* 7.
165. Hayden, *USGS 5th Annual Report,* 137.
166. Hague, "USGS Field Notebooks," box 55, Hague notebook, vol. 1, 1888, 19.
167. Hague, *Geology of Yellowstone,* 282–3; Iddings, "USGS Field Notebooks," box 53, Iddings notebook, vol. 21, 1886 (1889), #3893-R, 113–4.
168. *USFWS Annual Project Report 1977,* map.
169. French and Knight, "Grizzly Bear," 389–99.
170. Hayden, *USGS 6th Annual Report,* 253–4.

"Idyllic Falls" and Mount Chittenden; Photo by Mike Stevens

Bibliography

Albright, Horace Marden. *The Birth of the National Park Service.* Salt Lake City: Howe Brothers, 1985.

Allen, E.T., and A.L. Day. *Hot Springs of the Yellowstone National Park.* Publication No. 466. Washington: Carnegie Institution, 1935.

Atwood, John H. *Yellowstone Park in 1898.* Kansas City, Missouri: Smith-Grieves, 1918.

Bach, Orville, Jr. *Exploring The Yellowstone Backcountry.* San Francisco: Sierra Club Books, 1973.

Baldwin, Kenneth H., ed. *Enchanted Enclosure: The Army Engineers and Yellowstone National Park, A Documentary History.* Washington: GPO, 1976.

Barber, John F. *Ribbons of Water: The Waterfalls and Cascades of Yellowstone National Park.* YNP: Yellowstone Library and Museum Association, 1984.

Barlow, J.W., and David P. Heap. "Report of a Reconnaissance of the Basin of the Upper Yellowstone in 1871." Senate Ex. Doc. 66, vol. 2., 42nd Cong., 2nd Sess., SN-1479. Washington: GPO, 1872.

Bauer, C. Max. "Place Names of Yellowstone National Park." YNP Research Library, Mammoth, Wyoming, File no. 924.4/B344.

Beal, Merrill D. *The Story of Man in Yellowstone.* Caldwell, Idaho: Caxton Printers, Ltd., 1956.

Birdseye, C.H. "Map of Cascade Corner Yellowstone National Park." USGS, 1922.

Bonney, Orrin H., and Lorraine G. *Battle Drums and Geysers.* Chicago: Swallow Press Inc., 1970.

—. *Field Book: Yellowstone Park and the Absaroka Range.* Chicago: Swallow Press Inc., 1977.

Bornstein, Sam, and C. Wexler. *Hiking Through the Wonders of the World.* Chicago: N.p., 1926.

Brilliant, Ashleigh. *I Have Abandoned My Search for Truth and Am Now Looking for a Good Fantasy.* Santa Barbara: Woodbridge Press, 1985.

Brooks, Charles. *The Living River.* Piscataway, New Jersey: New Century, 1979.

Brower, David. *Gentle Wilderness: The Sierra Nevadas.* New York and Toronto: Ballantine, 1976.

Brust, James S., and Lee H. Whittlesey. "Thomas J. Hine: One Of Yellowstone's Earliest Photographers." *Montana: The Magazine of Western History,* Summer 1999.

Bryan, T. Scott. *The Geysers of Yellowstone.* Niwot, Colorado: University Press of Colorado, 1995.

[Bumpus, H.C.] *Trailside Notes for the Motorist and Hiker.* Number one. N.p.: U.S. Dept. of Interior, National Park Service, 1935.

Campbell, Reau. *Campbell's New Revised Complete Guide and Descriptive Book of the Yellowstone National Park.* Chicago: H.E. Klamer, 1909.

Carroll, Lewis. *The Complete Works of Lewis Carroll.* Edited by John Tenniel. New York: Random House, 1978.

Carter, Thomas B. *Yellowstone Backcountry Basics and Trail Guide.* Edited by Lee H. Whittlesey. Bozeman, Montana: Color World of Montana, Inc., 1978.

Chapman, W.S. *Yellowstone Back Country.* YNP: Yellowstone Library and Museum Association, 1964.

Charlton, Robert E. *Yellowstone Fishing Guide.* Portland, Oregon: Flying Pencil Publications, 1990.

Chittenden, Hiram M. *The Yellowstone National Park, Historical and Descriptive.* Cincinnati: Robert Clarke Company, 1895, 1903.

"Climbing a Height in the Park," *Livingston* (Montana) *Enterprise,* August 31, 1889.

Coleridge, Samuel Taylor. *The Collected Works of Samuel Taylor Coleridge, Vol. 1.* Edited by Lewis Patton. Princeton, New Jersey: Princeton University Press, 1970.

Conly, Marc. *Waterfalls of Colorado.* Boulder, Colorado: Pruett Publishing Company, 1993.

Cook, C.W. [David Folsom]. "The Valley of the Upper Yellowstone." *Western Monthly,* 4:60–67, July 1870.

Cramton, Louis C. *Early History of Yellowstone National Park and its Relation to National Park Policies.* Washington: U.S. Dept. of Interior, National Park Service, 1932.

Crowder, David L. *Tendoy: Chief of the Lemhis.* Caldwell, Idaho: Caxton Printers Ltd., 1969.

Davis, John C. "Yellowstone Park—An Interview with a Man Who Visited that Region as Far Back as 1863," *Louisville* (Kentucky) *Courier Journal,* April 13, 1884, p. 12. Reprinted in *Livingston* (Montana) *Enterprise,* April 21, 1884.

DeLacy, Walter Washington. "A Trip Up the South Snake River in 1863." *Contributions to the Historical Society of Montana,* 1:113-143, 1876.

Dominic, David. "The Sheepeaters." *Annals of Wyoming,* 36: 131–168, October 1964.

Dunraven, Windham T.W.-Q., 4th Earl of. *The Great Divide: Travels in the Upper Yellowstone in the Summer of 1874.* New York: Scribner, Welford, and Armstrong, 1876. London: Chatto and Windus, 1876.

Evermann, Barton W. "A Reconnaissance of the Streams and Lakes of Western Montana and Northwestern Wyoming." House Ex. Doc. vol. 20, 52nd Cong., 2nd Sess., SN-3129. Washington: GPO, 1893.

Ferguson, Gary. *Walking Down the Wild: A Journey Through the Yellowstone Rockies.* New York: Harper Collins West, 1995.

Frazer, Elizabeth. "The Land of the Whopper." *Saturday Evening Post,* 192:40, 42, 44, 46, 49–50, 53–54, 57, May 1, 1920.

French, Steve; Marilyn French; and Richard Knight. "Grizzly Bear Use of Army Cutworm Moths in the Yellowstone Ecosystem." *International Conference of Bear Research and Management,* 9 (1) 389–399, 1994.

Friedman, Irving; Daniel R. Norton; and Roderick Hutchinson. "Monitoring of Thermal Activity in Southwestern Yellowstone National Park and Vicinity, 1980–1993." *U.S. Geological Survey Bulletin 2067.* Washington: GPO, 1993.

Fritz, William J. *Roadside Geology of the Yellowstone Country.* Missoula, Montana: Mountain Press Publishing Co., 1989.

Fuller, Steven, and Jeremy Schmidt. *Yellowstone Grand Teton Roadguide.* Jackson Hole, Wyoming: Free Wheeling Travel Guides, 1990.

Gayley, Charles Mills. *The Classic Myths: In English Literature and in Art.* New York: Ginn and Company, 1911.

Grant, John. *An Introduction to Viking Mythology.* New York: Shooting Star Press, 1995.

Gregg, William C. "Cornering Cascades." *Saturday Evening Post,* 193:11, 78, 83, November 20, 1920.

—. "The Cascade Corner of Yellowstone Park." *Outlook,* 129: 469–476, November 23, 1921.

Guerber, H. A. *Myths of the Norsemen: From the Eddas and Sagas.* New York: Dover Publications, 1992.

Gunnison, Almon. *Rambles Overland: A Trip Across the Continent.* Boston: Universalist Publishing House, 1884, 1891.

Hague, Arnold. Unpublished personal papers and notebooks, in National Archives, Record Group 57, in the record series "Arnold Hague Papers" and "USGS Field Notebooks."

—; et. al. *Geology of the Yellowstone National Park, Part II, Petrography and Paleontology.* U.S. Geological Survey, Monograph 32, Part II, 893 pp. Washington: GPO, 1899.

Haines, Aubrey L., ed., *The Valley of the Upper Yellowstone.* Norman, Oklahoma: University of Oklahoma Press, 1965.

—. *The Yellowstone Story.* 2 vols. Boulder: Colorado Associated University Press, 1977.

—. *Yellowstone National Park: Its Exploration and Establishment.* Washington: GPO, 1974.

—. *Yellowstone Place Names: Mirrors of History.* Niwot, Colorado: University Press of Colorado, 1996.

Hamilton, Edith. *Mythology.* Boston: Little, Brown, and Company, 1942.

Hamilton, W.T. *My Sixty Years on the Plains.* New York: Forest and Stream Publishing Company, 1905.

Haupt, Herman, Jr. *The Yellowstone National Park.* St. Paul: J.M. Stoddart, 1883.

Hauser, Samuel T. "Diary of Samuel T. Hauser, Aug. 17 to Sept. 4, 1870." Ms. no. 249, Coe Collection, Beinecke Library, Yale University. Microfilm to author.

Hayden, F.V. *Preliminary Report of the U.S. Geological Survey of Montana and Portions of Adjacent Territories: Being a Fifth Annual Report of Progress.* Washington: GPO, 1872.

—. *Sixth Annual Report of the U.S. Geological Survey of the Territories . . . for the Year 1872.* Washington: GPO, 1873.

—. "The Wonders of the West—II. More About the Yellowstone." *Scribner's Monthly,* 3:388–396, February 1872.

—. *Twelfth Annual Report of the U.S. Geological and Geographical Survey of the Territories: A Report of Progress . . . for the Year 1878. In Two Parts. Part II. Yellowstone National Park. Geology—Thermal Springs—Topography.* Washington: GPO, 1883.

Haynes, Jack Ellis. *Haynes Guide* (all editions). YNP: Haynes Studios, Inc., Bozeman, Montana, 1890–1966.

—. *Yellowstone National Park—Photo-Gravures From Nature.* Fargo, North Dakota: 1887.

—. *Haynes Bulletin,* February and April, 1922. Copies at YNP Research Library, Mammoth, Wyoming.

—. Personal files of Jack Haynes (containing park tidbits such as place names, animals, plants, and history, used by Haynes for the annual updatings of his park guidebook) in Special Collections, Montana State University, Bozeman, Montana.

Hedges, Cornelius. "Journal of Judge Cornelius Hedges." *Contributions to the Historical Society of Montana,* 5:370–394, 1904.

—. "The Great Falls of the Yellowstone," *Helena Daily Herald,* October 15, 1870.

Henderson, A. Bart. Typescripts of his diaries in the Yellowstone country, 1866–1872, YNP Research Library, Mammoth, Wyoming.

Henderson G.L. "Park Notes," *Livingston* (Montana) *Enterprise,* June 25, 1887.

—. *Yellowstone Park Manual and Guide.* Mammoth Hot Springs, Wyoming: Privately printed, 1885. Second edition, 1888.

Herzberg, Max J. *Myths and Their Meaning.* Allyn and Bacon: New York, 1931.

Hoyt, John. "Report of the Governor of the Territory of Wyoming." House Ex. Doc. #1, 47th Cong., 1st Sess., part 5, SN-2018, pp. 1003–1079. Washington: GPO, 1881. Also published in the Secretary of Interior's Annual Report for 1881.

Hutchinson, R. A., and Michael J. Thompson. "The Travertine Totem Forest of Yellowstone National Park, USA: Geologic Controls and Geochemistry." *Water-Rock Interaction.* Rotterdam: A.A. Balkema, 1992.

Iddings, Joseph P. Unpublished notebooks in National Archives, Record Group 57, in the record series "USGS Field Notebooks."

Jackson, William H. *Time Exposure: The Autobiography of William Henry Jackson.* New York: G.P. Putnam's Sons, 1940.

Jones, William A. "Report Upon the Reconnaissance of Northwestern Wyoming Including Yellowstone National Park Made in the Summer of 1873." Washington: GPO, 1875. Also appeared as House Ex. Doc. #285, 43rd Cong., 1st Sess., SN-1615, Washington: GPO, 1874.

Jordan, David Starr. "A Reconnaissance of the Streams and Lakes of the Yellowstone National Park, Wyoming, in the Interest of the United States Fish Commission." *U.S. Fish Commission, Bulletin,* 9 (1889): 41–63. SN-2881,(1889), 1891.

—. "The Story of a Strange Land." *Popular Science Monthly,* 40:447–458, February 1892.

Killian, Michael. "Mythical Shangri-La Found, Explorers Say," *Los Angeles Daily News,* January 8, 1999.

Langford, Nathaniel Pitt. *Diary of the Washburn Expedition to the Yellowstone and Firehole Rivers in the Year 1870.* St. Paul: [J.E. Haynes], 1905.

—. T*he Discovery of Yellowstone Park 1870.* St. Paul: J.E. Haynes, 1923

—. *The Discovery of Yellowstone Park.* Lincoln: University of Nebraska Press, 1972.

—. "The Wonders of the Yellowstone." *Scribner's Monthly,* 2:1–17, 113–128, May, June, 1871.

"Leatherman's Lost Falls," *Livingston* (Montana) *Post,* April 25, 1901.

Manns, Tim, North District Naturalist, Memo to Superintendent, February 4, 1987, YNP Archives.

Marschall, Mark C. *Yellowstone Trails: A Hiking Guide.* Yellowstone National Park (YNP), Wyoming: Yellowstone Association, 1990.

Maynard, Charles. *Waterfalls of Yellowstone.* Seymour, Tennessee: Panther Press, 1996.

National Park Service. *Ranger Naturalists' Manual of Yellowstone National Park.* YNP: Dept. of Interior, National Park Service, 1928.

National Park Service. *Monthly Report of Superintendent of Yellowstone National Park,* unpublished bound editions, YNP Research Library, Mammoth, Wyoming, July 1947.

Norris, Philetus W. *Annual Report of the Superintendent of the Yellowstone National Park to the Secretary of the Interior for the Year 1880.* Washington: GPO, 1881. Also published as House Ex. Doc. 1, Pt. 5, vol. 2, 46th Cong., 3rd Sess., SN-1960.

—. *Fifth Annual Report of the Superintendent of the Yellowstone National Park by P.W. Norris, Superintendent.* Conducted Under the Authority of the Secretary of the Interior. Washington: GPO, 1881. Also published as House Ex. Doc. 1, Pt. 5, vol. 2, 47th Cong., 1st Sess., SN-2018.

—. "Meanderings of a Mountaineer, or, The Journals and Musings (or Storys) of a Rambler over Prairie (or Mountain) and Plain." Ms. prepared from newspaper clippings and handwritten additions. Huntington Library, San Marino, California. [1885]. Original newspaper articles published as series, "The Great West," *Detroit Post,* 1870–75.

—. *Report Upon the Yellowstone National Park to the Secretary of the Interior by P.W. Norris, Superintendent, for the Year 1877.* Washington: GPO, 1878.

—. *Report Upon the Yellowstone National Park to the Secretary of the Interior by P.W. Norris, Superintendent, for the Year 1878.* Washington: GPO, 1879.

—. *Report Upon the Yellowstone National Park to the Secretary of the Interior by P.W. Norris, Superintendent, for the Year 1879.* Washington: GPO, 1880.

—. *The Calumet of the Coteau and Other Poetical Legends of the Border . . .* Philadelphia: J.B. Lippincott and Company, 1883, 1884.

Norton, Harry J. *Wonderland Illustrated: Or, Horseback Rides Through the Yellowstone National Park.* Virginia City, Montana: Harry J. Norton, 1873.

O'Neill, Howard. "The Falls of the Yellowstone." *Southern Magazine,* August 1871.

Owen, W. O. "The First Bicycle Tour of the Yellowstone National Park." *Outing,* June 1891.

Parks, Richard. *Fishing Yellowstone National Park.* Helena, Montana: Falcon Publishing Inc., 1998.

Paull, Caroline. "Notes on Yellowstone National Park, June 28–August 4, 1897," YNP Research Library, Mammoth, Wyoming.

Peacock, Doug. *Grizzly Years.* New York: Kensington Publishing Corporation, 1990.

Peale, Albert C. Photostat and typewritten copies of personal diaries, 1871–1872, YNP Research Library. Originals at USGS, Denver, Colorado.

Pickett, Col. William D. *Hunting at High Altitudes, the Book of the Boone and Crockett Club.* Edited by George B. Grinnell. New York and London: Harper and Brothers, 1913.

Pierce, Flora Chase. Letter dated August 8, 1897. YNP Research Library, Mammoth, Wyoming.

Pierce, Steve. *The Lakes of Yellowstone.* Seattle: The Mountaineers, 1987.

Plumb, Gregory A. *A Waterfalls Lover's Guide to the Pacific Northwest.* Seattle: The Mountaineers, 1989.

Rees, John E. *Idaho: Chronology, Nomenclature, Bibliography.* Chicago: W.B. Conkey Company, 1918.

Richards, Alonzo V. "Field Notes of the Survey and Establishment of the Western Boundary of Wyoming Territory by A.V. Richards, U.S. Astronomer and Surveyor, 1874." Ms. with maps, Bureau of Land Management, Cheyenne, Wyoming.

Robinson, Herbert Spencer, and Knox Wilson. *Myths and Legends of All Nations.* Totowa, New Jersey: Littlefield, Adams & Co., 1990.

Rubinstein, Paul. "A Journey to the Fairyland Basin." Internet, 1997.

Russell, Osborne. *Journal of a Trapper.* Edited by Aubrey L. Haines. Lincoln: University of Nebraska Press, 1965.

Saltus, J. Sanford. *A Week in the Yellowstone.* New York: The Knickerbocker Press, 1895.

Schneider, Bill. *Hiking Yellowstone National Park.* Helena, Montana: Falcon Publishing Co., Inc., 1997.

Schullery, Paul. *Mountain Time.* Boulder, Colorado: Roberts Rinehart Publishers, 1995.

—. *Searching for Yellowstone: Ecology and Wonder in the Last Wilderness.* Boston: Houghton Mifflin Company, 1997.

Seamans, John E. "A Report on a Survey of Some of the Trout Streams of Yellowstone National Park." YNP Research Library, Mammoth, Wyoming, March 21, 1940.

Shaw, Richard J. *Plants of Yellowstone & Grand Teton National Parks.* Salt Lake City: Wheelwright Press Ltd., 1981.

Simpson, Ross W. *The Fires of '88: Yellowstone Park and Montana in Flames.* N.p.: American World Geographic Publications, 1989.

Smith, F. Dumont. *Book of a Hundred Bears.* Chicago: Rand McNally and Company, 1909.

Smith, Hugh M., and William C. Kendall. "The Fishes of the Yellowstone National Park." *U.S. Fish Commission, Annual Report,* 1921, Appendix III. Bureau of Fisheries Document No. 904. Washington: GPO, 1922.

Stanley, Edwin J. *Rambles in Wonderland: Or, Up the Yellowstone . . .* New York: D. Appleton and Company, 1878.

Stoddard, Charles Warren. "In Wonder-Land." *Ave Maria,* Notre Dame, Indiana. 47:6–11, August 6, 1898.

Strahorn, Robert. *The Enchanted Land or an October Ramble Among the Geysers, Hot Springs, Lakes, Falls, and Cañons of Yellowstone National Park.* Omaha, Nebraska: New West Publishing Company, 1881.

T.E.S. [Thomas E. Sherman]. "Across the Continent. II—The National Park." *Woodstock Letters,* 11:25–42. Maryland: Woodstock College, 1882.

Thayer, William M. *Marvels of the New West.* Norwich, Connecticut: The Henry Bill Publishing Company, 1891.

Thomas, Thomas H. "Yellowstone Park Illustrated." *The Graphic,* August 11, 18, 1888.

Thwaites, Reuben Gold. *Original Journals of the Lewis and Clark Expedition.* 7 vols. and Atlas. New York: Dodd, Mead, and Company, 1904–1905.

Toll, Roger. *Annual Report of the Superintendent of Yellowstone National Park,* National Park Service, unpublished bound volumes, YNP Research Library, Mammoth, Wyoming, 1931.

"Topographic Map of the Yellowstone National Park, Wyoming-Montana-Idaho," 1922. Partial revision, 1921.

"Citadel of Asgard Falls;"
Photo by Paul Rubinstein

Topping, E.S. *Chronicles of the Yellowstone . . .* St. Paul: Pioneer Press Company, 1888.

Trenholm, Virginia Cole, and Maurine Carley. *The Shoshonis: Sentinels of the Rockies.* Norman: University of Oklahoma Press, 1964, 1972.

Trumbull, Walter. "The Washburn Yellowstone Expedition, No. 1." *Overland Monthly,* 6:431–437, May 1871.

Turrill, Gardner Stilson. *A Tale of the Yellowstone or In a Wagon Through Western Wyoming and Wonderland.* Jefferson, Iowa: G.S. Turrill Publishing Company, 1901.

U.S. Board on Government Names, Reston, Virginia. Folder files of place names for YNP, various dates.

U.S. Dept. of Interior, Fish and Wildlife Service, Division of Fish Resources, Fishery and Aquatic Management Program, *Annual Project Technical Report.* Utilized 1939–1999 reports that are housed in the Yellowstone Research Library. In all cases, calendar year date is one year prior to the July release date.

Van Dyke, Henry. "A Meadow That Belongs to the People." *Outlook,* 145:79–80, January 19, 1927.

Varley, John D. "A History of Fish Stocking Activities in Yellowstone National Park Between 1881 and 1980." Information paper number 35. YNP: U.S. Fish and Wildlife Service, January 1, 1980.

Wheat, Carl. *Mapping the Transmississippi West.* 5 vols. San Francisco: Institute of Historical Cartography, 1957, 1958, 1959, 1960, 1963.

Wheeler, Olin D. *Wonderland '97.* St. Paul, Minnesota: Northern Pacific Railroad, 1897.

Wheeler, William F. "The Late James Gemmell." *Contributions to the Historical Society of Montana,* 2:331–336, 1896.

White, John G. "Souvenir of Wyoming (Being a Diary of a Fishing Trip in Jackson Hole and Yellowstone Park with Remarks on Early History and Historical Geography)," 3 vols., Cleveland, Ohio, typewritten, 1926. Only eight copies of this work were made—five were given to party members and the other three are at YNP Research Library, Missouri Historical Society, and Wyoming Historical Society.

Whittlesey, Lee H. *Death in Yellowstone: Accidents and Foolhardiness in the First National Park.* Boulder, Colorado: Roberts Rinehart Publishers, 1995.

—. "Discovery of a Waterfall," YNP Library, 1980.

—. "Everyone Can Understand a Picture: Photographers and the Promotion of Early Yellowstone." *Montana, The Magazine of Western History,* Summer 1999.

—. *Wonderland Nomenclature: A History of the Place Names of Yellowstone National Park.* Helena: Montana Historical Society microfiche, 1988.

—. *Yellowstone Place Names.* Helena, Montana: Montana Historical Press, 1988.

Whittlesey, Lee H., and Rocco Paperiello. "A Visit to Joseph's Coat Springs, Coffee Pot Hot Springs, and 'Fairyland Basin.'" *Transactions of the Geyser Observation and Study Association,* vol. 3, 1993, pp. 193–202.

Wineman, Mode. "Through Yellowstone National Park into Jackson Hole Country . . ." Ms. with photos, YNP Research Library, Mammoth, Wyoming, 1908.

Wingate, George W. *Through the Yellowstone Park on Horseback.* New York: O. Judd Company, 1886.

Wister, Fanny Kemble, ed., *Owen Wister Out West: His Journals and Letters.* Kingsport, Tennessee: University of Chicago Press, 1958.

Wuerthner, George. *California's Wilderness Areas, The Complete Guide. Vol. 1,* Englewood, Colorado: Westcliffe Publishers, Inc., 1997.

Wylie, W.W. *Yellowstone National Park, or the Great American Wonderland.* Kansas City: Ramsey, Millett, and Hudson, 1882.

Yellowstone Card File (abbreviated "YCF"). These lengthy card files of park place names are housed in the office of the Yellowstone Park Museum Curator, Mammoth Hot Springs, Wyoming.

Zipes, Jack., ed. *Complete Fairy Tales of the Brothers Grimm.* New York: Bantam, 1992.

"Dancing Water Cascade;" Photo by Mike Stevens

INDEX

Paul Rubinstein

A former air traffic controller, Paul Rubinstein holds a degree in geography, specializing in land-based and aerial cartography. He has spent the last 11 seasons in Yellowstone National Park, amassing thousands of miles of off-trail exploration. During this time, he has filmed and edited seven full-length Yellowstone videos and photographed thousands of images from some of Yellowstone's remotest locations. His photos have been featured in *American Heritage Magazine, Death In Yellowstone,* and the upcoming, revised *Yellowstone Placenames.* Rubinstein is currently working on his next book, *10 Years In Wonderland: A Collection of Yellowstone Backcountry Adventures,* a true account of some of his more harrowing experiences in Yellowstone's deepest wilderness. Come winter, he and girlfriend Barbara can be found in Calabasas, California.

Lee H. Whittlesey

Lee H. Whittlesey is archivist for the National Park Service at Yellowstone National Park, Wyoming. A historian who has published five other books on Yellowstone, Whittlesey has spent 27 summers and 15 winters in the "Grand Old Park." In his many years at Yellowstone, he has worn the hats of bus tour guide, snowcoach driver, communications specialist, law enforcement ranger, ranger-naturalist, and technical writer. A backcountry expert, he has hiked all 1,200 miles of Yellowstone's marked trails and hundreds of miles off-trail. Whittlesey holds a law degree from the University of Oklahoma and lives year-round in the park at Mammoth with his wife, Tami, and daughter, Tess.

Mike Stevens

A high school mathematics teacher for 30 years, Mike Stevens has had the opportunity to enjoy many a summer in the great outdoors. He has worked 17 seasons in Yellowstone National Park, often as a national park service volunteer or tour guide. An avid hiker and nature photographer, Stevens has had several of his nature photographs published in *A Yellowstone Album,* and, after logging more than 5,000 miles, has developed the reputation among his peers as the best foot soldier in all of Yellowstone. When he isn't traversing the park, Stevens makes his home in Simi Valley, California.